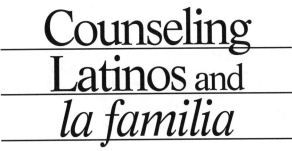

Counseling
Latinos and
la familia

MULTICULTURAL ASPECTS OF COUNSELING SERIES

SERIES EDITOR

Paul Pedersen, Ph.D., *University of Alabama at Birmingham*

EDITORIAL BOARD

VOLUMES IN THIS SERIES

1. **Increasing Multicultural Understanding (2nd edition): A Comprehensive Model**
   by Don C. Locke
2. **Preventing Prejudice: A Guide for Counselors and Educators**
   by Joseph G. Ponterotto and Paul B. Pedersen
3. **Improving Intercultural Interactions: Modules for Cross-Cultural Training Programs**
   edited by Richard W. Brislin and Tomoko Yoshida
4. **Assessing and Treating Culturally Diverse Clients (2nd edition): A Practical Guide**
   by Freddy A. Paniagua
5. **Overcoming Unintentional Racism in Counseling and Therapy:
   A Practitioner's Guide to Intentional Intervention** by Charles R. Ridley
6. **Multicultural Counseling With Teenage Fathers: A Practical Guide** by Mark S. Kiselica
7. **Multicultural Counseling Competencies: Assessment, Education and
   Training, and Supervision** edited by Donald B. Pope-Davis and Hardin L. K. Coleman
8. **Improving Intercultural Interactions: Modules for Cross-Cultural
   Training Programs, Volume 2** edited by Kenneth Cushner and Richard W. Brislin
9. **Understanding Cultural Identity in Intervention and Assessment** by Richard H. Dana
10. **Psychological Testing of American Minorities (2nd edition)** by Ronald J. Samuda
11. **Multicultural Counseling Competencies: Individual and Organizational Development**
    by Derald Wing Sue et al.
12. **Counseling Multiracial Families** by Bea Wehrly, Kelley R. Kenney, and Mark E. Kenney
13. **Integrating Spirituality Into Multicultural Counseling**
    by Mary A. Fukuyama and Todd D. Sevig
14. **Counseling With Native American Indians and Alaska Natives: Strategies for
    Helping Professionals** by Roger D. Herring
15. **Diagnosis in a Multicultural Context: A Casebook for Mental Health Professionals**
    by Freddy A. Paniagua
16. **Psychotherapy and Counseling With Asian American Clients: A Practical Guide**
    by George K. Hong and MaryAnna Domokos-Cheng Ham
17. **Counseling Latinos and *la familia*: A Practical Guide**
    by Azara L. Santiago-Rivera, Patricia Arredondo, and Maritza Gallardo-Cooper

Counseling
Latinos and
la familia
A Practical Guide

Azara L. Santiago-Rivera
State University of New York at Albany

Patricia Arredondo
Arizona State University at Tempe

Maritza Gallardo-Cooper
Circles of Care, Inc.

Multicultural Aspects of Counseling Series 17

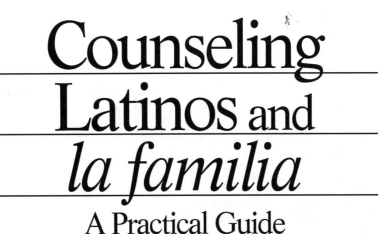
Sage Publications
International Educational and Professional Publisher
Thousand Oaks ▪ London ▪ New Delhi

For information:

Sage Publications, Inc.
2455 Teller Road
Thousand Oaks, California 91320
E-mail: order@sagepub.com

Sage Publications Ltd.
6 Bonhill Street
London EC2A 4PU
United Kingdom

Sage Publications India Pvt. Ltd.
M-32 Market
Greater Kailash I
New Delhi 110 048 India

Printed in the United States of America

Library of Congress Cataloging-in-Publication Data

Santiago-Rivera, Azara L. (Azara Lourdes), 1952-
  Counseling Latinos and *la familia:* A practical guide / Azara L.
Santiago-Rivera, Patricia Arredondo, Maritza Gallardo-Cooper.
      p. cm. — (Multicultural aspects of counseling; v. 17)
  Includes bibliographical references and index.
   ISBN 0-7619-2329-2 (c) — ISBN 0-7619-2330-6 (p)
   1. Hispanic Americans—Mental health services. 2. Hispanic
Americans—Counseling of. 3. Hispanic American families—Counseling of.
4. Hispanic Americans—Family relationships. 5. Hispanic
Americans—Mental health services. I. Arrendondo, Patricia. II.
Gallardo-Cooper, Maritza. III. Title. IV. Multicultural aspects of
counseling series; v. 17.
   RC451.5.H57 S28 2002
   362.2'04256'08968073—dc21
                                            2001004074

     06 07 08 10 9 8 7 6 5 4

Acquiring Editor:	Nancy S. Hale
Editorial Assistant:	Vonessa Vondera
Production Editor:	Diana E. Axelsen
Editorial Assistant:	Candice Crosetti
Copy Editor:	Jacqueline A. Tasch
Typesetter/Designer:	Denyse Dunn
Indexer:	Rachel Rice

Contents

Series Editor's Introduction

Going Beyond the Individual

The psychological sciences have traditionally been based on the notion of the individual as a basic building block of society. That is all being changed, in part by the demographic shift toward cultures, such as the Latinos, where the unit, and particularly the family unit, is central. This shift has enormous consequences for changing the way that counseling psychology functions as a scientific discipline, modifying the textbooks now being used, rewriting lectures for classes now being taught, redirecting professional guidance to students, and changing the rules of counseling practice. This book will help readers survive all those changes by increasing their awareness of why *la familia* is so important.

The remarkable growth of Hispanic and Latino populations in the United States has promoted changes in the way counseling is provided. Given the huge demographic shift, there is no avoiding those changes. Those who do not get on the train now will be left behind at the station. There is some urgency for providers of counseling to catch up with their multicultural consumers to maintain relevance and display competence. Although catching up is not going to be easy or simple, this book will provide considerable help to readers toward that goal through systematic and practical suggestions.

In the past, the notorious underutilization of counseling services by Latinos and other minority groups was tolerated or ignored by counseling professionals. That is no longer a viable choice. In the past, underutilization resulted in continued suffering for the minority client. In the present and future, under-utilization will result in continued suffering for the majority counseling provider and for the profession as a whole. It is not just increased competence for a specialized group that is at stake here but rather the validity of counseling as a human service resource.

Several specific changes in counseling practice will be addressed in this book. First, the importance of a multidisciplinary approach, which moves beyond the narrowly defined boundaries of counseling, will reflect the variety of relevant factors in counseling. Second, there is the integrative perspective of bringing in whole networks of individuals in the enlarged family group as the client rather an isolated individual. Third, understanding the indigenous worldview and perspective of Latinos, recognizing the extreme diversity of viewpoints within that broadly defined population, will require inclusive thinking. Fourth, balancing the unique advantages and disadvantages that impact the Latino client will provide a balanced perspective from the Latino standpoint.

The chapters of the book begin with a historical understanding of the Latino cultures and the way counseling is perceived from that perspective. Part I discusses how individualistic counseling has often minimized the importance of history with negative consequences for clients where historical roots are essential. The book then helps readers understand the complexities in defining Latino cultural identity from an insider's perspective. The primary values of Hispanic culture are discussed to help counselors avoid misunderstandings with their Latino clients. Demographic trends help readers project these changes into the future of multicultural counseling, particularly in the family context. Part II of the book reviews counseling intervention models, both from textbook counseling theory and from models indigenous to the Latino context. Key assumptions and concepts are highlighted. These strategies will have profound practical relevance for counselors working with Latinos. Finally, the book describes a balance between clinical and cultural dimensions that has generic relevance far beyond the Latino cultural group.

The **Multicultural Aspects of Counseling** series has evolved into an encyclopedia of volumes on different aspects of multicultural counseling. Throughout the series the books have taken an inclusive perspective, recognizing both within-group and between-group differences. Each volume has taken a very practical and applied perspective so that readers can immediately use the ideas they have just read. This book helps fill in an essential gap in the published books on multicultural counseling.

Paul Pedersen
University of Hawaii

Preface

Demographic changes and shifts, most notably, the rapid growth of the Latino population in the United States, can no longer be ignored. It is estimated
that Latinos will number 59 million by the year 2025, when one in five people
in the United States will be of Latino heritage (U.S. Bureau of the Census,
1993). Moreover, the number of Latino children ages 0 to 14 increased from
4.7 million in 1970 to 8.8 million in 1997; this population is expected to double
in size by 2025 (Estrada, 2000). Likewise, the traditional Latino family unit
has changed. Recent data indicate that the percentage of children living in intact families has declined from 74% in 1980 to 64% in 1995 (Estrada, 2000).
Undeniably, the growing presence of the Latino population throughout the
United States and the rapidly changing structure of the Latino family unit
have attracted the attention of the mental health profession. For instance, the
negative experiences associated with discrimination in education, employment,
and health care, as well as poverty, the migration experience, the process of
adaptation, and the language barrier may place Latinos at risk for physical
and mental health problems.

   It is well recognized that Latinos have historically underutilized mental
health services. As a result, proponents of multicultural counseling have ad-
vocated for the development of culturally responsive approaches to increase
effective use of such services (Altarriba & Santiago-Rivera, 1994; Santiago-
Rivera, 1995; Sue, Arredondo, & McDavis, 1992). Others propose that we
need to work with Latino individuals and their families using an integrative
and multidisciplinary approach (Zambrana, 1995). This is important because

there are a variety of factors (e.g., economic, sociopolitical, and cultural) interacting with each other that not only contribute to the underutilization of services but also influence treatment outcomes.

The first aim of this book is to present an integrated approach to understanding Latino individuals and their families. There are few resources available on counseling with Latino families (e.g., Falicov, 1998). The next aim, which fills a void in the literature, is to offer students and professionals-in-training, as well as professionals in the field (e.g., social workers, clinical and counseling psychologists, educators), essential background information about this heterogeneous population, as well as practical counseling approaches leading to culturally competent strategies in the assessment and treatment of Latinos and their families.

A third aim of this text is to broaden the scope of knowledge so that mental health professionals can begin to see how many Latino families are constrained by larger societal and institutional structures. We hope that mental health professionals will develop new ways of working with Latino families and take on more advocacy roles in breaking down these structural barriers that have impeded access to appropriate health care.

In terms of the book's layout, each chapter begins with a common Spanish proverb or a phrase that the authors have used in their work with Latinos, a set of objectives, and general competencies as outlined by Arredondo et al. (1996). Each chapter offers a set of Latino-centered competencies for each component of the three domains: awareness, knowledge, and skills. A set of statements, designed as a self-assessment, is located at the beginning of each chapter, with the correct answers provided at the end. Where appropriate, a rationale is given to explain a particular answer along with a reference to the pages in the text of the chapter.

This book is divided into two parts. Part I provides a discussion of critical background information about Latinos and their families. Part I consists of five chapters, each with a specific focus. Chapter 1 offers the reader an historical overview of the development of the Multicultural Counseling Competencies (Arredondo et al., 1996) and describes how this framework can be applied to Latino-specific competencies. This chapter also describes Latino-specific identity models that can serve as reference points when working with Latino clients. Following the personal identity dimensions framework (Arredondo & Glauner, 1992), Chapter 2 provides an overview of historical, sociopolitical, and geographical contexts (e.g., migration patterns) that are critical to understanding the heterogeneity of this population. We highlight the differences and similarities among the three largest Latino groups in the United States—Mexican, Puerto Rican, and Cuban—and give some attention to Central and South Americans. In addition, Dominicans, a strong presence in the Northeast, are highlighted in this chapter because of the dramatic increase in their numbers within the last decade. Particular attention is given to describing key historical events that have shaped, directly or indirectly, the lives of this heterogeneous cultural group. Chapter 3 discusses specific concepts, frames of reference, and issues that focus on identity, adaptation and change, family values, religion and spirituality beliefs, health and illness beliefs, language, and gender socialization. This chapter describes how these various dimensions are important in shaping the lives of Latino people. Chapter 4 provides an overview of specific demographic trends, particularly socioeconomic and family characteristics that are redefining the Latino family. Chapter 5 presents the characteristics and challenges of four types of Latino families (e.g., intact, bicultural/biracial, single parent, and immigrant) and describes the demands and stressors that push individuals and their families to cope in ways that may be maladaptive. Through case illustrations, some of the issues and challenges are highlighted.

Part II consists of three chapters that focus on counseling issues and interventions. Chapter 6 begins with a discussion on issues to consider before meeting the Latino client such as how the client-therapist match with respect to language and culture may affect the initial stages of counseling. This chapter also describes the role of Latino cultural values such as *personalismo* and *simpatía* and social etiquette in enhancing a positive counselor-client relationship. With respect to the important dimension of assessment in counseling, this chapter reviews relevant issues and provides an example of a Latino culture-centered clinical interview. Chapter 7 describes helping strategies that can be used during the counseling process, such as language switching, and the use of narratives and metaphors. Chapter 8 briefly reviews a variety of family therapy models that have been used successfully with Latino families and introduces Latino-centered approaches in clinical practice such as the use of a cultural and ecological approach to assessment (i.e., genogram). In Chapter 8, a number of important recommendations to enhance a balance between clinical and cultural dimensions are also presented. Finally, Chapter 9 provides a synthesis of critical issues covered in the preceding chapters, outlines implications for counselor training and supervision, and offers a set of culture-specific competencies. Chapter 9 ends with a discussion of the challenges ahead.

It is important to note that the term *Latino* instead of *Hispanic* is used throughout the text. It is the opinion of the authors that the term Latino represents a renewed sociopolitical consciousness and ethnic pride about one's heritage. Evidence of the term's popularity is reflected in preliminary 2000 Census reports in which Latino is used to describe demographic profiles of this population. Chapter 2 provides a rationale for the use of the term.

Acknowledgments

A special acknowledgment is extended to several individuals whose scholarly contributions inspired us to write this book. These individuals are Celia Jaes Falicov, Ph.D, whose pioneering work on counseling Latino families set the stage for us to pursue this challenging project, given that there is a paucity in the literature on this topic; Freddy Paniagua, Ph.D., who provided detailed comments on ways to improve earlier versions of the book manuscript (we also thank him for his invaluable contributions to the field, particularly his work on assessment and treatment guidelines for different cultural/ethnic groups); and Paul Pedersen, Ph.D., Series Editor, for believing in us and for being instrumental in initiating this project. He also provided us with suggestions on how to strengthen aspects of the book.

Our heartfelt thanks go to our clients, whether through direct service delivery or through supervision of our students and staff. This work is the product of their courage and survival and the many lessons they have taught us.

We wish to thank our friends, colleagues, and families for encouraging us to pursue this project. These individuals are Barry Hensel, Ph.D., clinical director of Circles of Care, Inc., for his continued support throughout the project; and James Braun, Ed.S., staff member at Circles of Care, Inc., in Florida, who provided resource materials.

We are truly indebted to the many people who helped us during the preparation of the book manuscript. A special thanks goes to Jeannette Gordon Reinoso and Shannon Adams, graduate students in the Department of Counseling Psychology at Arizona State University, for their skillful work in compiling and reviewing references for the book and to Solmerina Aponte, graduate student in Latin American and Caribbean Studies at the University at Albany, who crafted a concise glossary of terms and assisted in obtaining demographic information on the Latino population. We also want to thank the students enrolled in the Counseling Latinos course at Arizona State University, who offered new perspectives that were integrated into the book.

Finally, we are indebted to our immediate and extended families who were supportive during the book's preparation. Our sincere gratitude goes to George Cooper for his constant encouragement; Nisa Pilar Cooper for her enthusiasm in providing clerical assistance; Jonathan Gallardo-Cooper for his wit and help in locating library resources; and Lourdes, Damaris, Alexis Diana, and Carlos Santiago for their patience and love.

Para nuestros padres y familias . . .
la fuente de nuestra alegría, motivación y orgullo

(To our parents and families . . .
the source of our joy, motivation, and pride)

Apolinar Arredondo y Eva Zaldivar de Arredondo
Ignacio Lorenzo Gallardo y Otilia Reinosa de Gallardo
Jacinto Rivera y Jenny Rodriguez de Rivera

PART I

Overview

1

Understanding Latino Perspectives

The Multicultural Counseling Competencies

Cuando una puerta se cierra, otra abre.
When one door shuts, another opens.

Rovira, 1984, p. 158

Objectives

- To examine the Multicultural Counseling Competencies (MCCs) (Arredondo et al., 1996; Sue et al., 1992) and other culture-specific guidelines as frameworks for understanding Latino perspectives in counseling.
- To review the Dimensions of Personal Identity Model (Arredondo & Glauner, 1992) and its adaptation to Latino Dimensions of Personal Identity.
- To examine *Mestizo* and Latino-specific models and frameworks.

Competencies

As a result of studying this chapter, counselors will:

- Have knowledge of the historical and political context for the development of multicultural and culture-specific competencies and guidelines in the fields of counseling and psychology.

Latino-Specific Competencies

AWARENESS

- Culturally skilled counselors are aware of competency-based models and guidelines relevant to working with clients in general and with Latinos specifically.

KNOWLEDGE

- Culturally skilled counselors have knowledge about the historical and political context for the development of multicultural and culture-specific competencies and guidelines in the fields of counseling and psychology.
- Culturally skilled counselors are able to describe Latino-specific models and frameworks that can serve as reference points when working with Latino clients.

SKILLS

- Culturally skilled counselors are able to conceptualize the Dimensions of Personal Identity Model for working with individuals from different Latino groups.
- Culturally skilled counselors can identify specific MCCs and guidelines that can be resources for their work with Latino clients and institutions that serve them.

Self-Assessment

Directions: Answer True or False. The correct responses are at the end of the chapter.

T	F	1. The MCCs are ethnic specific.
T	F	2. The MCCs are a product of the National Association of Social Workers.
T	F	3. There is a Hispanic/Latino-based psychology.
T	F	4. The MCCs specify guidelines for counselor racial awareness.
T	F	5. There are dimensions of personal identity that are relevant to Latino groups.
T	F	6. The Dimensions of Personal Identity Model can be applied to both the individual and family.
T	F	7. A *Mestizo* model of identity development includes the individual's phenotype.
T	F	8. A culturally skilled counselor is aware that sociopolitical influences play a role in understanding the life experiences of Latino clients.

T   F   9. Awareness, knowledge, and skills are the components of the MCCs.

T   F   10. The Latino-Specific Competencies were developed at the same time as the MCCs.

Introduction

Both individual and institutional histories are valuable resources to draw on in recapping the evolution of the counseling profession's increasing prioritization of multicultural and culture-specific education, research, and practice. Although many of today's more recently graduated counselors and psychologists may have an appreciation of and may actually have been schooled through multicultural counseling coursework and research, it still seems appropriate to describe briefly how we arrived at today's status quo. In this introduction, historical Latino touchstones in this evolutionary process are also presented.

The counseling and psychology professions' limited focus on multiculturalism and on ethnic- and racial-specific groups has been acknowledged in the literature since the 1960s, when Gilbert Wrenn (1962) used the term *culturally encapsulated counselors.* Although publications were sparse and psychologists and counselors from ethnic and racial minority backgrounds were few, there was a grassroots effort to make culture and race more visible and legitimate areas of study within the fields of counseling and psychology. Influenced by the civil rights movement of the 1960s, a handful of ethnic and racial minority professionals assumed their personal power in both the American Counseling Association (ACA) (formerly the American Personnel and Guidance Association) and the American Psychological Association (APA). As a result of the efforts of such pioneers as Martha Bernal, Amado Padilla, Manuel Ramirez III, and Art Ruiz in the 1970s, Latino-based research began to be published alongside studies of African Americans, Asian Americans, and American Indians, and to be conducted by individuals of those ethnic and racial heritage backgrounds.

In the mid to late 1970s, articles on counseling the culturally different appeared in ACA publications, primarily in special issues of the *Personnel and Guidance Journal.* Under the editorship of Derald Wing Sue, the topics of culture, ethnicity, and race received deliberate attention. Featured articles by ethnic and racial minority researchers and educators provided an opening to descriptive and empirically based studies about different groups. Counselor educators such as the late Art Rene Ruiz offered contributions about Latino experiences and worldviews. After all, it was the post-civil rights era; segregation had ended, bilingual education was offered in public schools, and community counseling centers were flourishing. Federal funds from the National Institute of Mental Health, the Department of Education, and other agencies were allocated for Latino-based research centers in New York, Michigan, and Los Angeles, and Title VII fellowships were available for Latino doctoral students.

The special multicultural-focused counseling publications and articles sprinkled in *The School Counselor, Counseling and Values, and The Counseling Psychologist* affirmed the need to develop greater understanding and skills for education and training, research, assessment, and clinical practice in cross-cultural counseling, as it was then called. Although it was the late 1970s, the profession-at-large was still not ready for the cultural focus. This was manifested through conference presentations and training programs that had low attendance and a minimalist approach. It was what many multicultural specialists described as the "cookbook" or "tell us about them" mindset. Essentially, the focus was on the culturally different client. Whether the clients were Puerto Ricans or African Americans, helping professionals would ask the same type of question: What do I need to know to work with _____?

In the early 1980s, this cookbook tendency began to change. The term *competencies* was used in ACA and APA publications (Arredondo-Dowd, 1981; Sue et al., 1982) to promote culturally relevant counselor preparation. In addition, through the leadership of Allen Ivey, then president of Division 17 (Counseling Psychology) of the American Psychological Association, an Education and Training Committee promulgated a document (Sue et al., 1982) that is a benchmark in the burgeoning field of cultural and multicultural competencies and guidelines today. This publication outlined an historical and sociopolitical rationale for cross-cultural competencies; it was and continues to be the reference point for subsequent and contemporary publications.

In 1992, under the leadership of Thomas Parham, then president of the Association of Multicultural Counseling and Development (AMCD), "Multicultural Counseling Competencies and Standards: A Call to the Profession" (Sue, Arredondo, & McDavis, 1992) was published. These 31 competencies were organized into three domains: Counselor Awareness of Own Values and Attitudes, Counselor Awareness of Client's Worldview, and Culturally Competent Strategies and Interventions, and into three learning dimensions: awareness, knowledge, and skills. Aside from the ethical standards of both the ACA and the APA, few competency documents have been developed to guide education and practice and to give emphasis to holistic approaches. The Multicultural Counseling Competencies (MCCs) began to fill this void because historically, cultural, ethnic, and racial factors had been ignored. It should be noted that the Association of Marriage and Family Therapy, National Association of Social Work, and National Association of School

Psychologists have also included multicultural sensitivity in their ethical standards.

In addition, two other premises were advanced. One highlights the fact that all individuals, institutions, and training programs are culture bound. The other recognizes the need not only for broad-based multicultural guidelines but also for culture-specific perspectives, for example, African American, Caucasian, and Latino.

In 1996, the AMCD Professional Development Committee added depth to the 31 competency statements. "Operationalization of the Multicultural Counseling Competencies" (Arredondo et al., 1996) provides 119 behavioral statements addressing awareness, knowledge, and skills in the three domains. This document serves as a springboard for curriculum development, research and assessment, and the development of competencies in other areas of counseling practice, for example,, school, family, gay and lesbian concerns, and so forth. In effect, the MCCs have catalyzed new thinking and changes at various levels and in different institutions.

Related Guidelines

The important role of culture, race, and language, as both personal and institutional phenomena, has been addressed in several ways by the APA. Examples include (a) the establishment of Division 45, the Society for the Psychological Study of Ethnic Minority Issues; (b) support for the National Hispanic Psychological Association and other ethnic-specific associations; (c) publication of *Guidelines for Providers of Culturally and Linguistically Sensitive Services* (American Psychological Association, 1990); (d) interdivisional collaboration and publication of a presentation on "Best Practices for Promoting Diversity" (Arredondo, 2000); and (e) the publication of *Guidelines for Research in Ethnic Minority Communities* (Council of National Associations for the Advancement of Ethnic Minority Issues, 2000). Under review at this time are *Guidelines for Multicultural Counseling Proficiency for Psychologists: Implications for Education and Training, Research and Clinical Practice* (American Psychological Association, in press). This document is designed to offer guidelines for awareness, knowledge, and skills in the three previously specified areas. If accepted, the guidelines will parallel *Guidelines for Psychotherapy With Gay, Lesbian, and Bisexual Clients* (American Psychological Association, 1999) and specific guidelines for addressing women in counseling developed by Division 17, Counseling Psychology, entitled, "The Division 17 Principles Concerning the Counseling/ Psychotherapy of Women: Rationale and Implementation" (Fitzgerald & Nutt, 1986). Together, these documents provide guidance to educators and clinicians in both broad and specific ways.

Contemporary Perspectives on
Multicultural Counseling Competencies

Multicultural counseling has been described as the fourth force in counseling (Pedersen, 1999). The proliferation of literature in this area has erupted since the early 1990s. Multicultural counseling paradigms, racial identity models, ethnic-specific identity models, and instruments designed to assess multicultural competency (Arredondo et al., 1996; D'Andrea & Daniels, 1995; Ponterotto, 1988; Ponterotto & Pedersen, 1993; Sodowsky, Taffe, Gutkins, & Wise, 1992) are among the topics under discussion. In addition, research to assess multicultural competency (Holcomb-McCoy & Myers, 1999) with instruments specific to counselor attitudes and awareness, as well as outcome-based studies, are beginning to identify competencies that may be most predictive of culturally effective practice. There is new empirical research, described in such journals as the *Hispanic Journal of Behavioral Sciences and the Journal of Multicultural Counseling and Development.* These publications take ethnicity and race into account as well as such factors as acculturation, biracial identity, and other constructs that have historically been neglected in traditional psychology.

Culture-specific competencies for culturally informed education and practice are being promoted through ethnic-specific literature and videotapes. One example is *Innovative Approaches to Counseling Latina/o People,* a film that includes a demonstration of bilingual (Spanish-English) counseling (Microtraining Associates, 1999). Specific to Latinos, there is the *Psychology of the Americas: Mestizo Perspectives in Personality and Mental Health* (Ramirez, 1983), *Research With Hispanic Populations* (Marín & Marín, 1991), *Theoretical and Conceptual Issues in Hispanic Mental Health* (Malgady & Rodriguez, 1994), *Hispanic Psychology: Critical Issues in Theory and Research* (Padilla, 1995), *Latino Families in Therapy: A Guide to Multicultural Practice* (Falicov, 1998), *Psychological Interventions and Research With Latino Populations* (Garcia & Zea, 1997), and *Family Therapy With Hispanics: Toward Appreciating Diversity* (Flores & Carey, 2000). There are special issues on current directions in Chicano/a psychology (*The Counseling Psychologist,* 2001) relating to various issues among Latinos and across different sectors of the heterogeneous Latino population, underscoring the importance of the development of Latino-specific competencies. Throughout this book, Latino-specific competencies will be recommended.

Multicultural and culture-specific lenses broaden our understanding because they draw on history, anthropology, sociology, political processes, economics, and phenomena about human development from both etic and emic perspectives. The latter inform educators and practitioners about the relevance of culture specificity and relativity versus cultural universality. Furthermore, as will be learned from this text, emic perspectives are not static or dogmatic. As attention is given to Latinos as a cultural group, the heterogeneity among Latino ethnic groups and within-ethnic group differences also emerge, leading to further deconstruction of beliefs and stereotypes that have been promulgated as facts. The evolution of culture- and ethnic-specific paradigms already suggests the possibility that competencies may be needed for effective practice with different Latino groups, for example, Dominicans, people of Mexican descent, Puerto Ricans, and so forth.

As the discourse about multiculturalism and multicultural competencies increases, so too do the viewpoints. There is no singular school of thought about multiculturalism (Arredondo, 1998; Fischer, Jome, & Atkinson, 1998; Fukuyama, 1990; Locke, 1992), which is also the case in other major areas within psychology, including behaviorism and humanistic/existential and psychoanalytic/psychodynamic theories. Rather, there are differing platforms based on a professional's preferences and biases. Thus, for some, multiculturalism is driven by race- and culture-based models, whereas for others it is driven by the MCCs, and yet another paradigm is called the common factors approach (Fischer et al., 1998; Frank & Frank, 1991).

To many who are unfamiliar with the multicultural competencies and culture-specific guidelines, all of this may be far too confusing because of the integrative concepts inherent in these distinctive approaches. However, the diversity is also a statement about the depth and breadth of multiculturalism as a framework for creating meaning about human behavior in counseling and psychology. The challenge remains for educators, researchers, and practitioners to determine how to best draw from the various models so that their work continually focuses on "becoming" competent in culture-specific ways.

Identity Paradigms

Multicultural and culture-specific foci in education and training have drawn considerable attention to identity paradigms. Theories of cognitive, social, moral, and identity development taught as universal models have not been inclusive of ethnic/racial minority groups or of the influence of culture. Even Erikson's (1968) model of identity development, which has been widely used to explain identity-related tasks over the lifetime, has been criticized as not being relevant to women's developmental processes nor culturally sensitive (McGoldrick & Carter, 1998). Essentially, most theories taught and research conducted are based on a limited slice of the population. Latinos rarely fit in because, heretofore, there has been a greater emphasis and comparative focus on Black and White cultural groups.

One of the challenges in the field of multiculturalism is to articulate the centrality of culture, ethnicity, and race as dynamic dimensions of identity that also interact with other identity statuses. More recently, there have been discussions in the literature about the phenomenon of multiple identities (D'Andrea & Arredondo, 2000; Robinson & Howard-Hamilton, 2000) and biracial and multiracial identity (Poston, 1990; Root, 1992; Wehrly, Kenney, & Kenney, 1999). Various stage models have been proposed similar to Racial Cultural Identity Development (RCID) (Sue & Sue, 1990), Nigresence identity (Cross, 1991), White identity (Hardiman, 1982; Helms, 1984, 1995; Ponterotto, 1988), and minority identity (Atkinson, Morten, & Sue, 1983). Specific to Latinos are the Mestizo multicultural/multiracial perspective (M. Ramirez, 1998), the psycho- socio-cultural experience model (Arciniega, Casaus, & Castillo, 1987), the Latino Identity Development Model (Ruiz, 1990), and other ethnic identity models (Arredondo & Santiago-Rivera, 2000; Bernal & Knight, 1993; Phinney, 1993).

In this section, three identity models will be introduced. They will be referenced throughout the text, among others, because of their applicability to understanding Latino perspectives, worldviews, and within/across-group differences.

Dimensions of Personal Identity Model

In an attempt to view individuals holistically, and as a means to demonstrate the interrelationship among different identity statuses, the Dimensions of Personal Identity Model (Arredondo & Glauner, 1992) was introduced in the 1996 MCCs (Arredondo et al., 1996). The model (see Figure 1.1) describes multiple identity constructs (A, B, and C dimensions) that allow individuals to define and determine which dimensions have greatest salience for them at a given point in time.

The A dimensions are conceptualized as those that are least changeable because they are the result of an act of birth or of a life-altering experience. These include age, culture, ethnicity, race, sexual orientation, language, physical disability, and social class. The majority of these dimensions are protected by some form of federal or state legislation. Because many of the dimensions are visible, they often become the focus of prejudice, bias, and discrimination. As might also be expected, individuals hold both positive and negative perceptions about these dimensions of themselves, and this affects their self-concept, self-esteem, and personal empowerment. In addition, bias about the dimensions is often reflexively applied to others based on stereotypes or other learned thinking. Counselors are not immune to this behavior. They, too, may attribute value to different dimensions based on their particular preferences and worldview. Counselors may assume that a client of Mexican descent prefers to speak Spanish only and is Catholic and of lower socioeconomic status. If this mind-set enters the counseling setting, the building of an authentic therapeutic relationship will suffer.

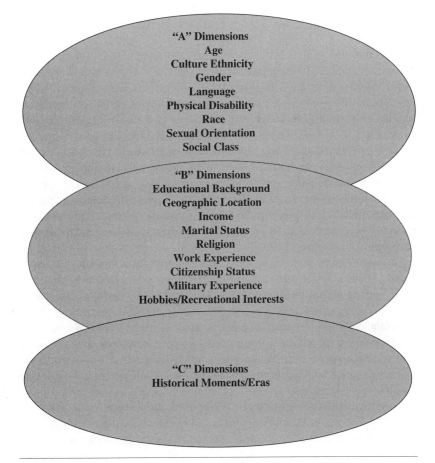

Figure 1.1. Dimensions of Personality Identity
SOURCE: Stevens (1973).

The B dimensions are less visible dimensions and might also be portrayed as developmental, although they are not necessarily age bound. They include educational background, geographic location, income, relationship status, spirituality/religion, work experience, citizenship status, military experience, and hobbies/recreational interests.[1] If a counselor does not get beyond the A dimensions, exploration of several of the B dimensions may be ignored. These dimensions seem to embody the consequences of A and C (Arredondo et al., 1996). For example, a phenotypically White Latino who left Cuba prior to, or as a result of the Castro regime likely benefited from supportive U.S. foreign policies at the time. Thus, economic and social support services facilitated occupation/work opportunities for many individuals. This does not continue to be so for refugees who fled Cuba in the early 1980s. Therefore, this example points out that the C dimension is an important element in people's lives.

The C dimension adds historical contexts and other external forces to the human experience. For example, immigration is a historical experience that comes about for a variety of reasons. As a result, an individual's and a family's sense of identity and self-efficacy are affected. The model invites counselors to view Latino immigrants beyond that status, which usually engenders a deficit perspective, to one that considers the A and B dimensions as well as the strengths required to leave one's homeland. In other words, the client needs to be understood in terms of multiple contexts. Immigrants from a rural Guatemalan town may be perceived as different, even in a Latino agency, because of their indigenous appearance (phenotype, dress, and differences in Spanish language dialects); to provide the proper services, historical and political data must be assembled to know why they left their homeland and to identify their coping strategies.

The model has been discussed as it applies to family counseling (Rotter & Casado, 1998), individual counseling (Robinson & Howard-Hamilton, 2000), and organizational consulting (Arredondo et al., 1996). For the latter, Arredondo has outlined the identity profile of different organizations drawing on the different dimensions. For example, in the majority of counselor and counseling psychology training programs, educators are primarily White; administrators are White males; all have a doctorate (educational experience), and many if not most have their academic position as their one and only work experience.

The utility of the Dimensions of Personal Identity Model is far-reaching because there are many starting points for conceptualizing individual and organizational issues. For educators and practitioners, the model offers ways to expand their thinking about themselves and others, in terms of their multiple identities, worldviews, and life experiences, and to bring a strength versus deficit or pathology perspective to interpersonal, helping encounters. Moreover, this model can also be useful for understanding within- and across-Latino group differences in agencies that are Latino- focused and staffed.

Latino Dimensions of the Personal Identity Model

It has already been posited that the within- and between-Latino ethnic group differences are considerable. To assume sameness about the different ethnic groups—such as Colombians, Cubans, Dominicans, and Puerto Ricans—would be tantamount to using stereotypes to know an individual and a group's worldview. The aforementioned groups have different histories, sociopolitical influences and relationships, forms of government, and economic resources and agendas. All of these factors and numerous others render the ethnic groups dissimilar on many contextual levels. Thus, in counseling, the individual's presenting issues and objectives have to be placed and viewed through various contextual lenses.

Through the use of the Latino Dimensions of Personal Identity Model (Arredondo & Santiago-Rivera, 2000), counselors have another reference point for conceptualizing the individual and family Latino experience. For example, a fifth-generation female college student of Mexican American heritage from California will have a different identity profile than a female student who grew up on the island of Puerto Rico and is attending a U.S. mainland educational institution for the first time. Although they may share some A and B dimensions, their C dimension will be quite different.

Another example relates to the provision of counseling to Latino families in which one parent is Mexican American, the other is first-generation Dominican, and the teenage children were born in the United States. What might be the shared and different dimensions of identity? (See Figure 1.2.) With this family, the factors of acculturation, language use and preference, gender differences in child rearing and expectations, social networks, and citizenship status may be important variables to consider. By referencing the A and B dimensions, a counselor may facilitate the exchange of information among family members while amplifying his or her own appreciation for working with individuals and the whole unit simultaneously.

These examples suggest that a counselor or counselor educator must step back and attempt to understand individuals and families holistically, not simply in terms of assumptions the counselor makes based on visible ethnic identity. This is not to suggest that ethnicity or ethnic identity should be overlooked; rather, this is to indicate that there may be different identity dimensions and contextual factors that are more salient to individuals at the time they present for counseling, including geographic location, distance and differences in environment from their primary home, work opportunities, and social class.

Mestizo Models of Identity Development

Mestizo refers to the synthesis of indigenous and European heritage. According to M. Ramirez (1998), most people in the Americas can identify themselves as *Mestizo* based on the history of European conquest of Mexico and the Caribbean and resulting intermarriage with American Indian peoples. A *Mestizo* automatically has a dual identity. Individuals carry with them and transmit a sense of pluralism "representing a synthesis of different lifestyles, values, perceptual and thinking styles, and coping techniques" (M. Ramirez, 1998, p. 22).

The *Mestizo* identity development paradigm is contrasted with the European, with the latter not embracing the coexistence of two or more cultures. Rather, bicultural or multiracial people face an identity crisis because they believe

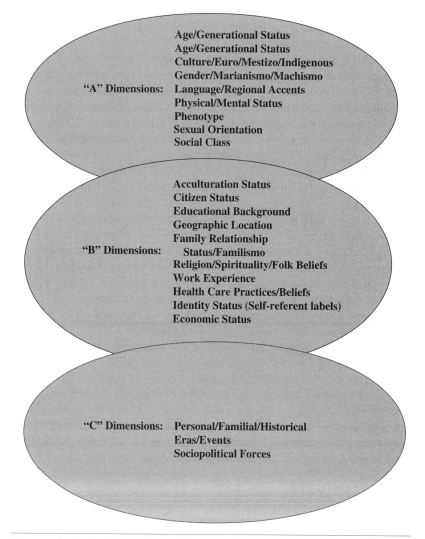

Figure 1.2. Latino Dimensions of Family and Personal Identity

that they must assimilate into the dominant or superior White culture (M. Ramirez, 1998). *Mestizo* heritage also introduces other salient and visible factors into consideration including phenotype, generational differences, social class, and socioeconomic status. Within a family of *Mestizo* heritage, it is not uncommon to have family members who look very different from one another in terms of color and indigenous versus European features. According to the literature, people with more European or Caucasian features enjoy benefits and privileges that visibly *Mestizo* individuals may not. One only needs to look at Latino performers, television anchors, or sitcom and soap opera actors to take note of the preponderance of lighter skinned, blue-eyed performers. These examples demonstrate the superiority of the Caucasian profile. Arciniega et al.'s (1987) psycho-socio-cultural experience model demonstrates the varying levels of contact of European and indigenous peoples. Counseling professionals, it would seem, need to be knowledgeable about the complexity of Latino identity and the different histories and backgrounds that influence and define this growing population in the United States (Comas-Díaz, 1996; Hayes-Bautista, 1978; Ruiz, 1990).

Framework for Latino-Specific Competencies

This section is designed to enhance the discussion about the need to develop and articulate competencies specific to working with Latino clients or with Latino-centered institutions and agencies. Another goal is to educate future professionals on a subject matter that has been minimally introduced, if at all, in counselor preparation and supervision and forms of clinical practice. It should be noted, however, that this discussion of proposed Latino-specific competencies is done with the understanding that there is great latitude and differentiation among individuals and within the different ethnic or nationality groups that might be categorized as Latino. In other words, within- and across-group differences need to be acknowledged as a starting point. The issue is further discussed in subsequent chapters.

In counselor training and practice, varying multicultural frameworks are being advanced, all with relevancy to Latino-referenced approaches and competencies. These include models for Whites, Blacks, and *Mestizos* (Carter, 1995; Cross, 1991; Helms, 1995; M. Ramirez, 1998); minority (Sue, 1978) and Hispanic ethnic identity (Phinney, 1993; Ruiz, 1990); multicultural counseling competencies (Arredondo et al., 1996; Sue et al., 1992); family life cycle (Falicov, 1999; Moore Hines, Garcia-Preto, McGoldrick, Almeida, & Weltman, 1999); and the common factors framework (Fischer et al., 1998). In this section, we shall recommend behavioral statements that reflect the three dimensions of awareness, knowledge, and skills and the three broad domains previously articulated.

The unifying concepts for the suggested Latino-based competencies are worldviews and value orientations, culture-specific historical knowledge about different ethnic groups that provides a context for understanding the variation and similarity of worldviews and value orientations, counselors' awareness of their own cultural values and biases, and, of course, identity models. The MCC framework provides the basis for the Latino-based competencies that follow.

Counselor Awareness of Own Values and Biases

Culturally competent counselors "believe that cultural self-awareness and sensitivity to one's own cultural heritage is essential" (Arredondo et al., 1996, p. 57). Culturally competent counselors "can identify specific attitudes, beliefs, and values from their own heritage and cultural learning that support behaviors that demonstrate respect and valuing of differences and those that impede or hinder respect and valuing of differences" (Arredondo et al., 1996, p. 57) *as this relates to clients, peers, instructors, and others in the community of Latino heritage.* "Culturally skilled counselors recognize their sources of discomfort with differences that exist between themselves and clients in terms of race, ethnicity, and culture" (Arredondo et al., 1996, p. 58) *and can describe those specific to individuals of Latino heritage based on real experiences and/or stereotypes they may hold.*

Counselor Awareness of Client's Worldview

Culturally competent counselors "possess specific knowledge and information about the particular group with which they are working" and "understand and can explain the historical point of contact with dominant society for various ethnic groups" (Arredondo et al., 1996, p. 64), *including all Latinos of varying nationalities, such as Mexican, Cuban, and Puerto Rican heritage.* "Culturally skilled counselors understand and have knowledge about sociopolitical influences that impinge on the life of many Latinos. Immigration issues, poverty, racism, stereotyping, and powerlessness may affect self-esteem and self-concept in the counseling process" (Arredondo et al., 1996, p. 65). *Culturally skilled counselors also have knowledge about the impact of language differences.*

Culturally Appropriate Intervention Strategies

Culturally skilled counselors "can describe concrete examples of how they may use intrinsic help-giving networks from a variety of client communities" (Arredondo et al., 1996, p. 68), *including networks for clients of Latino heritage and from varying socioeconomic and educational backgrounds.* "Culturally skilled counselors share knowledge of the potential bias in assessment instruments and use procedures and interpret findings in a way that recognizes the cultural and linguistic characteristics of the clients" (Arredondo et al., 1996, p. 69). *With Latino clients, culturally skilled counselors also inquire about preferences for language use and experiences with standardized testing practices, reviewing the relevancy of test norms, clarifying how test results will be used, and having supervision from culturally competent counselors. In this process, counselors know the limits of interpreters and translated tests.*

Latino-Specific Competencies

These are broad areas and specific competencies that may apply. However, in getting more culture-specific, we might have culture-specific competencies in working with Latinos,

1. Understand the concepts and terms of *personalismo, familismo, respeto, dignidad,* and *orgullo* and their meaning for relationship building with clients of Latino heritage.
2. Recognize the role of spirituality and formalized religion for individual Latino clients.
3. Can determine the counseling approach that may be most suitable for the individual client based on the presenting issue(s) and expected outcomes from counseling, previous experience in counseling, levels of acculturation, migration issues, gender role socialization, socioeconomic status, educational attainment, language proficiency (e.g., level of English language-speaking ability), and ethnic/racial identity status.
4. Can describe their own level of ethnic/racial identity as it may facilitate or impede the counseling alliance with individuals of varying Latino heritage and phenotype.
5. Can identify and modify approaches to be culturally effective.

Summary

This chapter provided a variety of springboards for understanding the heterogeneity of Latino perspectives. In particular, it summarized the evolution of multiculturalism as a force in counseling and psychology, briefly described the various documents that are serving as guidelines, discussed the development and increasing application of MCCs for purposes of education and practice, reviewed several identity models to help us understand the complexity of the human experience in context, described the Dimensions of Personal Identity for Latinos framework, and offered a variety of suggestions of possible Latino-Specific Competencies. This foundational discussion is further explored throughout subsequent chapters

Correct Answers to Self-Assessment

1. False. The MCCs were developed as general guidelines for all ethnic/cultural groups. (See pages 6-7.)
2. False. The MCCS were developed under the auspices of the Association of Multicultural Counseling and Development of the American Counseling Association. (See page 6.)

3. True. Several classic works have been written about the psychology of Latinos. (See page 8.)

4. True. Racial awareness is an important dimension of identity. (See pages 9-10.)

5. True. The Dimensions of Personal Identity Model incorporates an expanded repertoire of individual characteristics to include historical contexts and external forces. (See pages 10-12.)

6. True. The Latino Dimensions of Personal Identity Model can assist in conceptualizing the individual and Latino family experience. (See pages 12-13.)

7. True. *Mestizo* refers to the blending of indigenous and European heritage resulting in a bicultural identity. (See pages 13-15.)

8. True. Counselors are aware of such issues as immigration, poverty, language difference, racism, and stereotyping that encroach on the lives of many Latinos. (See pages 13-15 and Figure 1.2.)

9. True. The MCCs consist of three components: awareness, knowledge, and skills. (See page 6 and throughout chapter.)

10. False. The MCCs provide the basis for the Latino-Specific Competencies framework. (See pages 15-16.)

NOTE

1. The B dimensions have been modified by Arredondo to be more inclusive. Relationship status replaces marital status, spirituality has been added to religion, and income has been removed. For the latter, this is seen as a further consequence of the interactions among A and B dimensions.

2

Understanding Latino Families

Historical and Sociopolitical Multicultural Contexts

La familia es el corazón y espíritu de la cultura Latina.
The family is the heart and soul of Latino culture.

Objectives

- To provide historical perspectives about the different Latino groups, including their means and point of entry into the United States.
- To review the role of situation, region, neighborhood, and other contexts that affect an individual and family's experiences in the United States.

Competencies

As a result of studying this chapter, counselors will:

- Be knowledgeable about the varying historical experiences of the three largest Latino groups and the more recent immigrant and refugee groups.

Latino-Specific Competencies

AWARENESS

- Culturally skilled counselors can identify biases and assumptions, both positive and negative, they have about Latino clients and their families that may affect a counseling relationship.

KNOWLEDGE
- Culturally skilled counselors can describe the regional, situational, and sociopolitical contexts that have influenced Latino clients.
- Culturally skilled counselors can discuss the differences among Latino groups based on national identity and migration patterns and other historical experiences.

SKILLS
- Culturally skilled counselors can differentiate among the various Latino groups and incorporate specific knowledge about the migration experiences of a particular Latino group in understanding the family's concerns and problems.
- Culturally skilled counselors can identify specific historical events that may have directly or indirectly affected family functioning.

Self-Assessment

Directions: Answer True or False. The correct responses are at the end of the chapter.

T   F   1. In the early part of the 20th century, rapid industrialization of the United States increased the flow of migration from Mexico.

T   F   2. The southwestern states such as Texas, Arizona, and California were once Mexican territory.

T   F   3. The Puerto Rican presence in the United States has a much longer history than the Mexican presence in this country.

T   F   4. Because Puerto Ricans have U.S. citizenship status, they do not experience oppression in this country.

T   F   5. Cuban migration to the United States is said to have occurred in waves.

T   F   6. Dominicans are considered one of the newest immigrant groups.

T   F   7. Central and South Americans are a mixture of Indian, African, and European cultures.

T   F   8. A significant number of immigrants from El Salvador and Guatemala came to this country seeking political asylum.

T   F   9. The migration patterns of the Mexican, Puerto Rican, Cuban, Dominican, and Central and South American populations are similar.

T   F   10. Central Americans are more likely to have emigrated as political refugees.

Introduction

To be culturally competent when working with a Latino client and family, counselors must have knowledge about the different modes and points of entry that brought people of Latino heritage to the United States as well as the roots of the minority status that is still attributed to them. For the three major groups, those of Mexican, Puerto Rican, and Cuban heritage, there are three different story lines. In addition, for more recent immigrant and refugee communities from Central America, for smaller groups such as Dominicans, and for immigrants from South America and Spain, there are different historical and political backgrounds that can inform a counselor's understanding.

This introductory section is not meant to supplant the accounts of historians, political scientists, and others who have written on the experiences of one of the specific Latino groups, for example, Puerto Ricans. However, through discussion in this chapter that focuses on historical, sociopolitical, and geographical contexts, readers will acquire new knowledge about a very heterogeneous cultural group.

Before a discussion of such contexts, a brief explanation is provided for the selection of the term *Latino* instead of *Hispanic* for use in this text.

Latino Versus Hispanic

In the multicultural literature, the terms *Latino* and *Hispanic* have been used interchangeably. In the present text, the term Latino is preferred for the following reasons. First, the group term Hispanic was created by a federal order in 1978 by the Office of Management and Budget. Hispanic is defined as a "person of Mexican, Puerto Rican, Cuban, Central or South American, or other Spanish culture of origin" (Marín & Marín, 1991, p. 20).[1] The primary purpose of this label was to categorize a group of people not by specific country of origin with unique history, religion, indigenous roots, cultural traditions, and foods but rather by a common language, namely Spanish. Unfortunately, the term has led many to believe that Spanish-speaking individuals from these countries of origin have one common culture and that the term refers to a racial category.

Another reason is that some consider the word Hispanic offensive, whereas others merely see it as a bureaucratic term with very little personal significance. Thus, many do not define themselves as Hispanic but rather prefer to be called by their country of origin (e.g., Puerto Rican, Dominican, Cuban, Mexican). Finally, use of the terms *Latino* for a male and *Latina* for a female is growing in popularity among U.S.-born Latinos, representing a political consciousness and a sense of ethnic pride. Falicov (1998) noted that the term Latino is more representative of people from Latin America who have indigenous roots, whereas the term Hispanic, which comes from Spain, excludes such influences. These observations explain why the term Latino is preferred in this text.

Historical and Sociopolitical Background

History has to be turned back nearly 500 years to understand the historical context of events that have resulted in today's varying Latino experiences in the United States. As written, history recounts the travels of Christopher Columbus and Spanish and Portuguese navigators to the New World in search of riches and new territorial acquisitions for their respective royal families. Conquest, enslavement, persecution, conversion, and disempowerment are all words that speak to the treatment of the ancestors of today's Latinos in the United States. The indigenous people of what is today considered Mexico, Central and South America, Puerto Rico, Cuba, and the American Southwest were overpowered by the *conquistadores* and the religious persuasion of the Catholic missionaries who accompanied them. Intermarriage led to the evolution of mixed races and cultures, with the union of European and American Indian evolving into a *Mestizo* culture and the union of European and American Indian and African to the *criollo* or *mulatto* groups. In essence, the three major Latino ethnic groups in the United States, Cuban, Puerto Rican, and Mexican, are multicultural and multiracial beings.

Embedded in the history of Latinos are experiences of domination and subjugation in their homelands to the point of extinction. The Taíno Indians of Puerto Rico, the Dominican Republic, and other Caribbean islands constitute an example of a native people no longer in existence. The Southwest, home of American and Mexican Indian people for centuries, became the site of a holocaust for many when European *conquistadores* and some of the first American White settlers moved to the new Western frontier. Families were displaced, land was lost, and the native peoples became prisoners in their own homelands. Even today, people of Mayan heritage in southern Mexico are marginalized and therefore take up arms to defend the little they have left as an indigenous people.

The history of Latinos also involves African slavery. Cristóbal Colón, it is reported, settled the island of *Hispaniola,* known today as the Dominican Republic and Haiti. The phenotype of *Dominicanos* and *Haitianos* spans the color spectrum, indicative of the synthesis of European and African heritage. African slaves were also taken into Mexico to work in the silver mines of the states of *Zacatecas* and *Guanajuato.* The oppression of the African slaves is rarely discussed. However, in artwork at the Granery in the state of *Guanajuato,* the site of the Mexican revolution of 1821, there are depictions of the deplorable conditions that were experienced by African slaves in the Mexican silver mines.

Although it is not often reported, Latinos may also be of Asian heritage. The Philippine islands, conquered by Spain, were populated by people of Asian heritage. Whereas the native language of the islands is Tagalog, Spanish surnames are commonplace, and in the United States, Filipinos may claim either Asian or Latino heritage. In South America and Mexico, there are settlements of Chinese families as well. Peru is one such example.

Migration Patterns and Geographic Overview

From this early historical backdrop, the clock of time can be fast-forwarded to the 19th century and a number of historical incidents that surround discussions about mode of entry and the contemporary condition of the three largest Latino groups in the United States. Most of this information is not taught in U.S. history courses; therefore, counselor educators and practitioners must accept responsibility for acquiring this knowledge. The brief accounting here can assist in further understanding the differences among Latinos in terms of privilege, access or lack thereof to power, and other consequences of their settlement in this country.

Mexicans

The Mexican population is by far the largest of the Latino groups, with an estimated 20 million residing in the United States (U.S. Bureau of the Census, 2001a). The majority of Mexicans, about 89%, live in Texas, California, New Mexico, Arizona, and Colorado and trace their roots to the Southwest states that were once Mexican territory.[2] Also, in areas such as Chicago, Illinois, Gary, Indiana, and Cleveland, Ohio, there are long-established communities of Mexican families whose employers have been steel and automobile manufacturers.

Since the early 1900s, the ebb and flow of migration has varied depending on the economic and political forces both within Mexico and the United States. For instance, one of the main triggers of migration to the United States during the early 1900s before the Great Depression was the need for cheap labor. Mexican labor was favored because of Mexico's proximity and the willingness of Mexicans to work long hours at low wages.

During the early 1900s, the rapid industrialization of the United States, particularly in agriculture, and the demand for cheap labor dramatically increased the flow of migration from Mexico. Mirandé (1985) ascertained that as much as one eighth of the Mexican population came to the United States between 1910 and 1930. Likewise, between 1942 and 1964, the *Bracero* Program provided a continuous supply of contract workers.[3] During this period of time, thousands of Mexicans were recruited and hired to serve as seasonal farm and industrial laborers throughout the United States. In the 21st century, discussions about new types of guest worker programs have ensued between the Mexican and U.S. governments.

In essence, Mexican immigration has been historically tied to changes in the U.S. economy. During times of growth, migration increases, and when there is economic contraction, the demand for Mexican labor decreases. Nonetheless, migration from Mexico continues at a steady pace. Between 1961 and 1980, 14% of all immigrants were from Mexico. From 1981 to 1990, the Mexican proportion of immigrants increased to 23% (Acosta-Belén & Santiago, 1995). The U.S. Department of Justice reported increases of immigration from Mexico at a percentage change of 81.9%. At the end of the 20th century, Mexico remained one of the largest sources of new immigrants to the United States.

It is also well recognized that economic conditions in Mexico, coupled with the need for cheap labor in the United States, prompted significant numbers of people to leave their homeland without going through legal channels, such that the flow of undocumented Mexicans has increased over time. It is difficult to accurately estimate the number of undocumented individuals in this country because most live in Latino communities where they blend in, and friends and neighbors often protect them from being discovered and deported. For instance, in 1996, the undocumented immigrant population residing in the United States was estimated at 5 million, of which 54% were of Mexican heritage (Immigration & Naturalization Service, 2000).

Accounts of U.S. history and portrayals of this history through the popular media, films as well as television, have often omitted or distorted events that have affected people of Mexican heritage. For instance, Mexico's independence from Spain in 1821 is today widely celebrated both in the United States and in Mexico on September 16, and this has important meaning for the relationship between the two countries. Specifically, Mexico's emancipation was short-lived; although Spanish rule was ended, the neighboring United States was beginning its expansionist movement West. Unrest in what was then the northern part of Mexico and is now the U.S. Southwest seemed an invitation for U.S. politicians and the military to view Mexico as the enemy and a threat. Two wars ensued: the War for Texas Independence in 1835 and the Mexican American War of 1846 (Locke, 1992). The outcome of these wars was the Treaty of Guadalupe Hidalgo of 1848 between the United States and Mexico. As a result of its military defeat, Mexico ceded the entire Southwest and California to the United States. This included territory that is now the states of Oklahoma, New Mexico, Nevada, Colorado, Arizona, and Texas. Essentially, Mexican families became disenfranchised in their own homeland as a result. Farms or ranchos were lost, and the White conquerors again had the right to rule and suppress the original landowners.

Further military invasions of Mexico occurred during the time of the Mexican Revolution of 1910 to 1920. The U.S. government saw this internal struggle as an opportunity to continue to gain control of Mexico. Two noteworthy incidents were the occupation of Veracruz by U.S. forces in 1914 and the "Punitive Expedition" into the state of Chihuahua by General Pershing (Locke, 1992). The Mexican foe was Pancho Villa, who had led forces against conquered Mexican towns. Although Villa eluded the Americans in pursuit, many other Mexican people suffered as a result. Again, land and other natural resources in Mexican territory were claimed by the Americans, leading to economic oppression, a contributor to the condition of many descendants of Mexican heritage today.

Loss, disrespect, and psychological and economic oppression were the consequences of these conquests. Mexicans became migrant farm workers in their own homeland. Others, who had been landowners, now worked for White men, and the Spanish language became the "out" language as English-only became the mode of school instruction.

The history of the Southwest likely yields other historical accounts varying from state to state. However, because of the way U.S. history books are written, the impression conveyed is that Mexicans lost to a more powerful American military force fairly and squarely.

Political power among people of Mexican heritage occurs primarily in the Southwest and California, where they have been senators and congressional representatives, cabinet appointees and state legislators. Even today, the number of elected officials of Mexican heritage is not representative of this increasing population. Perhaps the one glimmer of inspiration in the midst of centuries of loss and oppression at multiple levels is the powerful icon known as Cesar Chavez. Chavez is credited not only for spearheading the United Farm Workers in the United States, but also for raising the political consciousness of contemporary Latinos. He is well known for his lifelong commitment to advocating for the rights of migrant farm workers and supporting the civil rights movements of gays, lesbians, women, and African Americans (Novas, 1994).

Puerto Ricans

The Puerto Rican population is considered to be the second-largest Latino group, with an estimated 3 million living in the United States (U.S. Bureau of the Census, 2001a). Specific characteristics of their migration pattern and historical events make this group considerably different from the Mexican population. Moore and Pachon (1985) argued that Puerto Ricans have had a much shorter period of contact with the United States as compared to Mexicans. Specifically, in 1508, Ponce de Leon arrived from Spain and began the colonization of the island of Puerto Rico, which lasted until 1897 (Locke, 1992). Enslavement of the Taíno and Carib Indians was commonplace when the Spaniards took possession of the island. They also introduced African slaves to shoulder the burden of labor.

Puerto Rico had been under Spanish rule for 400 years when, in 1898, the United States took possession of the island after the Spanish American War. With the rising threat of World War I and the political uneasiness surrounding Puerto Rico's status as a U.S. territory, Puerto Ricans were granted U.S. citizenship in 1917. Today, Puerto Ricans who are born and reside on the island are U.S. citizens, making them subject to the military draft. They are also eligible for government-sponsored federal programs such as public assistance; however, they do not pay U.S. income tax and cannot participate in U.S. elections. Interestingly, Puerto Ricans residing on the island participate in U.S. census data collection, but these statistics are reported in separate government documents (Rivera-Batiz & Santiago, 1996).

U.S. citizenship status has allowed Puerto Ricans to travel to and from the United States with no restrictions. This back and forth movement, known as *circular migration,* is considered common among a significant number of unskilled and blue-collar workers who stay in the United States for short periods of time in search of employment, then return to the island (Rivera-Batiz & Santiago, 1996). The available research, although limited, indicates that in extreme cases, this back and forth movement may disrupt schooling and long-term job opportunities for members of a household, suggesting that families may be negatively affected by this migratory pattern.

Although there was a Puerto Rican presence in the United States by 1910, the greatest migration occurred after World War II. Significant numbers settled in the northeastern states, most notably in New York City, where about a 30% of the population lives. About 35% of Puerto Ricans are found in Connecticut, New Jersey, and Massachusetts, and about 20% in the southern states, primarily Florida (Rivera-Batiz & Santiago, 1996; U.S. Bureau of the Census, 2001a). The remaining 15% live in the Midwest and the West, in cities such as Chicago and Los Angeles.

Today, the relationship between the island and the U.S. government continues to be tense. The island of Vieques in Puerto Rico is the site of military testing; many Puerto Ricans believe this is a practice that must cease. A second issue is that of Puerto Rican nationals who want their independence (statehood) and those who prefer to maintain the Commonwealth status. These ideologies have led to referendum votes, with the pro-Commonwealth status prevailing as of this writing.

Cubans

Cubans are the third-largest Latino group, totaling about 1.3 million people (U.S. Bureau of the Census, 2001a). Cuba, an island 30 miles off the coast of the United States, shares many experiences with Puerto Rico, beginning with the arrival of the Spanish *conquistadores.* Cuba's Indian population was oppressed, and slaves from Africa were also brought in to labor in the sugarcane fields and in other ways that exploited the island's natural resources. In 1898, Cuba was also acquired by the United States as a result of the Spanish American War. However, it remained a U.S. territory for a short 3-year period and in 1902 became an independent country.

Although the largest migration movement occurred after the Cuban Revolution in the late 1950s, a significant number of immigrants settled in Key West, Florida, in the early 1900s, establishing cigar manufacturing companies there. Mass migration of Cubans to the United States coincided with the rise to power of Fidel Castro (1956-1959). The threat of communism and the seizure of American-owned sugarcane plantations, oil refineries, and other businesses prompted the speedy departure of many Cubans, particularly the more highly educated and affluent.

Social scientists often describe the Cuban migration pattern as occurring in waves (Masud-Piloto, 1988; Moore & Pachon, 1985). Specifically, the Cuban Revolution triggered what many called the first "mass exodus" of Cubans, who were well-educated, upper class, and fair skinned. Members of this first wave had the economic means to leave Cuba, as well as the educational and professional background to quickly transition into mainstream American society. These individuals are credited with making significant contributions to the economic growth of Key West and Miami (Masud-Piloto, 1988).

The second wave of emigration occurred after the Cuban missile crisis in 1962, when thousands of Cubans fled in small boats and rafts, while others were airlifted; this wave totaled 273,000 people by 1973. Scholars studying this migration phenomenon report that this group, as a whole, received substantial aid from the U.S. government and private sponsors, as well as from fellow Cubans who were already well established in Florida.

The third wave of emigration was triggered by an incident at the Peruvian Embassy in Havana in 1980.[4] Once again, thousands of Cubans left via the port of Mariel in Cuba and thus were given the name *marielitos*. Unfortunately, these refugees were not as well received by Americans as the first two waves of Cuban immigrants had been. At the time of their arrival (1980), fewer resources were available to them, and investigators note that their arrival placed a heavy burden on the city of Miami. Another factor was that these new arrivals did not possess the educational and economic status enjoyed by their earlier counterparts. There were also comments suggesting that the new group comprised individuals that the Cuban government wanted out of Cuba. Nonetheless, Cubans, as a group, were granted refugee status and provided with resources and assistance to resettle in the United States. Another, more recent wave of Cubans, known as the *balseros,* arrived in 1994, and they resembled members of the Mariel boat wave. These Cubans were confronted with a hostile reception by American society (Gonzalez, 2000).

It is well recognized that the first wave of Cuban immigrants, who had financial means and education, were able either to establish their own small businesses or to become employed in their given professions. Also, one of the first bilingual education programs in this country was established in Coral Gables, Florida, in an attempt to speed up the English language acquisition process among Cubans. This strong foundation contributed to the fact that people of Cuban heritage today have the most wealth and are the most educated of all of the Latino groups in the United States and are perceived as the most mainstream group. Cubans have made more economic and educational gains than any other Latino group in the United States. It is also important to point out that the proximity of Cuba and the United States has contributed to a steady flow of individuals wishing to seek asylum. Best known for these attempts have been baseball players, who now enjoy both financial and social status for their athletic accomplishments.

People of Cuban heritage are dispersed across the United States, but it can readily be said that Miami is the *alma* (soul) for Cubans. The evolution of Little Havana as a center for small business owners, housing, and other community practices is indicative of this culture-specific phenomenon. Cubans have elected their own as mayors, congressional representatives, and other officials in the state of Florida.

According to the Cuban American National Council (Boswell, 1994), about 65% of all Cubans reside in Florida, with significant numbers in New Jersey, New York, and California. Interestingly, the Cuban population is steadily declining, unlike the Mexican, Puerto Rican, and Dominican groups. Specifically, in 1970, the Cubans represented 6% of the total Latino population; by 1990, their proportion had declined to 4.7% (Boswell, 1994). As such, they have experienced the lowest growth rate among the various Latino groups. The fact that Cubans are older and have fewer children, as well as the imposed restriction in migration from the home country, contributes to this decline in the population.

Dominicans

The Dominicans are considered one of the newer Latino immigrant groups, and their numbers have reached well over half a million. About 65% of all Dominicans live in the state of New York, with a significant number of the remaining 35% residing in states such as New Jersey, Florida, and Massachusetts (Boswell, 1994; Torres-Saillant & Hernández, 1998).

Dominicans come from the Dominican Republic, which is a country that occupies two thirds of the island of Hispaniola, located in the Caribbean. Haiti occupies the remaining third, which is on the western side of the island. According to historians, this island is where Cristobal Colón first dropped anchor. Equally important, this island witnessed the importation of African slaves. Thus, Dominicans reflect this mixed African and European heritage (*criollo* or *mulatto*) through a range of phenotypes.

What was the mode of entry for Dominicans to the United States? Like other immigrant groups, Dominicans arrived seeking better economic and educational opportunities. This small island has limited natural resources, and although tourism has increased with new resorts and golf courses, this does not provide sufficient employment.

According to Torres-Saillant and Hernández (1998), a series of events occurring in the late 1960s, such as the fall of agricultural production, rise in unemployment, and deteriorating living conditions in the Dominican Republic, triggered a mass exodus of Dominicans, many of whom were coming to the United States illegally. Thus, it is virtually impossible to determine with complete accuracy the total number of Dominicans in the United States.

Novas (1994) argued that significant numbers went to Puerto Rico first because with their similar physical features and characteristics, they easily blend in to Puerto Rican society. Dominicans then gain entry into the United States through Puerto Rico; residents of the island are not required to have passports when traveling to the United States. Although this migration pattern is noteworthy, there has also been a steady increase in Dominicans entering the United States legally, with the number growing from 3,045 in 1961 to 41,405 in 1991 (Torres-Saillant & Hernández, 1998). Equally important, the number of Dominicans in New York City alone rose from about 125,000 in 1980 to 207,000 in 1990, representing a 165% increase in the population in just a 10-year period (Hernández, Rivera-Batiz, & Agodini, 1995).

As previously stated, the largest settlements of Dominicans are the New York City area and Lawrence, Massachusetts. In the latter area, Dominicans have become the largest ethnic/racial minority group in the school system. In both cities, Dominicans have entered the political process and successfully won elected positions as school board members, city council representatives, and state legislators.

Central Americans

Central Americans are people whose countries of origin are Belize, Guatemala, El Salvador, Honduras, Nicaragua, Panama, and Costa Rica. These countries were also part of the Spanish conquest; however, there is considerable heterogeneity in culture and language among the people of this region. For example, Guatemalans have a strong Indian influence and speak a variety of indigenous languages, whereas Costa Ricans have more European ancestry and in some parts of the country speak only English.

It is probably fair to say that there have always been immigrants from Central America to the United States. Again, for reasons of geographical proximity, migration has occurred. This did not become noteworthy until the 1980s, when civil wars in El Salvador, Guatemala, and Nicaragua, in particular, caused many to flee *al norte,* with many settling in the Washington, D.C., area, California, the Southwest states, and other urban areas. Individuals fled torture, imprisonment, impoverished living situations, and other life-threatening conditions, leading many to develop and manifest symptoms of post-traumatic stress disorder. It is reported that those who escaped were primarily from rural areas and undereducated, with fewer skills to obtain employment in contemporary technological workplaces (Leslie & Leitch, 1989).

South Americans

The Spanish-speaking countries of South America consist of Argentina, Bolivia, Chile, Colombia, Ecuador, Paraguay, Peru, Uruguay, and Venezuela. The largest immigrant groups from these countries are from Colombia and Ecuador. In particular, Colombians as a group are well-educated professionals, fluent in English and Spanish, and they have been successful in the U.S. economy. Robinson (1998) noted that about 66% of Colombians in this country have a median income comparable to that of non-Hispanic Whites.

The relationship between the United States and South American countries is different than the U.S. relationship with Cuba, Mexico, Puerto Rico, the Dominican Republic, and the Central American countries previously discussed. Perhaps this is because of the geographical distance, the fact that South America is home to many individuals of European descent who came from England in the 18th century or who fled Nazi oppression, or the fact that the military and dictatorships have until recently been the form of government in many countries. These factors have contributed to a different type of historical and sociopolitical relationship with the United States. Regardless, South American countries and their citizens have not had the same U.S. colonization experience as the other countries previously discussed. Rather, the mode of interaction has more often been driven by economics, including the import and export of products, by military training, and by other less visible, political arrangements.

Although people from Colombia, Argentina, Venezuela, and other countries are heterogeneous, those who have emigrated to the United States from South America have a more privileged profile. The majority who have come to the United States are educated, entrepreneurial, bilingual, and bicultural individuals (Flores & Carey, 2000). These attributes allow individuals and families to cross cultures more readily and to leave their country in times of economic crisis, which is not easily done by unskilled immigrants.

The Central and South American countries have several historical factors in common with Cuba, Mexico, and Puerto Rico. All were visited and colonized by Spanish or Portuguese navigators and *conquistadores*. Although some indigenous groups remain in Peru, Ecuador, Guatemala, Mexico, and even Argentina, most groups were extinguished as a result of colonization. When it comes to mode of entry to the United States, the experiences of South Americans are quite different than those of the other groups previously discussed. None of these areas have been colonized or held as U.S. territories.

Central and South Americans are also a mixture of Indian, African, and European cultures. Each Latin American country has its unique political, social, and economic history that influenced the outmigration of its people. The trends of migration vary among these countries. For instance, during the 1980s, the civil war and violations of human rights in Central America triggered a massive migration from El Salvador and Guatemala. Thousands of Salvadorans and Guatemalans sought refuge to escape war-related violence, such as torture, rape, and the killing of family members. Exact figures for this population are not known because many have not become documented residents out of fear of deportation. The second- and third-largest groups of undocumented Latinos came from two Central American countries: El Salvador and Guatemala (Immigration and Naturalization Service, 2000).

Summary

Initial 2000 census reports indicate that the Latino population is nearly equal to the Black/African American population (Armas, 2001), with new growth in the Southwest and southern states, in particular (U.S. Bureau of the Census, 2001a). These trends, the proximity of the United States to Mexico and Latin American countries, and the long-term historical relations based on imperialistic and adversarial experiences create an interesting dynamic for contemporary relations between the U.S. government and people of Latino heritage, regardless of their generational status.

Working from a competency-based framework, educators and counselors must become knowledgeable about both historical and current contexts for Latinos. If we accept the premise that worldview is influenced by values and beliefs, then we must be cognizant of how history influences people's perspectives and outlooks on a number of interpersonal experiences. For example, if an individual's grandparents left Mexico to reside in the Southwest, say Arizona, before it had statehood, that family's lived experiences would be different from Mexican families who arrived after World War II and more recent immigrants. In this case, uniqueness rather than sameness must be assumed.

Corresponding to this historical backdrop are other critical dimensions that have always been important to the identity and life of Latino families. In the next chapter, there is a discussion of important dimensions such as religion and spirituality, health and illness beliefs, gender socialization, and language. These dimensions are significant to explore in counseling because they are always relevant within this family-centered culture.

Correct Answers to Self-Assessment

1. True. Migration patterns are closely tied to the economic and political climate of the country of origin. (See all of chapter.)

2. True. Much of what we know today as the Southwest states was once Mexican territory. (See pages 24-25.)

3. False. The Mexicans have a much longer period of contact with the United States. (See pages 23-25.)

4. False. Despite their citizenship status, Puerto Ricans like other Latino groups have experienced oppression. (See pages 25-26.)

5. True. There are distinct migration periods where significant numbers of Cubans left Cuba. (See pages 26-28.)

6. True. Dominicans are a new group of Latino immigrants. (See pages 28-29.)

7. True. Indian, African, and European strains are mixed in people of these areas. (See pages 29-31.)

8. True. Many of these immigrants are political refugees. (See pages 29-31.)

9. False. The migration patterns are distinct in that migration not only occurred during different periods of time but also originated in different parts of the Americas. (See all of chapter.)

10. True. Political motives are more common among Central American immigrants. (See pages 29-30.)

NOTES

1. There is considerable confusion about who should be considered Hispanic. Some believe that the term covers individuals from 21 Spanish-speaking countries and two with the native language of Portuguese (Flores & Carey, 2000), whereas others argue that individuals from countries speaking Portuguese are not part of this group (Novas, 1994). Nonetheless, the government created a term that would put them into one group, as it did in categorizing other ethnic groups such as Black/African American, Asian American, and American Indian.

2. Mexicans claimed the Southwest area that is known today as Texas, New Mexico, California, Arizona, Nevada, Utah, and a part of Colorado. About 73,000 early Mexicans settlers lived along the modern Mexican border in the early 19th century (Moore & Pachon, 1985; Novas, 1994).

3. During World War II, there was a desperate need to replace American workers who had gone to war, particularly in the agricultural industry. The *Bracero* Program was established by the United States and the Mexican government to address this labor shortage. Thousands of Mexicans came to the United States as seasonal workers. The term *bracero* literally means "working with one's arms" (Novas, 1994).

4. In April 1980, six Cubans crashed through the gates of the Peruvian Embassy seeking asylum. During the incident, a Cuban guard was killed. The Cuban government wanted to prosecute the men, but the Peruvian government did not want to release them. Before this incident, the U.S. and Cuban governments had been negotiating the release of political prisoners and family reunification efforts. To avoid further political problems, the government announced that anyone wanting to leave should go to the Peruvian Embassy. Unexpectedly and within 78 hours, 10,000

Cubans showed up at the doorstep of the Peruvian Embassy wanting to leave Cuba. A number of prominent Cuban exiles from Miami negotiated with Castro's government to transport them to Florida. This group is known as the Havana 10,000. The negative press often sensationalized the events that led up to this massive migration out of Cuba. The composition of this group was vastly different from previous migratory Cuban groups, consisting of prisoners, homosexuals, and working class people with lower socioeconomic backgrounds and darker skins. Consequently, it has been argued that their transition and process of adaptation has been difficult (Masud-Piloto, 1988).

3

Understanding Latino Families From Multiple Contexts

Essential Frames of Reference

De padres sanos, hijos honrados.
From wholesome parents, honest children.

Rovira, 1984, p. 68

Objectives

- To review conditions and factors such as acculturation, generational differences, ethnic identity, phenotypes, language use and preference, and several other relevant dimensions of the Latino Dimensions of Family and Personal Identity Model (adapted from Arredondo & Glauner, 1992) that render each individual and family as unique.
- To examine the influence of religion as a factor in colonization and its role in worldview formation, gender socialization, and transgenerational values.

Competencies

As a result of studying this chapter, counselors will:
- Be able to describe the influence of religion on Latino worldviews and family relationships and expectations.

- Be able to discuss conditions and factors of acculturation, ethnic identity, socioeconomic differences, phenotypes, and other experiences that contribute to the uniqueness of individuals and Latino families.
- Be sufficiently skilled to prepare a presentation describing the historical, multicultural, multiracial experiences and context that surround Latino families.

Latino-Specific Competencies

AWARENESS
- Culturally skilled counselors can recognize the expectations they hold about family values and interpersonal relationships that may be different from Latino values and practices.

KNOWLEDGE
- Culturally skilled counselors can describe a variety of factors, such as the impact of migration and generational differences in Latino value orientation, that may influence the dynamics of a Latino family.
- Culturally skilled counselors can understand the concepts of *personalismo, respeto, orgullo,* and *compadrazco,* and their meaning for the Latino individual.

SKILLS
- Culturally skilled counselors can identify specific cultural beliefs and practices such as the use of health-related folk remedies that help a family cope with illness.
- Culturally skilled counselors can incorporate specific historic, social, economic, and familial characteristics to accurately conceptualize a family seeking support.

Self-Assessment

Directions: Answer True or False. The correct responses are at the end of the chapter.

T   F   1. Latino identity is multidimensional.
T   F   2. Latino ethnic identity does not change as a result of the acculturation process.
T   F   3. The migration experience affects all family members in the same way.
T   F   4. Kinship systems are not found in Latino culture.
T   F   5. Familistic values remain strong regardless of the level of acculturation.

T   F   6. *Compadres* have an important social function in
                 contemporary society.
T   F   7. The concept of *personalismo* refers to the valuing of
                 personal relationships.
T   F   8. The Catholic religion is not as important as *familismo*.
T   F   9. Latino health beliefs are a combination of religion and
                 native Indian influences.
T   F   10. *Marianismo* refers to female dominance in Latino families.

Introduction

This chapter focuses on describing key frames of reference and value-based concepts that help to understand the Latino family from a multidimensional perspective. Borrowing from such fields as anthropology, sociology, psychology, history, and political science, a variety of culture-based concepts are described to help counselors capture the complexity of people's experiences. The goal is not to create a separate vocabulary but rather to help counselors understand, respect, and work effectively with Latino clients and their families.

In this chapter, we describe terms, concepts, frames of reference, and issues that focus on (a) identity; (b) adaptation and change; (c) family values; (d) religion, spirituality, and beliefs; (e) health and illness beliefs; (f) language; and (g) gender socialization. Particular attention is given to how these areas are interrelated and have become defining forces for the Latino family in times of distress and normal life cycle change. The impact of these dimensions in generating conflict within an individual and/or family system is also described.

Identity and Race

As noted in Chapter 2, Latinos are heterogeneous in national origin and migration histories. Massey, Zambrana, and Alonzo-Bell (1994) wrote that variations are clearly evident in the generational and legal status of Latinos:

> They may be fifth generation Americans descended from Spanish colonists or new immigrants just stepping off the jetway; they may be native-born children of immigrant parents or naturalized citizens; they may be legal immigrants driving across the Rio Grande on a bridge or undocumented migrants swimming underneath. Depending on when and how they got to the United States, Hispanics may know a long history of discrimination and oppression, or they may perceive the United States as a land of opportunity where origins do not matter. (p. 193)

The distinct migratory perspectives outlined in Chapter 2 have important implications for the way in which Latinos self-identify. For instance, the term

Hispano is used in places such as southwestern Colorado and the northern part of New Mexico, reflecting a Latino population that has been in the United States for several centuries and claims origins from Spain. Likewise, it is not uncommon for Latinos of Mexican origin living in the Southwest to call themselves *Mexican, Chicano, Mexican American,* or *Spanish American.*

Puerto Ricans may call themselves *Boricua,* which comes from the word *Borinquen,* the name given to the island of Puerto Rico by the aboriginal *Taíno* Indians. An identity as a *Boricua* reflects a strong connection with the island, whereas Puerto Ricans born in New York may proudly call themselves *Nuyorican* as a statement about their bicultural identity.

Fundamentally, these descriptors point not only to different ways in which individuals from these groups see themselves but also to the importance of using a label that traces their cultural roots to the countries of origin. Also, these labels reflect distinct histories. According to Moore and Pachon (1985), Latinos choose to use such labels to affirm their identity as different from other groups in American society. Others such as M. Ramirez (1998) call the Latino population *La Raza Cosmica,* referring to the within-group diversity.

Scholars from a variety of disciplines have written extensively about the notion of Latino identity. For instance, psychologists such as Falicov (1998) have called it a hybrid identity, whereas political scientists such as Maria de los Angeles Torres (1998) describe the unique characteristics of a border identity in which there is a blending of many cultures. Regardless of the terminology created to explain this phenomenon, the definitive feature of these various conceptualizations is that Latino identity is multidimensional.

Related to identity is the issue of race. The Latino population as a whole is considered a racially mixed group. From a historical perspective, this mixing of races began with the Spanish colonization of North and South America dating back to the 1400s.[1] Until the first settlers arrived in the new land, the inhabitants were indigenous people. The Spaniards explored and settled in the New World, bringing new traditions, language, customs, and most notably Catholicism. The decimation of the indigenous population produced a need for labor; thus, African people were brought as slaves and populated the Spanish colonies. African slaves were primarily brought to the Caribbean and parts of Central and South America. In fact, Santo Domingo, the capital of the Dominican Republic, was the port of entry for the first African slaves brought to the New World in 1502 (Torres-Saillant & Hernández, 1998). The intermingling of Spanish, Indian, and African people over hundreds of years has created a racially mixed Latino population. Acosta-Belén and Sjostrom (1988) stated,

> The *mestizaje* (race mixture) produced by the fusion of the White, Indian and Black races and cultures is one of the most distinctive features of the Spanish conquest and colonization of the Americas, and hence the Latin American and U.S. Hispanic cultures. (p. 85)

In sum, Latino ethnic identity is complex, involving historical migratory patterns from countries of origin, as well as the process of adaptation. Although ethnic labels vary across Latino groups, a strong sense of ethnic identity remains constant, regardless of generations in the United States. It has been argued by leading researchers that bicultural identity is increasingly becoming the norm for Latinos in this country (e.g., Hurtado, Rodriguez, Gurin, & Beals, 1993; Marín, 1993). Latinos have found that although they maintain ties and share common ground with their respective homelands, there are also important differences in their identity and identification with their countries of origin. Latinos in the United States have learned to navigate in what is essentially a multicultural environment in which various cultures coexist. The process of acculturation and mainstreaming into U.S. culture provides sources of identity and loyalties that are incorporated into a new identity. The movement toward a bicultural identity as a consequence of acculturation has its benefits, such as maintaining strong family ties and positive psychological well-being (Flores & Carey, 2000).

Adaptation and Change

Acculturation

The concept of acculturation has been widely studied in a variety of disciplines, primarily anthropology, sociology, and psychology, to explain how individuals adapt to and change in new environments. Our preference is to view acculturation as a sociopsychological phenomenon that is an ongoing process, and thus dynamic in nature. Gerardo Marín (1992), a pioneer in the study of acculturation among Latinos, defined it as

> a process of attitudinal and behavioral change undergone . . . by individuals who reside in multicultural societies (e.g., the United States, Israel, Canada, and Spain), or who come in contact with a new culture due to colonization, invasion, or other political changes. (p. 236)

According to Marín, the process of acculturation depends on (a) the degree to which the individual identifies with the culture of origin, (b) the importance given to having contact with individuals from other cultures, and (c) the "numerical balance" between the people who are part of the majority culture and those who are part of the Latino's culture of origin.

Important dimensions to this process of new learning are changes in attitudes and behaviors. At a basic level, Latinos may forget important historical events or traditions of their culture of origin, Marín thought, while learning new histories and traditions from the host culture. At an intermediate level, Latinos may lose proficiency in the Spanish language, and at a more profound level, there may be changes in core values, beliefs, and norms that guide behavior. For example, Marín (1993) postulated that specific behavioral scripts such as *simpatía* (charming and sociable) may become less important when interacting with people from other cultures; however, these scripts may be more salient when interacting with other Latinos. Likewise, Bernal and Flores-Ortiz (1982) noted that although Latinos are involved with traditions and customs of the home country to varying degrees, they remain committed to their culture of origin, and their connectedness depends on such factors as the pressure to acculturate and the degree to which they are able to return to their homelands.

Although this sense of connectedness may remain, recent data show that Latinos, especially those who arrive at a young age and are educated in this country, have values and beliefs that are more similar to White Americans. A recent survey of more than 2,000 Latinos conducted by *The Washington Post* ("Latinos in America," 2000) and a number of researchers at the Henry J. Kaiser Family Foundation and Harvard University supports earlier research that the process of adaptation and mainstreaming varies widely depending on such factors as the age of migration, level of education, and bilingual (Spanish and English) language abilities. Interestingly, the survey found that Latinos who retained dominant use of the Spanish language have a more traditional value structure than those Latinos who are bilingual.

Falicov (1998) also outlined a variety of theoretical perspectives on this issue, illustrating the complex process of adaptation. First, she theorized that acculturation is a process whereby individuals gradually lose their culture of origin as they adopt the values and behaviors of the new culture. Individuals who undergo acculturation may experience marginalization by the host culture, which often leads to stress. Moreover, stress reactions to this process may have different effects on individuals within a family, and these distinct reactions lead to conflict. Second, Falicov introduced the notion that individuals may learn to navigate or "alternate" between the host culture and culture of origin, depending on the context of the situation. Such an approach allows for the maintenance of cultural traditions, particularly the Spanish language within a family. Third, Latinos may combine aspects of the host culture and native culture to produce what Falicov considers a hybrid culture. Large urban settings allow for such a blending of cultures, which is often reflected in the first and subsequent generations of U.S.-born Latinos. Such contexts allow for interpersonal interaction in a much more pluralistic and multiethnic setting compared to their homelands. Finally, Falicov suggests that individuals within a family who follow an alternation or hybridization model appear to have a wider range of coping behaviors at their disposal and can successfully manage the environment in which they live. However, individuals within such families may experience stress associated with unresolved conflicts concerning their identity, changing value structure, and linguistic differences

(Cervantes, Padilla, & Salgado de Snyder, 1991). Moreover, adolescents, who are undergoing developmental changes, may experience added stress associated with the process of acculturation. This occurs particularly among recent immigrants (Diez de Leon, 2000).

Another way to capture the complexity of the adaptation process is by examining its various manifestations. Gallardo-Cooper (2000) offers a framework that describes this process using three dimensions: complete assimilation, acculturation, and rejection of the American culture. As outlined in Table 3.1, language use and preference, ethnic identity, family dynamics, cognitive and coping styles, and affective, interpersonal, and sociopolitical behaviors are examined in the context of these three dimensions. For example, one may examine the adaptation process of individuals who reject the dominant American culture in that they may refuse to speak English, may identify by ethnic heritage only, may have a strong preference for Latino traditions and friends, and may be critical and distrustful of American institutions. What is important about this framework is that it describes how and in what ways complete assimilation to the American way of life or rejection of American culture may result in negative consequences for the individual and family.

With respect to the measurement of acculturation, a variety of instruments are available for use. Acculturation measures have been developed for Cubans (e.g., Szapocznik & Kurtines, 1980), Mexicans (e.g., Cuellar, Arnold, & Maldonado, 1995; Cuellar, Harris, & Jasso, 1980), and a variety of Latino groups (e.g., Marín, Sabogal, Marín, Otero-Sabogal, & Perez-Stable (1987). Appendix A provides a description of such measures.

Impact Of Migration

Little is known about the psychological impact of migration, as well as the process of change that individuals within a family undergo as each member adjusts and adapts to a new way of life (Lorenzo-Hernandez, 1998). Zúñiga (1992b) outlines various stages in the migration process that are important sources of information about the individuals and influence a family's experience and subsequent ability to adapt. Specifically, she describes these stages as (a) the preparatory stage, which refers to the decision making, the involvement of family members and others, the family's ability to say good-bye to loved ones, and the degree to which emigration was planned or sudden; (b) the act of migration, which refers to the quality of the migration experience itself; (c) the period of overcompensation, during which individuals undergo such dramatic shifts in their lives that they may become "entrenched" in traditions to maintain a sense of stability; (d) the period of decompensation, in which conflicts arise and crises within the family may occur, including tra-

Table 3.1 Manifestations of Acculturative Process by Different Domains

	Assimilation	*Acculturation*	*Rejection*
Language preference	Monolingual English; if bilingual, prefers English.	Bilingual; uses language-switching.	Monolingual Spanish: refuses to learn English; prefers only Spanish.
Ethnic identity	Embraces only Euro American traditions, food, music, and leisure activities; identifies as an American.	Dual-self: embraces Latino and Euro American traditions, food, music, leisure activities; identifies by ethnicity or as a Latino/Hispanic and supports American national sentiment.	Embraces only Latino traditions, food, music, leisure activities; identifies by ethnic heritage only.
Family dynamics	Moves away or rejects Latino family traditions, rules, and members tied to Latino sentiment; in conflicts with family elders and pull toward family "tightness"; separates from family early, seeks independence; prefers democratic/equalitarian role positions in the family.	Engages and supports family traditions and rules; members have American and Latino values; practices *familismo* and encourages self-reliance; can apply democratic as well as hierarchical family structure.	Prefers Latino traditions and rules; conflicts with younger or more acculturated members (e.g., dating); seeks family as major source of socialization and support; highly hierarchical in family structure; elders and authority figures highly respected *(respeto)*.
Cognitive style	Rigid; American way is the only way; is individualistic in thinking style; does not seek consensus from family.	Flexible and resourceful with multiple systems to access multiple realities and views; is both individualistic and collectivist in thinking style; seeks consensus from family depending on the issue.	Rigid conflict resolution; problems with Euro Americans or more acculturated individuals; only thinks in collectivist (Latino-centered) ways.
Coping style	Adapts only among Americans; difficulty negotiating with Latinos or any other minority group.	Dual adaptation, accommodation in both cultures; doubles amount of options generated, ease in conflict resolution and negotiation.	Adapts only with Latino ways; fights American institutions and rules, conflict resolution problems with more acculturated individuals.
Affective behaviors	Angry, anxious, critical, frustrated when Latino self may be identified; ridicules Latinos and their ways to separate self from Latino self; defensive and guarded with threat of being associated with Latino culture.	Full range of emotions but not linked to cultural rejection. Can express emotionally strengths and weaknesses of both cultures.	Impatient, critical, complains of current society's realities; longs to return to native country; lives in the past when life was more Latino oriented; is distrustful of non-Latinos.
Interpersonal behaviors	Chooses Euro Americans or assimilated Latinos for friends; avoids Latino leisure activities.	Has mixed friends from different cultural groups; engages in a wide range of activities with Latinos and Euro Americans.	Prefers Latinos only for friends; engages only in Latino community activities.
Sociopolitical behaviors	May or may not get involved in civic or political activity (vote); refuses to learn about Latino concerns and history; rejects native country's system.	Supports civic activities regardless of cultural affiliation; can recognize flaws and strengths in sociopolitical systems.	Refuses to vote; does not believe in American system; is distrustful of institutions and public servants.

SOURCE: Gallardo-Cooper (1999).

ditional role conflict between women and men that may result in marital problems; and (e) the transgenerational impact, which refers to differences in values and behaviors between the younger and older generations that may lead to conflicts within the family.

In a similar framework, Arredondo-Dowd (1981) conceptualized the migration process as involving three stages: premigration, migration specific, and postmigration. During each stage, a variety of conditions and factors affect the way an individual responds to the migratory experience and subsequently adapts to the new country. For instance, an important factor to take into consideration in the premigration stage is whether the decision to leave the homeland was based on desired goals such as to improve economic conditions, pursue education, or reunite with family members. On the other hand, the decision to leave the homeland may have resulted from the need to flee the country because of a life-threatening situation. Thus, Arredondo-Dowd speculated that the adaptation process in the postmigration stage is influenced by these differing conditions, including other important dimensions such as the individual's ethnic/racial membership and language background.

Immigration of Latinos continues to grow at a rapid pace, particularly from countries such as El Salvador and Nicaragua, yet, mental health service providers know very little about the psychosocial needs of this group. It has been suggested (as outlined in Chapter 2) that the migration experience of Latinos from Central America is vastly different from the experience of Mexicans, Puerto Ricans, and Cubans (Cervantes, Salgado de Snyder, & Padilla, 1989; Espín, 1987, 1999). For instance, many Central American immigrants come from war-torn countries and may be more likely to experience posttraumatic stress disorder. Specifically, Leslie and Leitch (1989) found that their sample of 91 Central American immigrants, who had arrived in the United States within a 3-year time period, reported these as the most frequent stressors: (a) "increase in cost of living," (b) "started or changed to a new job," (c) "birth of a child," (d) "lost or quit a job," and (e) "increase in parents' time away from home" (p. 322). Furthermore, Leslie and Leitch found that women not only reported more stressors than men but also were more likely to disclose conflicts within their families.

Family-Centered Values and Systems

Familismo

Although Latino groups are heterogeneous, some common themes can be traced to the Spanish colonial period. One of these common themes is *familismo*, a preference for maintaining a close connection to family. In general, Latinos have a strong familistic orientation in that they value close relationships, and stress interdependence, cohesiveness, and cooperation among family members. These ties go beyond the nuclear family and extend to such relatives as aunts, uncles, cousins, and grandparents, as well as close friends. *Familismo* stems from a collectivist or allocentric worldview in which there is a willingness to sacrifice for the welfare of the group (Marín & Triandis, 1985). This worldview is manifested in a shared sense of responsibility to care for children, provide financial and emotional support, and participate in decision-making efforts that involve one or more members of the family (e.g., Falicov, 1998; Marín & Marín, 1991; Moore & Pachon, 1985). Furthermore, there is evidence to support the notion that perceived family closeness has not declined as a result of acculturation or as a result of living in urban-industrial settings, even though other aspects of familismo, such as an obligation to provide financial assistance to immediate and extended family members, have decreased (e.g., Baca Zinn, 1982; Keefe & Padilla, 1987; Sabogal, Marín, Otero-Sabogal, Marín, & Pérez-Stable, 1987). Likewise, Hurtado (1995) pointed out that because Latinos are more likely than non-Latino Whites to live near their families, they are more apt to engage in frequent face-to-face contact, particularly with family members, and give less importance to other forms of communication such as telephones and letters.

Given that a familistic orientation remains strong, even among highly acculturated Latino families (e.g., Sabogal et al., 1987, "Latinos in America," 2000), there are important implications for the role of *familismo* in the positive psychosocial development of children. For example, Vega, Gil, Warheit, Zimmerman, and Apospori (1993) found that among 6th- and 7th-grade Cuban adolescents, family pride and cohesion buffered the negative consequences of conflict associated with acculturation. More recently, Frauenglass, Routh, Pantin, and Mason (1997) reported that a strong sense of family social support was associated with lower levels of deviant behaviors (e.g., tobacco, marijuana, and alcohol use) among Latino adolescents.

Unfortunately, because the concept of *familismo* has not been well understood, counselors have erroneously diagnosed behaviors as pathological when in reality they are quite normal when viewed with a cultural lens. Diagnostic labels such as *enmeshed* and *codependent* have been widely used to describe Latino families. With this in mind, Falicov (1998) urges clinicians to "examine their own personal and professional values and philosophies about family structure and connectedness, while exploring the specific meanings of closeness and attachment for each family" (p. 164).

Likewise, counselors are encouraged to view familismo and its many dimensions as strengths within families. For instance, the extended family, particularly *los compadres* (the godparents), can be an important resource in providing needed support during times of crisis.

Compadrazco

The familistic orientation is also manifested in the selection and role of godparents in a child's life. *Compadrazco* (godparentage) has historical significance and remains an important tradition among Latinos. A Spanish tradition that dates back to the colonization period, it was quickly adopted by the various indigenous populations. As stated earlier, the indigenous populations were quickly decimated, leaving many orphaned children. These children were often adopted by other families. Thus, *compadres* served as a substitute for the biological parents. Whereas this role was predominant and necessary during that historical period of time, *compadres* in contemporary Latino culture have more of a "social function than one of parent substitute" (Mirandé, 1985, p. 155). What is most striking about this phenomenon is that *compadres* (godfathers) and *comadres* (godmothers) may be prominent leaders or older people who hold some position of authority and respect within the Latino community. Such individuals play an important role in the Latino family's life and are included in all traditional celebrations. The practice of godparentage formalizes relationships between the child's parents and the *compadres,* and promotes a sense of community.

Personalismo

The cultural trait of *personalismo* (valuing and building interpersonal relationships) is also characteristic of a collectivist worldview (Levine & Padilla, 1980) where there is a great deal of emotional investment in the family. Moreover, high importance is given to the qualities of positive interpersonal and social skills such that family members, both nuclear and extended, maintain mutual dependency and closeness for a lifetime. The valuing of warm, friendly, and personal relationships has important implications for how Latinos perceive and respond to environments (e.g., hospitals, mental health agencies) that are quite often impersonal and formal. For instance, the way that a receptionist greets the family seeking help and the personal communication style of the therapist will determine whether or not the Latino family returns (Flaskerud, 1986).

Spirituality and Religion

Contemporary discussions about spirituality and religion also hearken back to the days of early contact between the indigenous people and the *conquistadores*. Flores and Carey (2000) discuss the Latino spiritual soul, whereas M. Ramirez (1998) discusses the philosophy of cultures of indigenous people as influencing the spiritual belief system of its descendants, *Mestizos*. The interrelationship between faith, religion, and spirituality (Flores

& Carey, 2000) is fundamental for Latinos and for what are often described as Latino value orientations and beliefs. In most instances, this synthesis is not easy to tease apart.

Latinos often invoke their belief in higher powers as a way of making meaning, particularly of unfortunate events, such as an untimely death, an illness, and so forth. The expression *si Dios quiere* (if it is God's will) is often used. This is a form of acceptance or an indication that individuals have no control over what God has willed. Culturally unaware and insensitive social scientists have often referred to these statements pejoratively as fatalistic. They often go on to say that Latinos, therefore, have an external versus an internal locus of control. To interpret these statements without reference to the spiritual context often leads to wrong assumptions about individuals and Latinos as a whole. Furthermore, it introduces an imbalance of power between the therapist and the client if judgment is made about the individual's spiritual orientation around externalizing to a higher power.

In terms of organized religion, people of Latino heritage continue to be primarily Roman Catholic and, to varying degrees, practice the religion.[2] This is not surprising because from the beginning of the conquests by Spaniards such as Hernán Cortés, Ponce de Leon, and others, priests and friars were part of the mission. Historical accounts point to the active role that the missionaries had in the conquest. Although they were not necessarily involved in conquering by combat, they had a contributing role, conquering through baptism and conversion to the Catholic religion.

The diversity among Latino groups is also evident in the practice of various religious ceremonies. These practices are a unique and fascinating blend of Catholicism, native Indian influences, and in some Latino groups, African elements. For instance, one of the most cherished and beloved religious figures among Latinos, particularly Mexicans, is *la Virgen de Guadalupe* (Virgin of Guadalupe), the patron saint of Mexico. The belief in *la Virgen* is a clear example of how Mexicans have combined Catholicism with indigenous Aztec elements. Symbolizing hope and love, the Virgin is portrayed as having brown skin and, according to legend, appeared in Mexico in the mid 1500s to a poor priest, Juan Diego (Falicov, 1998). People of Latino heritage are known to make pilgrimages to her shrine, either requesting help or expressing gratitude for answer to their prayers.

Important religious figures among Cubans, Puerto Ricans, and Dominicans are Christ, the Virgin Mary, and other Catholic saints, such as Our Lady of Mercy. Among these Latino groups, the practice of *Santeria* exemplifies the fusion of Catholicism and African traditions. For example, African gods such as *Changó* and *Obatalá* are worshipped at the same time as Our Lady of Mercy, a Catholic saint (Gonzalez-Whippler, 1989). The point to be made here is that these religious symbols may represent the Latino family's belief that a cure for physical or mental illness is possible only for supreme powers.

The devotion to religious deities is commonly seen in the home, where there is an *altar* (altar) with statues of favorite saints, pictures, and lit candles. Religion and religious practices such as attending church services may play a central role for the family in times of crisis and in times of celebration. Examples are the Catholic *bautismo* (baptism) of an infant and *Día de los Muertos* (Day of the Dead), which is a widely celebrated annual event among Mexicans, a day to remember loved ones who have passed away. Altars with photographs of the deceased are mounted and adorned with food and other gifts. Mummies or skeletons, in all types of attire, have become the icon for *El Día de los Muertos.*

Santos or saints are also prayed to for different intercessions and support. From Spain to Mexico to settlements of families of Latino heritage in the United States, religious holidays are times of great celebration. During Holy Week, there are week-long processions through the streets of Spain's cities and towns. Images of Jesus Christ and the Virgin Mary are carried on shoulder-high floats yearly by lay societies of men well rehearsed in the practice.

Of course, Latinos may also participate in other formal religions. There are Latino Protestants and Latino Jews. The latter may trace their origins to the Sephardic Jews who fled Spain in the 15th century at the time of the Inquisition; other Latino Jews escaped to South America from Europe during Hitler's reign.

For many Latinos, the interrelationship between spirituality and/or religion and cultural practices is extraordinarily close. In discussions about Latino worldviews, it is a challenge to separate the origin of beliefs and values. Among Latinos, there is often discussion about the emphasis on *respeto* or deference to authority or a more hierarchical relationship orientation. The question has also been asked whether this *respeto* or deference is a result of the dominant-subordinate relationship experienced through oppression and colonization, acknowledgment of higher powers from the indigenous spiritual paradigms, and/or the influence of the Catholic religion, which provides prescriptive guidelines for behavior. In the context of counseling, it is important to know that the hierarchical relationship orientation may be based on more than one explanation, for example, culture.

Health and Illness Beliefs

Knowledge about traditional beliefs concerning illness and health and understanding of their role are paramount in working with Latino families. Our intent is to provide a brief description of relevant cultural beliefs that influence the way in which individuals and their families interpret and respond to health and illness.[3]

There is a consensus among scholars that people develop ideas and beliefs about illness and disease from different aspects of culture such as religion, spirituality, family relationships, social roles, language, and values (Molina, Zambrana, & Aguirre-Molina, 1994). Thus, a number of forces operate to influence not only what is believed to cause illness but also ways to treat particular ailments.[4] Illnesses such as *empacho* (upset stomach), *susto* (fright), and *ataque de nervios,* which resembles a panic attack, are considered common among Latinos who adhere to traditional beliefs. These health conditions, known as folk illnesses, come from a combination of medieval Spanish and indigenous Indian beliefs. For some Latino groups, such as Cubans, Puerto Ricans, and Dominicans, these conditions have African roots.

According to Molina et al. (1994), cultural explanations of what causes illness also come from a variety of beliefs, some of which center on the natural environment (external), such as bad air, germs, dust, or excess cold and heat, and others that involve individual responsibility (internal) such as fear, envy, and shame. One of the most fascinating beliefs has to do with the supernatural world, in which spirits and witchcraft cause illness and disease. It is not uncommon for Latinos to believe in *brujos* (witches) and *brujeria* (the practice of witchcraft). The roots of these beliefs can be traced to precolonial times, when the indigenous people worshiped gods that had supernatural powers. It is important to note that witchcraft can also be seen as causing a breakup in a relationship or other forms of conflict between or among people (Falicov, 1998).

The belief that supernatural forces operate in causing illness is evident in what is known among Latinos as *mal de ojo* (evil eye). The symptoms are high fever, inability to sleep, crying, and headaches. It is believed that a person who is jealous of another (child or adult), will stare at the victim and cause the illness. According to folklore, women and children, considered weaker than men, are particularly vulnerable to *mal de ojo* (e.g., Molina et al., 1994).

It is important for counselors to know that Latinos may seek help from traditional folk healers such as *curanderos* (Mexican), *santeros* (Cuban), or an *espiritista* (Puerto Rican), who will perform special rituals using a variety of methods such as a massage with special ointments, prayers, candles, and herbal teas and baths. Quite often, these healers are viewed as having more authority and power than a physician or mental health service provider (Zea, Quezada, & Belgrave, 1997). As a result, Latinos may not comply with medical treatments prescribed by professionals who have different beliefs about the etiology of illness.

Many of the religious, health, and luck-related items needed to perform the rituals by the *santeros, curanderos,* and *espiritistas* are found in *botanicas,* which are small stores located in Latino communities. The fact that *botanicas* still flourish in so many of our Latino communities speaks to several important issues. First, these shops symbolize the blending of religious, primarily Catholic, and indigenous beliefs and traditions in the treatment of physical and psychological health states (Garzon & Siang-Tan, 1992). Second, their presence symbolizes the resistance to complete assimilation.

Although cultural influences can help explain particular health attitudes and practices, not all Latinos adhere to them as described above. As noted by Molina and Aguirre-Molina (1994),

> Some beliefs and behaviors are prevalent among certain subgroups but many operate at a minimum, if at all, among others. But while the strength of traditional health beliefs varies by degree of acculturation, educational attainment, and economic level, Latinos have nevertheless been described as being highly traditional in their health care practices; they maintain a distrustful attitude toward doctors and modern medical techniques, and believe that professional diagnoses are no better than self diagnoses. (p. 30)

It is well recognized that negative experiences such as the communication barrier due to language differences and culturally insensitive treatment approaches have contributed to skepticism about medical and mental health establishments. Thus, it is not surprising that Latinos will use informal methods that are more closely tied to traditional cultural values and beliefs. However, Zea et al. (1997) caution service providers to consider the influence of socioeconomic factors (e.g., educational attainment, geographic location) on health beliefs among Latinos. Their position is that although culture may play a significant role, so does socioeconomic status. In particular, Zea et al. argue that Latinos from higher socioeconomic backgrounds may resemble non-Latino Whites in their attitudes and behaviors about health and illness.

Nonetheless, informal methods of treating disease and illness are often reinforced by family members. These beliefs and traditions have been passed on from one generation to another, and typically, it is the older generation, particularly the grandmother, who may be the most knowledgeable about certain remedies and rituals to cure specific ailments. A more comprehensive description of the various folk illnesses mentioned in this chapter can be found in Appendix B.

Language

The United States now has the fifth-largest Spanish-speaking population in the world. In fact, the Spanish language is the second-most-often spoken language in this country (U.S. Bureau of the Census, 1993). Although a significant percentage of Latinos speak English well to very well, they may have a strong preference for speaking Spanish in the home. (See Chapter 4 for details.) The desire to maintain the Spanish language while increasing proficiency in English supports the argument that there is a movement toward bilingualism and biculturalism. In a recent study on the loss and maintenance of language among three generations of ethnic minorities (e.g., first generation, born in the homeland; second generation, first born in the United States; and third generation, second generation to be born in the United States), Schrauf (1999) found that the majority of Puerto Ricans, Cubans, and Mexicans were able to maintain the Spanish language because they live in Latino communities, frequently engage in cultural festivities, and practice religious rituals and traditions. More important, this pattern persisted throughout all three generations.

Whereas the bilingual population is growing, particularly among first and subsequent generations of U.S.-born Latinos, a large segment of recent immigrants have very limited skills in reading, writing, and speaking English. This presents a challenge for individuals in a Latino family. Numerous studies have shown that the language barrier is related to underutilization of mental health services (e.g., Cheung & Snowden, 1990; Leong, Wagner, & Tata, 1995), misdiagnosis (e.g., Malgady & Costantino, 1998; Marcos, 1994; Marcos, Alpert, Urcuyo, & Kesselman, 1973), and ineffective treatment (e.g., Bamford, 1991; Javier, 1989).

Latinos in both a nuclear and extended family may have varying degrees of Spanish and English proficiency, depending on where they reside, their number of years in the United States, and the degree to which cultural traditions are practiced. For instance, the parents may be more fluent in the Spanish language than their children, whereas the grandparents may speak only Spanish. On the other hand, the level of proficiency may also be related to socioeconomic levels. Hazuda, Stern, and Haffner (1988) found that Mexicans living in upper-class San Antonio, Texas, residential areas were more proficient in the Spanish language than those living in lower socioeconomic areas. In essence, counselors are urged to consider language issues when working with Latino families.

Gender Socialization

Discussions of gender socialization immediately reference to the concepts of *marianismo* and *machismo*. For example, the cultural value of *marianismo* has a religious association to the Virgin Mary. The term, associated with female gender socialization, suggests that girls must grow up to be women and mothers who honor the model of the Virgin Mary. In short, they must be pure, long-suffering, nurturing, and pious (Lopez-Baez, 1999). The concept of *marianismo* is also used to describe women as virtuous and humble, yet spiritually stronger than men.

Within traditional families, these madonna-like qualities ascribed to women are played out in interesting ways. For instance, mothers are viewed as selfless, self-sacrificing, and nurturing individuals who provide spiritual strength to family members. Also, the female children in the family must remain virgins until they marry.

This expectation also gives mothers an important yet challenging role in the family. If a woman is self-effacing and giving at all times, she may appear to outsiders to be more like a submissive doormat. However, those who know Latinas, especially mothers, often note that women are the silent power in the family.

In *The Maria Paradox* (Gil & Vazquez, 1996), the 10 commandments for women who subscribe to the paradigm of *marianismo* are listed. These include the following: Do not forget a woman's place; Do not forsake tradition; Do not be single, self-supporting, or independent-minded; Do not forget that sex is for making babies, not for pleasure; Do not be unhappy with your man, no matter what he does to you; Do not ask for help; Do not discuss personal problems outside the home; and Do not change. Although Latinas of varying generations may recognize the commandments, many report that as a result of acculturation, education, and involvement in relationships that do not reinforce the commandments, they experience less conflict about not living according to the commandments. It can be argued that many women, not just Latinas, have been socialized according to this belief system; however, *marianismo* is still considered a Latino cultural value.

In the discussion of gender socialization emerges the term *machismo,* popularized as a desirable yet negative Latino male characteristic. It has been defined as the "cult of virility . . . arrogance and sexual aggressiveness in male-to-female relationships" (Stevens, 1973, p. 315). However, Latino psychologists have taken issue with the anglicized interpretation of this concept and put forth other definitions. According to Morales (1996),

> *Machismo* refers to a man's responsibility to provide for, protect, and defend his family. His loyalty and sense of responsibility to family, friends, and community make him a good man. The Anglo-American definition of *macho* that describes sexist, male-chauvinist behavior is radically different from the original Latino meaning of *machismo,* which conveys the notion of "an honorable and responsible man." (p. 274)

In this context, the traditional family structure may be considered hierarchical with authority given to husbands and fathers. Father figures in particular command respect from others. These are all positive qualities; however, the popular use of the term in U.S. society has, to some extent, distorted its original meaning to one that is now associated with sexism and violence (Bacigalupe, 2000) and pathological behavior (Mirandé, 1985). Baca-Zinn

(1982) offered a strong argument for the need to redefine *machismo* by suggesting "that masculine roles and masculine identity may be shaped by a wide range of variables having less to do with culture than with structural position" (p. 35).

There is considerable debate over the extent to which Latinos adhere to traditional gender roles in contemporary U.S. society. Although evidence suggests that gender roles are undergoing transformation, the complexities surrounding this phenomenon are far from clear-cut. Specific concepts related to traditional gender roles that commonly appear in the literature concerning Latinos are described; however, we strongly suggest further study by referring to the work of Oliva Espín (1999), for example.

The traditional gender roles may be more apparent among recent immigrants; yet, they too will undergo change as the family adapts to a new way of life. However, Oliva Espín (1999) cautions that in the process of adaptation, men may be "allowed and encouraged to develop new identities in the new country . . . girls and women are expected to continue living as if they were in the old country (e.g., with regard to gender role norms and behavior, clothing, rituals, and so on)" (p. 7). She argues that the reason for this push toward preserving traditions stems from the need to remain connected to the homeland for psychological well-being because so much is lost during the migration and adaptation process.

When examining gender role-based behaviors among Latinos, one must consider a variety of influencing factors such as socioeconomic indicators (e.g., level of education, income), place of residency, migration experience, language, and family composition. These determinants significantly influence gender roles. For example, more Latinas are heading households and as a result must take on roles that were traditionally dominated by men. As single heads of households, women are responsible for making major decisions about the welfare of their families and for providing for and nurturing their children. Thus, the traditional ascribed role of women in *marianismo* is not evident in this case; however, the internal conflict about this expectation may persist.

Summary

The Latino family is undergoing change and continuously evolving as a unit influenced by the process of adaptation and environmental forces. In particular, Baca Zinn (1979) staunchly argued that Latino family patterns are a function of structural forces within U.S. society and not solely a function of cultural values. It is common knowledge that to buffer the negative consequences of discrimination in employment, education, and housing, for instance, Latinos have effectively relied on their families and community network

for survival. Thus, familistic beliefs, attitudes, behaviors, and, in some instances, traditional gender roles are reinforced to maintain a sense of control.

Our purpose was to describe general concepts and ideas; we emphasize
that the counselor must first work with the family's personal constructions of
life circumstances. One of the more difficult challenges is to understand how
social, political, economic, historical, and cultural forces intersect to help
explain individual and family functioning, while keeping in mind the uniqueness of each family's background, as well as the choices made by individuals
within that family. Equally important, counselors must decide how and when
to consider cultural contexts in treatment and at the same time avoid stereotyping, which often happens when considering broad and general characteristics about a given ethnic group.

Correct Answers to Self-Assessment

1. True. It is multidimensional. (See pages 31-38.)
2. False. The process of adaptation and change affects ethnic identity. (See pages
   38-40.)
3. False. The migration experience may affect men and women in different ways.
   Traditional gender roles may change within a family as individual family members acculturate. (See pages 40-42.)
4. False. Kinship systems are strong in Latino culture. (See pages 42-44.)
5. True. Research studies show that familistic values remain strong across Latino
   groups and generations. (See page 43.)
6. True. The role of godparents remains important. (See page 44.)
7. True. Personal relationships are highly valued. (See page 44.)
8. False. The Catholic religion is just as important as the concept of *familismo*.
   (See pages 44-46.)
9. True. Religious and indigenous beliefs both influence ideas about health. (See
   pages 46-48.)
10. False. *Marianismo* is a term used to describe Latinas as virtuous and humble.
    (See pages 49-51.)

NOTES

1. It is well documented that the Spanish conquest resulted in decimating most of the indigenous populations in the New World. War, famine, mistreatment, illness, and suicide played a role
in eliminating the population. African slaves were brought to the Caribbean islands, particularly
Puerto Rico and the Dominican Republic, to replace the quickly declining Indian population.
Africans mixed with the Spanish and the remaining indigenous groups to produce what many
refer to as *mestizaje* or a mix of races. However, it is important to note that this mixing of racial
groups occurred in varying degrees. For instance, the Spanish colonizers of Mexico mixed with
indigenous groups such as the Aztec, Maya, and Inca people, whereas in the Caribbean, there is a

stronger African ancestry (Acosta-Belén & Sjostrom, 1988; Novas, 1994; Torres-Saillant & Hernández, 1998).

2. The majority of Latinos are Roman Catholic; however, there are Protestant, Pentecostal, and Jehovah's Witnesses sects both in the United States and in Latin American countries (Abalos, 1986; Moore & Pachon, 1985).

3. For a comprehensive review of a broad range of issues related to the health status of Latinos, such as the influence of culture, class, and gender on health, access to health care, patterns of chronic diseases, and mental health concerns, refer to Molina and Aguirre-Molina (1994) and Falicov (1998).

4. Discussions about the influence of medieval theories of disease such as the hot/cold theory can be found in Currier (1966), Gregory (1978), and Harwood (1971).

4

Understanding Latino Families

Redefining Their Diversity

Más reluce el humo de mi tierra que el fuego de la ajena.
The smoke of my land is brighter than the fire of another.

Rovira, 1984, p. 72

Objectives

- To present demographic trends about each of the Latino groups to gain an appreciation for the diversity within them.
- To examine socioeconomic and family characteristics of each Latino group to gain an understanding of how these factors are redefining the Latino family.

Competencies

As a result of studying this chapter, counselors will:
- Be able to describe demographic profiles of the various Latino groups.
- Be able to discuss the differences within the Latino population as they relate to age, language, residence, education, occupation, employment, marital status, religion, and family composition.

Latino-Specific Competencies

AWARENESS

- Culturally skilled counselors can understand and appreciate the diversity and heterogeneity within the Latino population.
- Culturally skilled counselors are aware of the similarities and differences in demographic trends among the various Latino groups.

KNOWLEDGE

- Culturally skilled counselors can describe demographic and socioeconomic characteristics specific to each group (e.g., Mexicans, Puerto Ricans, Cubans).
- Culturally skilled counselors can discuss the impact of specific social, economic, and familial characteristics that have shaped the Latino family in the United States.

SKILLS

- Culturally skilled counselors can incorporate knowledge about specific social, economic, and familial characteristics in a cultural context and informed framework that leads to effective helping of families.
- Culturally competent counselors can advocate for a family in need of services.

Self-Assessment

Directions: Answer True or False. The correct responses are at the end of the chapter.

T	F	1. Mexican Americans are the largest Latino group in the United States.
T	F	2. The Dominican population has steadily grown in the United States.
T	F	3. Latinos live in primarily rural settings.
T	F	4. The Cuban population has the lowest educational attainment of all other Latino groups.
T	F	5. Overall, poverty levels remain relatively higher for Latinos than for non-Latino Whites.
T	F	6. One of the major changes in the Latino family structure is the dramatic increase in female heads of household.
T	F	7. In general, Latino families tend to be larger than non-Latino White families.
T	F	8. Among the Latino groups, Cubans have the largest number of people in a household.

T   F   9. As a group, Central and South Americans have achieved
                higher educational attainment, comparable to that of the
                Cuban population in the United States.
T   F   10. Overall, the divorce rate among Latino groups remains
                lower than for non-Latino Whites.

Introduction

Census figures indicate that the Latino population as a whole grew rapidly
from 22 million in 1990 to about 35 million in 2001; it now constitutes 12.5%
of the total population in the United States (U.S. Bureau of the Census,
2001a). Perhaps no other ethnic group in the United States is as heterogeneous in its ethnicity, physical appearance, cultural practices and traditions,
and Spanish language dialects as the Latino population. Latinos in the United
States are a diverse group of multigenerational immigrants from different
Spanish-speaking countries as well as long-term residents in the Southwest
United States. All have unique social, economic, and political histories.
Latino groups vary in their ancestry, blending indigenous (e.g., Aztec and
Mayan) and Spanish cultural traditions and, for some Latino groups, African
traditions.

As outlined in the previous chapters, different forces compel individuals and
their families to leave their home countries. Such motivations vary widely
from escaping political turmoil to seeking education and economic opportunities with the hope of improving their lives. Important differences were
described in Chapter 2 about the various groups in terms of geographic settlement areas and length of time living in the United States. To summarize,
Mexicans from Mexico settled in the southwestern area of the United States
as early as the 1700s, and thus, generations of families have lived in this
country. In contrast, Dominicans from the Dominican Republic, considered
one of the more recent immigrant groups, have immigrated in large numbers
within the last three decades, primarily in the Northeast (Torres-Saillant &
Hernández, 1998).

This chapter focuses on describing the demographic, socioeconomic, and
family characteristics of the three largest Latino groups in the United States:
Mexican, Puerto Rican, and Cuban. Although these four groups are emphasized, a summary of Dominican and Central and South American populations
is also provided, using available census data. Socioeconomic indicators such
as income, education, and employment, as well as family size of each group
are presented. Particular attention is given to how such indicators have influenced structural changes that are redefining the Latino family in the United
States.

Table 4.1 Latino Groups as Percentage of Total Latino Population (in thousands)

Group	Number	Percentage
All Latinos	35,306	100
Mexicans	20,641	59
Puerto Ricans	3,406	10
Cubans	1,242	3
Central Americans	1,687	5
South Americans	1,353	4
Dominicans	765	2
Other Hispanics[a]	6,211	17

SOURCE: U.S. Bureau of the Census (2001a).
a. This classification includes Spaniards.

Latino Groups

More than half or about 59% of all Latinos in the United States are of Mexican heritage. Puerto Ricans account for about 10%, and Cubans account for about 3% of the total population. Census figures also indicate that Central Americans and South Americans as a group make up about 9% of the total Latino population. Dominicans are one of the fastest-growing groups constituting about 2% of the Latino population. Table 4.1 represents these percentages.

Year of Immigration and U.S.-Born Latinos

Migration continues to be the driving force in the overall growth of the population, but it is important to note the within-group differences as they relate to time of migration and place of birth. Based on 1990 census data, two thirds of Mexicans were born in the United States, whereas the majority of Central Americans were born in their respective countries of origin. Less than a third of the Cuban and Dominican residents were born in the United States.

With respect to migration, more than two thirds of the Cubans and Dominicans arrived in this country during the period between 1960 and 1990. The greatest migration movement for Cubans was during the 1960s, whereas for the Dominican and Central and South American populations, the greatest influx occurred during the 1980s. These migration movements reflect periods of political and economic crises in their respective home countries. Table 4.2 represents the percentage of Latino groups who migrated to the United States from before 1950 to 1990, as well as those born in this country.

Table 4.2 Year of Immigration and U.S.-Born Latinos (percentage), 1950-1990

Year of Immigration	Mexicans	Puerto Ricans	Cubans	Dominicans	Central Americans	South Americans
Born in the United States	65.3	53.9	27.5	27.8	18.5	21.4
1980 to 1990	17.6	15.1	19.7	37.8	57.2	39.1
1970 to 1979	10.6	8.3	13.2	20.5	16.4	21.9
1960 to 1969	3.7	8.8	33.3	10.9	5.6	14.7
1950 to 1959	1.5	9.0	4.7	1.9	1.5	2.3
Before 1950	1.3	4.9	1.6	1.1	.8	.6
Total	100	100	100	100	100	100

SOURCE: Boswell, 1994; U.S. Bureau of the Census, 1990.

Demographic Characteristics

The following section provides a description of the population that helps those who want to understand Latinos as a group, as well as the diversity within their numbers. Comparisons are made across the various Latino groups on such factors as age, educational attainment, occupation, marital status, family size, and poverty level.

Age

Overall, the Latino population is younger than the total U.S. population. As shown in Table 4.3, a significant percentage of Latinos are under 19 years of age. Compared to the U.S. population as a whole, a smaller percentage of Latinos are 65 and older.

Cubans are clearly older than the other Latino groups, with South Americans the next oldest. As indicated in Table 4.4, the older median age of the Cuban population contributes to the lower birth rate (Boswell, 1994).

Table 4.3 Percentage Distribution of Latinos by Age Compared to U.S. Population

Age	Latino	U.S. Total
Under 19	39	29
20 to 29	17	13
30 to 44	24	24
45 to 64	15	22
65 and over	5	12

SOURCE: U.S. Bureau of the Census (2001b), Table 1.1.

Table 4.4   Median Age of Latino Groups

	Mexicans	Puerto Ricans	Cubans	Dominicans	Central Americans	South Americans	All Latinos Total	U.S. Population
Median age	24.2	27.3	40.7	29.5	29.2	33.1	25.9	35.3

SOURCE: U.S. Bureau of the Census (2001a).

Table 4.5   Ability to Speak English and Another Language (Percentage)

	Mexicans	Puerto Ricans	Cubans	Dominicans	Central Americans	South Americans
Speaks English language:						
Very well	61.9	67.5	50.1	40.2	40.5	50.9
Well	16.4	18.5	21.0	22.6	22.2	24.3
Not well	14.1	10.7	18.7	22.2	23.6	17.8
Not at all	7.6	3.3	13.1	15.0	13.7	7.0
Language spoken at home:						
English only	24.1	18.7	10.4	6.5	8.1	9.3
Another language	75.9	81.3	89.6	93.5	91.9	90.7

SOURCE: Boswell, 1994; U.S. Bureau of the Census, 1990.

Language

Table 4.5 represents self-report information on the ability to speak English and another language. Overall, the majority of Latinos across the various groups reported speaking English well to very well. According to Boswell (1994), almost all Latinos reported a preference for speaking Spanish at home. Although these figures clearly show the maintenance of the Spanish language, a significant number of Latinos are also able to speak English. Daily interactions through holding a job, purchasing goods, and seeking services such as health care require ability with the English language. Based on these figures, one can conclude that there is a bilingual (Spanish and English speaking) population of considerable size.

Residence

The tendency for Latinos to live in metropolitan areas, particularly in large cities, is primarily due to the type of job opportunities available to them.

Table 4.6 Latino and Non-Latino White Population by Metropolitan and Non-metropolitan Residence (Percentage)

Area	Latinos	Non-Latino Whites
Metropolitan area (inside central city)	46	21
Metropolitan area (outside central city)	45	56
Nonmetropolitan area	9	23

SOURCE: U.S. Bureau of the Census (2001b), Table 20.1.

Compared to non-Latino Whites, twice as many Latinos live in large cities. Interestingly, almost equal numbers live in metropolitan areas outside the city. In contrast, a small percentage of Latinos live in non-metropolitan areas as compared to non-Latino Whites. More recently, there have been reports of new immigrants settling in more rural parts of the country, including western Nebraska, Alabama, Arkansas, Maine, and Tennessee. Employment opportunities provide the impetus to move to these areas. However, as indicated in Table 4.6, Latinos continue to have an urban presence in the United States.

Socioeconomic Characteristics

Educational Attainment

Educational attainment is often used as a measure of an individual's or group's ability to succeed in the United States. Educational attainment is also linked to employment and income. As shown in Table 4.7, the profile for

Table 4.7 Educational Attainment of Latinos and Non-Latino Whites 25 Years Old and Older (Percentage)

Educational Level	Latinos		Non-Latino Whites	
	Male	Female	Male	Female
Less than 9th grade	27	27	4	4
9th to 12th grade (no diploma)	16	15	7	7
High school diploma	28	28	32	36
Some college or associate's degree	18	20	26	27
Bachelor's degree	7	7	20	18
Advanced degree	4	3	11	8

SOURCE: U.S. Bureau of the Census (2001b), Table 7.3.

Table 4.8   Educational Attainment of Latino Groups (Percentage)

Educational Level	Mexicans	Puerto Ricans	Cubans	Central and South Americans
Less than 9th grade	32	17	18	22
9th to 12th grade (no diploma)	17	18	9	13
High school diploma	26	30	33	30
Some college or associate's degree	18	22	17	17
Bachelor's degree	5	9	14	12
Advanced degree	2	4	9	6

SOURCE: U.S. Bureau of the Census (2001b), Table 7.1.

Latinos indicates that 27% have less than a 9th-grade education, compared to only 4% of non-Latino Whites. Twice as many Latinos compared to non-Latino Whites have a 9th- to 12th-grade education, but no high school diploma. Unfortunately, Latinos continue to lag behind in overall educational attainment. For instance, Latinos are less likely to enter college and complete a bachelor's degree, and even fewer have attained advanced degrees. Nonetheless, Latinos have made significant gains. For example, in 1980, 54% had less than a high school diploma, with about 8% earning college degrees. In 1990, about 50% had less than high school education, and college completion increased to 9% (Rivera-Batiz & Santiago, 1994; Zambrana, 1995). There is virtually no difference between men and women in educational attainment for Latinos; however, there appears to be a slight difference at the bachelor's level, indicating that more women than men have some college or an associate's degree.

Mexicans have the highest percentage of people with less than a 9th-grade education, whereas Cubans and Central and South Americans have had the most gains in education, particularly at the bachelor's and advanced degree levels. Table 4.8 shows that Puerto Ricans appear to have made greater gains at obtaining some college education or completing associate's degrees.

Occupation

As noted in Table 4.9, Latinos are heavily concentrated in jobs as machine operators, inspectors, and laborers or jobs in transportation and repair. In addition, a significant percentage have jobs in the service occupations. These two categories cover about 55% of the labor force. Ortiz (1995) noted that, in general, these types of jobs are considered low-status occupations requiring minimal education. In contrast, non-Latino Whites occupy executive, administrative, managerial, and professional specialty jobs in greater numbers. Such occupations are considered high status, requiring advanced levels of education.

Table 4.9   Occupations of Latinos and Non-Latino Whites, Percentage of Civilian
Population 16 Years Old and Older

Occupation	Latinos	Non-Latino Whites
Executive, administrative/managerial, and professional specialties	14	33
Technical and related support	2	3
Sales	10	13
Clerical and administrative support	13	14
Skills jobs[a]	36	23
Services	19	12
Farming, fishing, and forestry	6	2

SOURCE: U.S. Bureau of the Census (2001b), Table 10.4.
a. The largest category, consisting of jobs such as precision work, transportation, repair, inspectors, machine operators, and laborers.

Table 4.10 Percentage Distribution of Latino and Non-Latino White Income in 1999
(People 15 Years Old and Older)

Income	Latino	Non-Latino White
$9,000 or less	7	4
$10,000 to $19,000	37	15
$20,000 to $34,999	32	32
$35,000 to $74,999	21	38
$75,000 or more	3	11

SOURCE: U.S. Bureau of the Census (2001b), Table 11.1.

Income and Poverty

A variety of barriers limit the upward mobility of Latinos. Ortiz (1995)
noted that competition and discrimination have impeded Latinos from
achieving greater success in the labor market. Interestingly, she concluded
that wages have remained low for Mexicans and Puerto Ricans, in particular,
because they live in states with large concentrations of Latinos where they
compete for the same low-wage jobs. Table 4.10 represents the income distribution for Latinos and non-Latino Whites. Income levels remain low for
Latinos, with about 44% of the population earning $19,000 or less, compared
to about 19% of non-Latino Whites. About a third of Latinos have incomes in
the $20,000 to $34,000 range, a proportion comparable to the proportion of
non-Latino Whites in this category. However, the gap widens at the higher
income levels, where only 24% of Latinos earn $35,000 or more, compared to
about half of working non-Latino Whites. It is important to note that Cubans

Table 4.11 Percentage Distribution of Latino Groups and Non-Latino Whites by Marital Status (People 15 Years Old and Older)

Marital Status	Mexicans	Puerto Ricans	Cubans	Central and South American	Non-Latino Whites
Married, spouse present	50	42	56	47	57
Married, spouse absent	3	2	2	4	1
Widowed	4	4	9	3	7
Divorced	6	10	11	7	10
Separated	3	5	2	4	1
Never married	34	37	20	35	24

SOURCE: U.S. Bureau of the Census (2001b), Table 1.1.

have the highest income level of all Latino groups (U.S. Bureau of the Census, 2001b).

Given the high concentration of Latinos as a group in low-status and low-wage occupations, it seems reasonable to conclude that poverty rates would be high. Based on current population estimates, about 23% of Latinos are below the poverty level, compared to about 8% of non-Latino Whites. Overall, the poverty rate is three times higher for Latinos than for non-Latino Whites across all age groups. Based on 1999 income figures, about 30% of Latino children under the age of 18 were living in poverty, compared to only 9% of non-Latino White children (U.S. Bureau of the Census, 2001b).

Family Characteristics

Marital Status

The Catholic religion, because of its dominance among Latinos in the United States, has been a contributing factor to the low incidence of divorce among Latinos. However, in recent years, there has been a change in the marital status of Latino men and women, with a considerable increase in the divorced, separated, or widowed population.

Although different time periods are associated with these trends, it is clear that Puerto Ricans have been most affected by changes in marital status. Table 4.11 clearly shows that compared to other Latino groups and to non-Latino Whites, Puerto Ricans have the lowest percentage of people married with spouse present, and the highest percentage of people who never married. Cubans have a higher percentage of people who are married with their spouse present, a proportion comparable to that of non-Latino Whites, but they also

Table 4.12 Householder in Family by Family Type (Percentage)

Type of Household	Mexicans	Puerto Ricans	Cubans	Central and South Americans	Non-Latino Whites
Married couples	70	57	77	65	82
Female householder (no spouse present)	21	36	18	25	13
Male householder (no spouse present)	9	7	5	10	5

SOURCE: U.S. Bureau of the Census (2001b), Table 4.1.

Table 4.13 Family Size Among Latinos and Non-Latino Whites (Percentage)

Family Size	Mexicans	Puerto Ricans	Cubans	Central and South Americans	Non-Latino Whites
2 to 3 people	40	56	60	46	68
4 to 5 people	42	38	35	44	29
6 people or more	18	6	5	10	3

SOURCE: U.S. Bureau of the Census (2001b), Table 5.1.

have the highest percentage of divorced individuals, in comparison to all other groups. Mexicans have the lowest rate of divorce and separation in comparison to all other groups. Central and South Americans have the highest percentage of people married with their spouses absent; however, the overall number is small.

Family Composition and Size

One of the major changes in Latino families is the alarming increase in females heading households with no spouse present. This is particularly affecting Mexican and Puerto Rican families. As can be seen in Table 4.12, the Puerto Rican population has the highest percentage of females heading households with no spouse present, compared to other Latino groups and to non-Latino Whites. The proportion of males heading households with no spouse present is also higher among Mexicans, Puerto Ricans, and Central and South Americans than among Cubans and non-Latino Whites.

As noted in Table 4.13, Latino families tend to be larger than non-Latino White families. However, when examining within-group differences, Mexicans have the largest percentage of families with four or more people in a household, followed by Central and South Americans. Cubans have the fewest number of people in a family compared to all other Latino groups and more closely resemble the non-Latino White population on this characteristic. A plausible explanation is that there is a high correlation among such factors as income, education, and family size. Specifically, the higher the educational and income level, the smaller the family size. As noted earlier, Cubans have the highest educational attainment and income levels of all Latino groups; thus, it seems reasonable to conclude that Cuban family size would be smaller.

Summary

Overall, with the exception of Cubans, Latinos as a group are younger and have larger families than non-Latino Whites. The maintenance of the Spanish language remains strong among all groups. Most Latinos live in large cities, with a growing population of Latinos moving to metropolitan areas outside these cities. Although significant gains have been made in educational attainment over the past two decades, Latinos continue to have lower levels of education than any other racial/ethnic group in the United States. Puerto Rican women are more likely to head households and have considerably lower income levels than women of other Latino groups.

One of the major concerns with the rising number of minority women heading households is that the declining economic conditions of the family, particularly after a divorce or separation, create a vicious cycle of poverty. Ortiz (1995) noted that this phenomenon is unlike the "feminization of poverty," which has occurred primarily within non-Latino White families headed by women. Divorce or separation means less of a change in economic conditions for Latino families, because even with two parents present, they are poorer than the majority White families at the outset. Thus, when divorce or separation results in a Latina becoming the head of a household, it does not affect her economic status in the same way as it would for a non-Latina White woman. However, the shift from two-parent to one-parent households undoubtedly affects the economic stability of the family. Ortiz emphasized that "Coupled with the overall deteriorating economic conditions, we have seen a deterioration in the well-being of minority families. Latino families have experienced many of these changes, although the extent varies considerably by national origin, regional concentration, and other factors" (p. 19). Thus, counselors must recognize that although there are within-group differences in the demographic profile of the Latino population, there are also certain characteristics that prevail. More important, counselors should be aware that income and education level, employment status, and place of residence are powerful indicators of a family's quality of life and overall psychological and physical well-being.

Correct Answers to Self-Assessment

1. True. The largest proportion of Latinos are Mexican Americans. (See page 57.)
2. True. Dominican immigrants have increased in number in recent years. (See pages 56-57.)
3. False. Latinos live primarily in cities and adjacent metropolitan areas. (See page 60.)
4. False. Cubans have more education than other Latino groups. (See page 61.)
5. True. More Latinos are poor. (See pages 62-63.)
6. True. The number of female-headed households has increased, particularly in some groups. (See pages 63-64.)
7. True. Many Latinos have larger families. (See page 64.)
8. False. Mexicans have the largest number of people per household. (See pages 64-65.)
9. True. Central and South Americans have educational levels similar to Cubans. (See pages 60-61.)
10. True. Divorce is less common among Latinos than among non-Latino Whites. (See pages 63-64.)

5

_____
_____
___

Understanding Latino
Families in Transition

No hay mal que por bien no venga.
There is no evil from which some good cannot be derived.
Rovira, 1984, p. 168

Objectives

- To provide background information about different realities evident in Latino families today.
- To review a variety of Latino family characteristics and behaviors in the context of cultural and life experiences that may influence family relationships and human development.

Competencies

As a result of studying this chapter, counselors will:

- Be knowledgeable about the characteristics of four different realities or structures of Latino families—the intact, single-parent, bicultural, and immigrant—the challenges they face, and implications for counseling.

Latino-Specific Competencies

AWARENESS

- Culturally skilled counselors can recognize family-of-origin structure and functioning as one of many possible types of family organization without imposing the family of origin as the standard for assessing other Latino families.
- Culturally skilled counselors are aware of the developmental sequelae of a bicultural upbringing and can recognize differences and similarities with their own developmental course.

KNOWLEDGE

- Culturally skilled counselors understand the foundation and barriers of different Latino marriages and family compositions.
- Culturally skilled counselors can identify characteristics of Latino families at risk and the different forms and degrees of stress they experience (e.g., psychosocial, acculturation, trauma).

SKILLS

- Culturally skilled counselors incorporate information regarding "at risk" factors and protective variables into a culturally sensitive therapeutic intervention.
- Culturally skilled counselors appreciate, identify, and integrate clients' strengths in interventions regardless of the predicament of the family.

Self-Assessment

Directions: Answer True or False. The correct answers are at the end of this chapter.

T   F   1. In Latino families, marital satisfaction is secondary to the welfare of the children.

T   F   2. A traditional two-parent Latino family with low levels of acculturation may be described as having a hierarchical structure.

T   F   3. The parenting style among Latinos may be viewed as authoritarian.

T   F   4. Because children are the center of Latino families, parents may be perceived as lenient and democratic in their parenting approach.

T   F   5. Latina single women and recent immigrant family members may be at risk for some forms of mental health problems.

T   F   6. A Latino couple sharing the same heritage can experience cross-cultural conflict.
T   F   7. As long as the family members are from the same ethnic group, a bicultural approach to understanding family dynamics is not necessary.
T   F   8. The migration experience for a family can be considered a life-cycle stage.
T   F   9. Acculturation stress refers to the short-lived period of adaptation evident among immigrants immediately following the migration experience.
T   F   10. Social networks and social support are driving forces in the adaptation of immigrant families.

Introduction and Background

The study of the family continues to be a focus of interest for social scientists, who have found that family functioning is at the core of sociological and psychological health. Within the modern family, modifications in family structure, changes in parental roles, and new family lifestyles have resulted in a variety of mental health dilemmas. Moreover, the family of the new millennium encounters challenging new tasks not encountered by past generations, such as cyberspace relationships, birth by design, and time limitations (Papp, 2000).

Cultural diversity adds another dimension to the complexity of the family. Because culture is a constantly changing process (Szapocznick & Kurtines, 1993), Latino families need to be understood in the context of the acculturation process, migration experience, language, race, nationality, and socioeconomic background. In addition, the Latino family needs to be understood from a broad framework incorporating not only the value system but also the emotional style and communication patterns that shape the family's quality of life (Betancourt & López, 1993).

To understand the family, it is also important to appreciate marital dynamics. Unfortunately, the study of marriage has been skewed toward finding what is wrong or what is dysfunctional, overlooking what seems to work (Berg & Miller, 1992; Gottman, 1998). Deficit models have prevailed in research with ethnic minorities, resulting in negative biases (García Coll et al., 1998; Rogoff & Morelli, 1989). However, the multicultural movement has contributed to the understanding, acceptance, and validation of the strengths inherent in diverse cultures, even though these may clash with the dominant culture.

Strong Latino family values, in particular, contribute to overall marital satisfaction and lower incidence of divorce in the United States. Scholars concur that most Latinos, influenced by Catholicism for centuries, consider marriage a lifelong commitment. When marriage is forever, couples are expected to work out all conflicts and differences within the formal union without the option of terminating the relationship. For many Latinos, the purpose of marriage is childbearing, making the children a central motivating force in family dynamics. The couples' personal satisfaction with the relationship may take second place to the welfare of the children. In addition, staying together for the sake of the children appears to be a more common justification among Latinos. More than men, women are reported as pressured by their families to keep the family together (Lijtmaer, 1998); men's philandering, although not approved openly, seems to be more tolerated among Latinos (Penn, Hernández, & Bermúdez, 1997).

Because marriage is viewed as a long-term commitment, Latinos may seek to establish tolerance, increase acceptance, and avoid conflicts. They may conceptualize marriage as a "trading partnership" where individuals assume specific roles and duties to ensure benefits in several areas such as economic stability, sexual intimacy, procreation, and household responsibilities (Oropesa, 1996). For example, a 78-year-old Dominican woman, seen with her husband of 52 years, referred to her husband's history of philandering as a "blessing because after 12 births, I did not want to have any more children." At the same time, she described a caring, loving, and compatible relationship with her husband throughout her marriage.

Acculturation, Gender Roles, and Family Dynamics

Understanding the Latino family also requires knowledge of how the acculturation process influences gender roles. It is also well recognized that sociopolitical changes in American society supporting the rights of women have inevitably affected both Latino males and females residing in the United States. Coupled with the acculturation process, this trend creates potential for conflicts in relationships and intimacy.

It has been argued that Latinas undergo a faster (Hernández, 1996) and more dramatic (Espín, 1999) gender role transformation than males, which often creates significant relational, family, and identity conflicts. Yet, Latinas, as a group, still fall behind their American counterparts in their pursuit of an egalitarian relationship, and many partners discourage independence and self-reliance.

In older couples, wives may present themselves as highly dependent on their husband (e.g., errands, transportation) and commonly are labeled as passive-dependent (a trait often perceived as a characteristic of *marianismo*). Although husbands may complain about their wife's apparent dependence, they maintain this dynamic because it ensures their authority, competence, and role as protector of the family (a trait often perceived as a characteristic of *machismo*). In contrast, women, pressured to keep the family together, often sacrifice more autonomy to maintain the husband's sense of manhood. These women often report saying, "I let him do it, so that he can feel that he still can do something for his family." As men age, it is the fear of losing their place in the hierarchy, rather than the notion that women relinquish authority, that seems to create this dynamic. Therefore, empowering Latinas in the counseling process needs to be addressed contextually by exploring the reciprocity principle. The following case illustrates this point.

> A husband married 50 years complained to the therapist about how demanding his wife was: "I have to take her to all these places, and she cannot even keep track of appointments. . . . I have to do everything for her, I even have to make sure that she makes it to the appointment." As the therapist explored further, the husband could not identify any of the chores he did for the family, whereas the wife, who was a fastidious homemaker, spent a regimented daily schedule full of household chores. She then added, "You know what, I wanted to learn how to drive many years ago, but you never let me . . . now, I am too old to learn, at least you have something to do."

Attitudes About Marriage and Cohabitation

Attitudes toward marriage and cohabitation among Latinos may explain their expectations and anxieties about relationships. In particular, Oropesa (1996) investigated the beliefs about marriage and attitudes about cohabitation as a means to sexual intimacy, childbearing, and intention to marry among non-Latino Whites, Mexican Americans, and Puerto Ricans. Of the three groups, Mexican Americans gave marriage a higher value, followed by Puerto Ricans and non-Latino White individuals. Beliefs about cohabitation without plans for marriage and for childbearing were found to be the same between Mexican Americans and non-Latino White individuals (i.e., mild disapproval). Puerto Rican ratings indicated more neutral attitudes concerning a living arrangement for the purposes of sexual intimacy and childbearing, with or without intention of marriage. However, when Mexican Americans were asked to consider cohabitation with intentions of marriage, they were more accepting of this living arrangement reaching ratings similar to those of Puerto Ricans. In addition, being born in Mexico and being a woman led to stronger adherence to a marriage preference.

Even though these research findings demonstrate possible trends in attitudes about marriage, there may be conflicting values present. Because Latino families exert pressure for togetherness and maintain frequent contact, it is speculated that they also provide sanctions and directives to family members regarding marital and familial decisions. From this perspective, Oropesa's

(1996) findings suggest the need to explore with Latino clients internal dilemmas regarding their views of marriage and cohabitation, particularly the attitudes and beliefs held by more acculturated Latino youth. Clients may have dichotomous values that clash with religious orientation, family expectations, and contextual variables. For example, a Mexican American female college student may struggle with decisions about premarital sex when her support group's values clash with those of her family and religion.

Developmental Tasks in Latino Families

Latino families also need to be understood from the perspective of confronting developmental tasks across the life span. The family life-cycle model promoted by Carter and McGoldrick (1999) brings to light the realization that families are not static and are in a constant dance of adaptation. Falicov (1999) identifies eight stages of the Latino family life cycle. Although this paradigm allows for an understanding of expected transitions in the life of Latinos based on culturally relevant periods of expected change, it does not incorporate unexpected real life crisis or transitions encountered (Lyle & Faure, 2000), such as geographical separations, early deaths, divorce, stepfamilies, and the like.

When confronted with crises such as the disability of a child, Latinos have demonstrated different coping patterns compared to other populations in the United States. Mary (1990) found that Latino parents were able to cope better by not viewing the child's disability as a personal burden. Similarly, Heller, Markwardt, Rowitz, and Farber (1994) found that Latino mothers were not as distressed because they used religious attributions and coping strategies. Parents' distress revolved not around issues of loss and pain related to a child having a disability but around possible disruption or real effects the disability had on the family (Blacher, Shapiro, & López, 1997). Thus, work with Latino families requires an understanding of the characteristics and dynamics of special Latino groups as they respond and adapt to naturally occurring daily events as well as exceptional psychosocial stressors. For further understanding about how Latino families encounter life transitions based on Latino value orientations, see Falicov (1998, 1999) and García-Preto (1996a, 1996b, 1998), as well as an adaptation of this model in Lyle and Faure (2000).

It is important to underscore that even though Latino families share similar characteristics, each Latino family needs to be seen as a unique entity with idiosyncratic qualities. It is often challenging to tease out the many cultural variants, personality traits, family of origin influences, and contextual factors that affect family functioning. Moreover, it is the interaction of these forces that defines how the family reacts to life transitions.

With this perspective, the chapter explores different realities evident in Latino families today. Four Latino family realities will be covered: the intact *familia,* the single-parent *familia,* the bicultural *familia,* and the immigrant *familia.*Understanding the characteristics and realities leads to a discussion of relevant counseling implications. For purposes of organization, issues relevant to other family compositions are discussed under the intact *familia* section, such as working families, parenting, and human development.

The Intact *familia*

Characteristics

The intact family refers to parents who continue to live together either through legal or common-law marriages. Typically, this family includes the mother, the father, and the children. In many instances, the nuclear family may include a grandparent or another member of the extended family. Grandparents raising grandchildren may also represent an intact family. Children are generally seen as a blessing and a time of celebration for the entire extended family (Falicov, 1999). Following the Catholic tradition of not using birth control, families tend to have many children. However, with increasing acculturation, the trend is toward a reduction of family size. Siblings also compose a hierarchical structure with the oldest having the highest authority. Elders are held in high esteem among all family members.

The typical Latino family includes both parents, with the father employed full-time and the mother as a homemaker (Lichter & Landale, 1995). Traditional families, defined by low acculturation levels, have been described as patriarchal. The mother has the primary responsibilities of family management and child rearing. Because the Latino family system practices a hierarchical structure, mothers, regardless of their power within the family, may be submissive to the father and project to the children an image of being second in command. By maintaining this position for the sake of family harmony and the maintenance of cultural values such as *respeto* and family hierarchy, Latino parents inadvertently communicate solidarity to the children.

Typically, there are specific roles for the mother and father, with the mother assuming responsibilities for house chores and children's care and the father holding the ultimate authority in important family financial decisions or major discipline actions. The primary role of fathers is to be the primary breadwinner and a disciplinarian, and they may be distant from day-to-day family responsibilities. It is important to note that in our clinical experience, Latino fathers tend to be highly supportive of the mothers and are involved with child care and household responsibilities. However, Latino fathers may define their support to the wife and children differently than women would. Latino men may label themselves as competent fathers and husbands by describing themselves as *Yo soy un hombre de familia* (I am a family man), but men would differentiate their "family man" role from their wife's or daughter's role. For example, in a family session, a Latino father of two young daughters said in a humorous tone: "I *resent immensely* doing the dishes, I mean that's a woman's job . . . hey, hey . . . hey, but I do it anyhow." This comment reflects the affective and gender role-specific beliefs observed in many, but not all, Latino relationships.

Realities

Working Families

A recent study by the Institute of Political Economics indicated that Latino families make a significant contribution to the economic prosperity of the United States ("Dicen que prosperidad," 2000). However, this contribution comes at a high price. In particular, middle-class Latinos worked 5 hours extra per week compared to Anglo Americans and 9.4 hours extra per week compared to African Americans. Even Latino professionals with high socioeconomic status worked a median of 12.9 more hours per week than their counterparts. These findings contrast with the trends observed in the early 1990s, when married Latina mothers were the least involved in the labor market.

Based on data obtained by the 1990 Census, Lichter and Landale (1995) explored working patterns, living arrangements, and stage in the family cycle (i.e., family size, fertility years) among Latino groups. Interestingly, they found that, with both parents working, Mexican Americans were unable to surpass the poverty threshold. These findings suggest that Mexican American children may be twice jeopardized: once by their exposure to the concomitants of poverty and again by the negative effects of spending less time with parents who work full-time.

In this context, the stress level among working Latinos raising a family is expected to be high, considering their long hours and low wages. The daily pressures of raising children in two working-parent families have been well documented (Glickauf-Hughes, Hughes, & Wells, 1986; Hayghe & Bianchi, 1994), particularly among low-income families (Deater-Deckard & Scarr, 1996).

With respect to child care, it is not uncommon for grandmothers or grandfathers to come to the assistance of working parents; however, they are still young enough to work outside the home (Burnette, 1999). When mothers cannot depend on extended family for child care, they prefer home care from kin or a family friend. Older children are also given the responsibility of caring for the younger ones after school. Although well-educated or highly acculturated individuals tend to access preschool services or professional day care, they may still prefer family for child care. Latina mothers may also struggle with a strong desire to be home and raise the children while recognizing the need to seek outside employment. In these circumstances, they may consider part-time employment as an option to juggling family and financial responsibilities.

Because of low wages, discrimination, and inequality in the workplace, the efforts made by many Latina mothers who work full-time or part-time may have minimal overall benefits. Many choose to stay home and care for the children (Hayghe & Bianchi, 1994), especially if they lack work skills, familial support, or social networks.

Parenting

One of the major objectives in the parenting of Latino children is the acquisition of interpersonal skills, which include respect for authority (Gallardo-Cooper, 2001b) and social relatedness (Falicov, 1998). Obedience, *respeto,* humility, and affectionate behaviors are also encouraged in the socialization process. *Respeto* implies setting clear boundaries in human relationships and is central in socialization. Elders may discourage parents from "horsing around" with children to avoid problems setting the adult-child boundary of *respeto.*

Becoming *bien educado* (well educated) does not mean formal education but rather the process of learning adequate social graces and skills (Nava, 2000). Thus, how to be a *bien educado* and not to be a *malcriado* (lack of respect, rude, and spoiled) are primary guidelines in raising children. With this parenting worldview, Latino parents encourage interpersonal and prosocial behaviors. Children are taught to maintain a hierarchical approach in relationships. In some Latino cultures, children are taught to look down when being scolded, and any type of assertiveness is punished. The following case illustrates this point.

> One Argentinean mother related her discontent with raising her family in the United States: "In my country, you teach your children to respect and trust others . . . everyone knows each other and you know their family tree . . . but living in America now, I need to raise them to distrust others and not to reach out because they may get hurt. I do not want for them to hold back on being close to others either. . . . I don't like that they are learning to talk back to the teachers, but here, they tell me, they have to defend themselves. Here, schools teach children to say no; in my country, you teach them to say yes."

With respect to the practice of discipline, it is not uncommon for Latinos to use shame, threats (Garcia-Preto, 1996b), and mild corporal punishment (Falicov, 1998) as deterrents to inappropriate behaviors. Some mothers even claim they would spank an adolescent who may show disrespect. However, a sensible perspective on understanding parental behavior is necessary. Negy

(2000) warns against erring in clinical judgment when behavior that borders on abuse is normalized as "cultural." He gives an example of a common practice among Mexican American parents whereby children were punished by having them kneel for long periods of time on *fichas* (small metal objects such as bottle caps).

Latino parents have been identified as authoritarian, exerting control over their children (García-Preto, 1996b, 1998; Falicov, 1998). Important components of the parenting style of Latinos are control, high levels of supervision, and strict standards. Latino discipline practices that enforce obedience and *respeto* to authority figures have been linked to deterrence of delinquent behaviors (Pabón, 1998). In addition, close family involvement through supervision is considered a protective factor to child resiliency, especially when children are confronted with life event stressors (Tiet et al., 1998).

This parenting style has been found to be consistent among Latino parents with low-risk and high-risk adolescent boys. Florsheim, Tolan, and Gorman-Smith (1996) found that between Latino and African American inner-city families, Latino parents from both high-risk and low-risk groups exerted more control in their approach. It was observed that the more autonomy and assertiveness the Latino boys exhibited, the more their parents responded with authoritarian and punitive measures. Latino parents encouraged submissiveness whereas African American parents encouraged autonomy.

In counseling, this parental control, when combined with the child's strong loyalty to the family, is seen as an "enmeshed" family. However, it is important to closely examine the parent-child attachment and the family members' history before reaching this conclusion. For example, a Latina mother may provide extensive supervision to her adolescent daughter's male relationships, and it may be viewed as "good parenting," especially when raising daughters (García-Preto, 1998). However, these issues create intergenerational conflicts between parent and child, especially during adolescence, when Latino children compare their parents' parenting style with the more open standards of their American friends' parents.

Although the authority of the parent still prevails among Latino parents raising children in the United States, Latinos have been very open to change, and they improve their discipline practices as long as these are congruent with cultural values. However, the authors have found initial hesitation among parents to adopt behavioral strategies such as contracts or token economies when the counselor loses sight of the level of acculturation. For example, exploring the development of a behavioral contract as an intervention for a 15-year-old youth who failed to do his house chores, the counselor experienced a bold response from his mother. She was a high socioeconomic status, low acculturated Colombian who responded: "Hey, I am Latina and I parent my children the Latino way, not the American way . . . when I say do it, he just needs to do it." In this case, behavioral approaches, well proven in the professional and scientific literature, are based on a collaborative, democratic approach to parenting, which in this case clashed with the mother's parenting worldview (e.g., Shank & Turnball, 1993; Todd, 2000).

Child Development in Latino Families

Several theoretical models have been proposed that explain Latino developmental processes (Florsheim et al., 1996; Inclán & Herron, 1998). For instance, Inclán and Herron (1998) conceptualize Latino families between an agrarian and modern family model. In the former, children become adults, whereas in the latter, children become adolescents, then, adolescents become adults, creating three stages. It is possible that the perception of adolescents as "children" among traditional Latino families may also contribute to different parenting perspectives, expectations, and attributions.

Latino mothers with young children have been described as overprotective (Lijtmaer, 1998) and tend to prolong childhood stages by American standards (e.g., drinking from the bottle as a preschooler). There is also a tendency to see child development as an internal process that is self-directed (Falicov, 1998). This developmental perspective may relate to findings that Latino parents from low socioeconomic levels tend to have lower expectations of developmental milestones and abilities (Zepeda & Espinosa, 1988). Similarly, among immigrant Mexican mothers, children are seen as not actively generating learning experiences with the environment, and development is perceived as emerging slowly throughout childhood (Arcia & Johnson, 1998). Likewise, parents may label behaviors as problematic in children who do not meet their cultural expectations, especially when these behaviors contradict gender role expectations (Canino & Spurlock, 2000; Grossman & Shigaki, 1994). For example, overactive girls and those interested in sports or physical activity may be seen as more problematic than boys who exhibit similar behaviors (García-Preto, 1998).

Because these attitudes and beliefs lead to different child rearing practices, many developmental constructs may not apply to Latino individuals. For instance, separation and individuation are central constructs in developmental theory, but among Latino adolescents, the process of becoming an adult differs markedly from the process in the dominant culture. Separation and individuation from a Latino perspective are a fluid, slow process, not tied to a predetermined chronological period, as American society seems to understand it. With time, the Latino child moves through the vertical organization of the family structure, with the elder holding the highest status of all before advancing in the aging process. See Table 5.1 for a general description of Latino parent-child developmental tasks.

Moreover, children develop a sense of self and competence, not through independence and autonomy but through the process of socialization of collectivism and *familismo*. Self-worth is generated by giving, respecting, and helping the family and others in the community, not through individualistic tasks of mastery and independence. Even though Latino parents express pride for children's accomplishments and level of mastery, they simultaneously reinforce loyalty and social connectedness.

Another developmental construct, empty nest syndrome, does not typically apply to Latino families because adult children and their parents continue to have a very close relationship that transcends a separation and loss crisis. Intergenerational involvement encourages the recycling of Latino socialization values, solidifies the expansion of two families that join together through marriage, encourages intergenerational relationships, allows for a sense of competence in elders, and provides significant stability for the children.

The tendency among Latinos with adult children is to continue the frequency of contacts through daily communications, family rituals, and mutual support. This focus also includes sharing all celebrations with the entire family. When families live apart, it is interesting to observe that adult children use their vacation to visit family whenever financially possible. Frequent communication continues during periods of crises. Most adult children, when separated geographically, continue their support by sending money and needed items such as medicines. This sense of family obligation and support is also heightened during times of acute and chronic care (Magilvy, Congdon, Martinez, Davis, & Averill, 2000; Warda, 2000).

Care of Elderly Parents

Elder care presents challenging and difficult tasks for most Latino adults. The norm is to care for the elder until his or her death. Latino families expect health care professionals to discuss with them the elder's medical condition as Latinos hold a collectivist view of decision making in medical care. Blackhall, Murphy, Frank, Michel, and Azen (1995) studied the disclosure of medical diagnosis to the family with four different ethnic groups. They found that Mexican Americans and Korean American elders preferred to have their families make the decisions about life support and know the diagnosis rather than the patient. This expectation conflicts with the patient-physician practice of maintaining patient autonomy. Family members who experience the failing health of a family member may report a need to become involved in decision making about the medical treatment to minimize the patient's suffering and loss of hope (Martinez, 1999).

Placing elders in nursing homes is viewed negatively, often as abandonment, but hospital care is seen as justifiable. Adult children and the family are expected to carry on the responsibilities of rehabilitation, recovery, and daily care. In cases where nursing care is inevitable, Latino family caretakers have been described as delaying the access of medical care resources that could

Table 5.1 Latino Parent-Child Developmental Tasks

	Child	*Parent*	*Family*
Infancy	Attachment; meet developmental milestones	Provide safety and affection; define parental roles and support network; extend infancy; developmental milestones not generally seen as internally driven	Assign *padrino, madrina* roles; grandparents and extended family seen as resources of support and care for the infant; birth of child solidifies marriage
Preschool	Language and socialization; expected to develop affective and social skills: cariño, respeto; developmental tasks reflected by external events (e.g., birth of sibling, starting day care)	Focus is to teach social graces and bonding; developmental milestones seen as dependent on child's readiness and not norms; reinforces interpersonal connections versus independence/autonomy	Children incorporated in all adult social activities; home care preferred over day care: grandparents or extended family may be involved in child care. Family history used to confirm developmental milestones
School age	Adjustment to school; exposure to new system; challenges with language and academic demands; peers; may be "language broker" for family and "window to American culture"	Encourages *respeto* to other authority figures; discourages activities outside the family. Education level sets degree of school involvement and perception of school	Older child may be given responsibility to oversee younger siblings or relatives at school; older child given duties to care for siblings at home; encourages familial peers and socialization
Adolescence	Gender-defined family responsibilities; sexual interests and identity development, may prefer dominant culture; gender role conflicts with parents	Provides strict supervision, especially with daughters; parents hold to native culture standards and strategies of discipline; cultural values threatened	Culture and intergenerational conflicts; concerns with social problems (drugs, teenage pregnancy, gangs); gender expectations differ
Young adult	May or may not be "leaving home;" college, marriage; career development; incorporation of spouse's family; parenthood; seeks parental guidance and support	Continues to support adult children (financially, shelter, etc.); may share household with married children; loss of adult children not as drastic a transition due to continuity of "togetherness" (vs. "empty nest syndrome")	Encourages togetherness, family rituals, and frequent contacts; grandparents assume supportive role; marriage or college "acceptable" reasons to "leave home"; marriage seen as permanent, long-lasting decision; couple expected to have children
Middle age	Growth of family; illness or death of parent; care of elders; daughters seen as primary caregivers of elders while sons provide financial help; retirement less conflictual transition due to focus on family	Sought for guidance and help; extension of parental duties with adult children redefines own marriage and older adult developmental tasks; may long for old ties and return to native country	Duty to maintain cultural values; recycle lifespan developmental tasks; a *buen hijo* or *hija* (good son or daughter) "never abandons the family or parents"; nursing home may be seen as abandonment
Older age	Assumes responsibilities in the family; role defined through familial tasks or duties; reinvestment in old ties and cultural connections; practice of traditional religious, medical, and cultural rituals	Adult children and grandchildren seek elders' support, guidance; value their input (respeto); rituals practiced during terminal illness and after death	Family contributes with caretaking responsibilities of elders; religious and cultural rituals allow for expression of grief and sorrow (catharsis) and reconnection to the past

SOURCE: Gallardo-Cooper, 2001b.

assume more responsibility of the elder patient. Family caregivers often take on this role at the risk of jeopardizing their own health. Of interest, a study conducted with Puerto Rican families found that the home care they provided, although warm and caring, created monumental distress in these families. When the Latino elders were eventually institutionalized, they exhibited more impairment with basic activities of independent living (e.g., brushing teeth, dressing) than non-Latino Whites. The investigators concluded that the threshold of tolerance of the Latino families was higher, and their decision to institutionalize was excessively prolonged until the care of the elder became "nearly impossible" and at the high cost of extraordinary human effort (Espino as cited in Angel, 1998; Angel & Angel, 1997, 1998).

Angel and Angel (1998), who studied the health and care of Latino elders for a 10-year period, argued that Latino families believe that they are neglecting their dear ones by sending them away to assisted living facilities. They also recognize the need for more advanced care for elders, reflecting the realities of Latino families today (e.g., working couples, smaller families, high-cost quality health care), and they advocate for the development of culturally sensitive community-based programs including home-based care.

Counseling Implications

Based on the topics covered in prior sections, the following counseling implications are relevant to Latino families.

Keep abreast of the research on Latino families. For instance, the Latino family that remains close has been found to be the best predictor of mental health, despite barriers of low education and socioeconomic levels (Blank & Torrecilla, 1998; Gil, Vega, & Biafora, 1998). Similarly, Brook, Whiteman, Balka, Win, and Gursen (1997) studied a large sample of Latino and African American boys in New York City to identify risk factors for substance abuse based on parent-child attachment, parental control, and parental modeling. They found different "protector variables" related to attachment and control practices. For African American boys, the accessibility of the mother and father was important; in particular, a close relationship with the father deterred drug use. Interestingly, among Latinos, both parents were available, but a close attachment with the mother (closeness and communication) mediated their drug use.

Children also present complex challenges for the mental health provider because they are dependent on their caretakers and are undergoing critical periods of personality development. To work therapeutically with children implies working with multiple systems such as the family, the school, and the social group. The challenge is complex because the counselor must also consider the impact of negative labels used to describe them, such as *disadvantaged* and *at risk,* in addition to socioeconomic background, family structure, place of residence (i.e., urban vs. rural), language issues, and poor health coverage.

Parent-child conflicts with low-risk and high-risk male adolescents can be addressed within a family therapy mode of intervention as Latinos value communication, endorse the open expression of affection, and encourage family togetherness (Florsheim et al., 1996).

Gender roles within the family should be explored. The relationship of gender roles to family functioning should also be examined.

Latino families have been found to be receptive to professional support and to use specialized programs. However, offering programs without learning what Latino families need may jeopardize their participation. Educational and supportive programs may be helpful, but without a needs assessment, the programs may fail to attract potential participants (Bailey, Skinner, Rodriguez, & Correa, 1999).

Latino parents, especially from low socioeconomic groups, need to be educated about developmental processes. They should understand the role the environment exerts on early stimulation and development.

The Single-Parent *familia*

Characteristics

Latino single-parent families include a mother, father, or grandparent raising one or more children. Teen pregnancy, separation or divorce, and widowhood may explain the status of single mothers. Also, it is common to find single mothers or single fathers residing with their family of origin or with some other relative. Although there are a variety of single-parent family configurations, this section addresses the most common family composition, Latino single mothers.

One of the most salient factors having long-term effects on children is poverty, particularly among Puerto Rican mothers. Lichter and Landale (1995) found that Puerto Rican single mothers (42.8%) had the highest levels of poverty when compared to other Latino subgroups (e.g., Mexican American, 20.4%; Cuban, 21.3%; other Latino, 24.6%), and Anglo American (13.4%). Puerto Rican single mothers were slightly behind the poverty rate of African American women who are heading households (47.2%). Moreover, African American children raised by a single mother seemed to be most prone to poverty due to family structural factors (i.e., single-parent household) whereas Puerto Rican children seemed most prone to poverty through single parenthood *and* parental work patterns. One of the major concerns raised by this finding is that 20% of Puerto Rican single fathers were not working, more than twice the rate of unemployment when compared to Cuban and Mexican fathers. This suggests that the health and psychological development of many Puerto Rican children who live in single households may be seriously compromised.

Others have argued that there are higher rates of teen pregnancy and school dropout among children in single-parent households. Likewise, although the United States has the highest rate of single-parent families among industrialized nations, the United States also provides the least amount of government assistance to such families (Krauth, 1995).

On the other hand, clinicians as well as researchers have disputed the negative consequences of single parenting. For example, Battle (1997) compared the academic achievement of Latino students from single-parent and two-parent households and found that when controlled for socioeconomic status, there were no differences. He concluded that the problem is not the single-parent family structure but rather the inherent problems associated with poverty that are often found in single-parent homes. Similarly, clinicians and researchers have argued that children in single-parent households develop more adaptive traits such as autonomy and self-reliance as a result of taking on more responsibilities in the home environment (Featherstone, 1996; Krauth, 1995).

Nonetheless, this shifting of responsibilities in a Latino single-parent household may create special problems in family adaptation. Mothers may also report a sense of guilt concerning their failure to provide a traditional family structure, and they may feel stigmatized by their family of origin. This may contribute to the high incidence of mental health and medical problems reported by Latina single mothers in the literature.

The high rate of depression reported among Latina mothers adds to the risks of parent-child difficulties and poor child social-emotional development. For example, Koss-Chioino (1999) reports that the rates of depression among Puerto Rican women are twice those reported for Puerto Rican men. In particular, depression was related to fears of abandonment or rejection from a parent or a partner. Partner losses also reflected significant dependency and fear of survival without male companionship. Blacher et al., (1997) also report that whereas women in the United States have twice the risk of depression compared to men, the probability of mental health problems is increased by belonging to a lower socioeconomic group, lacking English language skills, and using primarily the Spanish language.

Another concern relates to Latina single mothers caring for children with special needs. For instance, comparative studies of children with severe mental illness (Jenkins & Schumacher, 1999) and mental retardation (Bailey et al., 1999; Magaña, 1999) consistently report the difficult tasks Latinas undertake by themselves. Latina mothers in particular have been found to experience depression and poor health (Magaña, 1999). One pervasive pattern found in these studies was that they were predominantly isolated from the community, suffered from poor health care, and did not master the English language.

Realities

In clinical practice, it has been observed that Latina single mothers may tend to suppress their own needs for adult relationships. These mothers deny themselves the opportunity to have healthy and supportive relationships but instead hold a position represented by *los niños vienen primero* (children come first). There is a sense of self-sacrifice that does not allow them to redirect their energies into other adult relationships. Adult relationships, if they occur, are often short-lived, and women have a strong intention to terminate if the relationship demands too much time or effort. In many respects, these single mothers prevent risky situations by minimizing the contacts of their children with questionable and multiple surrogate fathers.

Many of these single mothers become highly overprotective and may deter socialization of their children with nonfamily or non-Latino individuals. When isolated, Latina mothers tend not to allow their children to play outside with other peers from the neighborhood. The case of Clara illustrates this point.

THE CASE OF CLARA

Clara, a Dominican single mother of four children struggled to maintain complete control over her children. Her large family of origin lived in Massachusetts, and she had recently separated from her common-law husband due to severe jealousy. One of Clara's adolescent sons had spina bifida and the other leukemia. The third child, age 10, was diagnosed with attention deficit disorder. Only her youngest child, a daughter 8 years of age, did not exhibit any special needs. Clara's house was small but well organized and very clean. The representatives from medical and social agencies who frequently visited the family were always impressed by the spotless house Clara maintained despite her close attention to the needs of all her children. She was a dedicated mother, who spent considerable time providing medical support to the visiting nurses, bedroom upkeep with constant bed linen changes, and hygiene duties required of her two adolescents sons. The children were not allowed to play outside, to spend the night at friends' houses, or to visit peers. Peer visits were only permitted at home and were often discouraged.

The family received services from Hospice as well as from the local community mental health agency to address the older children's medical conditions. The counselor provided on-site services and recommended that Clara allow the younger children to play outside with other children to release some of their energy and to minimize their acting out at home. The daughter was placed in a position of authority to supervise her brothers. Clara rejected that recommendation consistently, and at times, the counselor met resistance whenever Clara was directed to use more "open" approaches leading Clara to exert less control over her children, especially as it related to playing outside and interacting with other children.

The counselor's pressure led Clara to request termination of counseling. She said, "In my country, children learn to play with their siblings and cousins. This way they learn proper manners and behaviors. They do not spend time overnight with friends in other people's houses where they can be exposed to bad habits *(malas mañas)* and bad situations. I do not let my children play outside because I do not know their friends' families and what they are like. My children may have problems, but they are good children because I am always supervising them. And here I am alone raising my children without a family to support me and you want me to let them go out."

As in all groups, some single mothers may engage in dysfunctional behaviors that place children at risk of serious problems. Substance abuse, poverty, trauma, criminal behaviors, teen pregnancy, indiscriminate sexual practices, and multiple partners take their toll on the psychological well-being of Latino children, or for that matter, any child raised in these conditions. Among middle-aged Latina women, the risks of substance abuse increases with poverty and unemployment (Markides, Ray, Stroup-Behnam, & Trevino, 1990). In these circumstances, children are often removed by family or state protective services, and the children are placed in foster homes or relatives' homes.

Placement of Children: Custodial Grandparents

The placement of children in foster homes or relatives' homes points to another situation found among single-parent households, namely the grandparent as a custodial caretaker. Latino grandparents have undertaken a major role as caretakers. However, they have received little clinical and empirical research attention. Burnette (1999) conducted a study among custodial grandparents in the New York City area and found alarming results. In her sample, only one of every five custodial grandparents was married, and only 18% were proficient in English. When compared to the general population, the investigator found that custodial grandmothers had high levels of poverty, poor health, and depression. Burnette (1999) concluded that "poverty, health decrements, and mental health problems are closely intertwined across the lifespan: in late life, these are usually the results of both cumulative and current disadvantage" (p. 314). This study points to a growing concern that grandparents who are placed in a caregiving role lack the most basic needs and are unable to access resources to ameliorate poverty; poor medical care and social limitations are commonplace.

An important repercussion of single grandparents' raising children is that, quite often, it is difficult to raise children at a time when the caregivers' own health dramatically deteriorates. A grandmother suffering from arthritis and heart problems may not have the energy and stamina necessary to raise a young child. Inertia and passivity counteract successful parenting because raising children requires an active approach. That is, having limited mobility (e.g., confined to chair or a bed) is in no way conducive to proper supervision and overall care. Due to these limitations, grandparents may use yelling more often as well as threats to control the children. They either lack transportation or cannot access transportation because of a medical condition, and this leads to an isolated lifestyle. Staying home also prevents these grandparents from becoming involved in the community and in the lives of their grandchildren. If the grandparent and grandchild have a close relationship, there may be a reversed role in which the children take on many adult responsibilities such as running errands, doing household chores, and translating for the grandparent in public places. In such instances, there is a tendency to be highly overprotective, to overlook discipline practices, and to become *ciegos* (blind) about the ramifications of the child's possible manipulation and acting-out behaviors. Therefore, careful attention needs to be given to the functioning level of the elder caretaker and the quality of his or her relationship with the child.

Counseling Implications

The above discussion leads to the following counseling implications.

The lack of perceived support and isolation are critical issues to consider with single parents. Therefore, counselors should identify barriers to the family's support network: professionals, friends, or family (Planos, Zayas, & Busch-Rossnagel, 1997).

The functioning level of the parent or elder should be assessed with respect to activity level, health status, and English language skills. Optimum parenting requires a highly active, psychologically stable, and self-sufficient individual who seeks supportive child-related community involvement.

Stress can occur as a result not only of major life transitions but also of daily hassles. Daily hassles are small but frequent annoying events that create cumulative effects and are highly correlated with health problems. After ruling out the resolution of potentially traumatic events such as divorce and death, counselors should address daily problems experienced in the Latino single-parent family.

The family's ecology must be explored. Having a mentor has been found to be a protective factor among Latino children at risk for mental health and behavioral problems (Rhodes, Contreras, & Mangelsdorf, 1994; Sánchez & Reyes, 1999). Most often, these mentors are family or family friends of the same ethnicity and gender, or *padrinos* (Sánchez & Reyes, 1999).

Contextual factors should be examined in the assessment of perceived deviant behaviors. For example, pregnant Latino adolescents at risk for alcohol abuse may engage in less prenatal substance abuse if they live with their family of origin or their boyfriends, husbands, or partner's families (Rhodes, Gingiss, & Smith, 1994).

The Bicultural *familia*

Characteristics

Biculturalism in marital and relationship counseling is relatively unexplored. Systemic biculturalism can be defined as the interaction of two cultural contexts in family relationships. Although Latino bicultural families come in many packages, most fall under two major categories: *acculturated bicultural* families and *cross-cultural bicultural* families. The first type represents the interplay of different acculturation levels functioning simultaneously within a family system, based on the degree of incorporation of host culture values. The second type of bicultural family is defined by intermarriage. These are cross-cultural unions involving differences by ethnicity, nationality, race, geographical area, language, religious preference, socioeconomic level, or a combination of these factors.

Acculturated Bicultural Families

In general, bicultural families have been mostly addressed as having intergenerational and intercultural conflicts due to different levels of acculturation in family relationships. Different factors affect the rates of acculturation, such as age and degree of exposure to the host culture. First, the difference in age between two individuals in a family may result in two different worldviews and life experiences. These differences often result in intergenerational conflicts. However, when individuals also experience acculturation, the age differences are compounded by cultural variants. Thus, discrepancies occur in adult-child relationships (i.e., parent-child, grandparent-grandchild). Second, the amount of exposure to the host culture correlates with acculturation levels and interacts with gender and generational status. For example, Latina homemakers may be less acculturated than Latinas who are employed outside the home; and first-, second-, and third-generation U.S.-born Latinos will have greater intercultural variance compared to foreign-born Latino family members.

Cross-Cultural Bicultural Families

Latinos have the highest rate of intermarriage in the United States (Garvin, 2000), and these trends are setting the stage for what has been called "the beginning of the blend" in our society (Suro, 1999). At the present time, slightly more than half (57%) of third-generation Latinos will cross-marry (Garvin, 2000) but other projections indicate that two thirds of the Latino population will marry a European American (Suro, 1999). These projections suggest that Latino families will experience greater and faster changes. Ignoring these unions in the professional literature, as is currently the case, will limit the knowledge necessary to develop effective clinical interventions with such families (Negy & Snyder, 2000).

Several conflicting findings have been reported on factors that predispose marriages outside the Latino culture. For example, Heubusch and Dortch (1996) indicated that gender, nationality, and generational level significantly influence Latino intermarriage rates. These authors reported that Latino men intermarry more than Latinas, and some Latino nationalities have different trends (e.g., Cubans intermarry more than Dominicans). As in other ethnic groups, time in the United States influences intermarriage; second-generation South American men are more prone to cross-cultural unions than are first-generation Latinos. On the other hand, in a study by Suro (1999), no gender differences were found in rates of intermarriage between Caucasian European American and Latino couples. Instead, three characteristics were identified as salient predisposing factors: partial or completed college education, higher socioeconomic status, and age younger than 35 years. Furthermore, U.S.-born Latinos were more likely to intermarry than immigrants. Interestingly, the national rate of Latino cross-cultural marriages was found to be twice as high in states with low Latino populations.

Because Latinos are a heterogeneous population, the potential exists for multiple types of unions. For instance, there may be intragroup unions, such as a Mexican marrying a Costa Rican, a Catholic Peruvian marrying an Argentinean Jew, and a Cuban Asian marrying a Puerto Rican. Although commonality in language and ethnicity as defined in the United States (i.e. Latino, Hispanic) does not guarantee compatibility, these two factors play a major role in such relationships. Examples of Latino intermarriages that could be defined as both acculturated and cross-cultural bicultural unions are Mexican American with Mexican born and Puerto Rican-born with U.S.-born Puerto Rican (e.g., *Nuyorican*). Again, in both examples, the partners share similar ethnicity, cultural values, and perhaps language, tastes, and interests, but there are distinct differences in their life experiences related to ethnic identity development and degree of contact with U.S. culture. Among many factors, the differences of being raised in two distinctly different parts of the world and within different sociopolitical structures reflect differential personality and identity formation processes.

In addition to the issues mentioned above, Latinas may be attracted to unions with European American men because they expect that these unions will provide a more egalitarian relationship. In some circles, there is a belief that Latinas "do better" marrying a European American because they will encounter less resistance to sharing family responsibilities with their partners, gain a sense of feminist liberation, and experience less incidence of male philandering. In contrast, Latino-Euro American marriages present in counseling with distinctive dichotomies regarding their opposing views of extended family loyalty. For example, a common complaint of Euro American spouses is that Latino partners seek more time and involvement with their family of origin than the Euro American spouses would prefer. Cross-cultural conflicts can be illustrated by the following case.

THE CASE OF CARMEN AND LUIS

Carmen and Luis were *LatiNegros* (Latinos who consider themselves to have African roots) who had been married for 12 years. Carmen was born and raised in New York City by a strict Puerto Rican father who became a widower when Carmen was a young girl. (Carmen's mother was Cuban.) Luis was born and raised in a small town in Puerto Rico, and he was the youngest son of a family of five sisters. The couple had three boys ages 3, 6, and 10. The 6- and 10-year-old children were diagnosed with learning disabilities. Carmen requested marital counseling to address her doubts about Luis's commitment in their relationship and possible infidelity. She complained that at social gatherings, he often ignored her, which made her feel hurt and alone. Reluctantly, Luis agreed to marital counseling to "help my wife."

The exploration of their marital history and cultural variants revealed that Carmen had prevailing themes of displacement and isolation, believing that she was not supported. Carmen never felt accepted by Luis's family because she was *Nuyorican* and had darker skin. Consequently, she felt threatened by the frequent contact Luis had with his family in Puerto Rico. Carmen thought that Luis's sisters were critical of her when Luis was not around and that his father was rude and disrespectful toward her. Yet, she denied addressing these issues with her father-in-law because of *respeto,* but she expected Luis to correct his father's behavior. However, Luis did not believe that his family was rude to or critical of Carmen. An argument would ensue between the two of them when Carmen raised this topic, each time resulting in her feeling more distressed and unsupported.

The couple was seen separately to further assess individual issues. In these sessions, Carmen openly discussed experiences with racism and discrimination that began early in her childhood. In addition, although Carmen was bilin-

gual, it was clear that her Spanish fluency was weak, and she made many gram-
matical errors. She also disclosed that she was self-conscious talking with
Luis's family in Spanish, but she did anyway "because it would be worse if I
didn't." In contrast, Luis did not report any experiences with discrimination as
a child.

The counselor recognized the cultural value of *respeto,* and gender role socialization conflicts as important and set the goal of helping the couple develop
more adaptive skills. For instance, Luis first preferred to take care of his father's
problem with his wife "because a woman cannot embarrass a man like this, not
a man with authority." However, Carmen's expectation that Luis would correct
his father, after the fact, was not a functional strategy, as it created potential
marital and family tensions. As other resolution options were explored, Carmen
became aware of her submissive position with male authority figures, as her
father was very strict and prohibited all confrontations with authority figures.
Because confrontation had such a negative connotation for Carmen, the counselor redefined confrontation as an opportunity to express her feelings toward
her father in law's behavior as well as an opportunity to improve her relationship with him, reinforcing the values of *respeto* and social connectedness. The
counselor also explored Carmen's perceptions of her own father, their relationship, and the way they resolved problems. The couple agreed that Carmen
could discuss with *respeto* any discomfort or misunderstanding whenever she
felt offended. Carmen also rehearsed different scenarios during joint sessions.
Direct communication in this situation was an effective strategy because it also
allowed Carmen to validate her perceptions and assumptions about her father-
in-law.

In addition, issues of male authority were also addressed when Luis refused
to have "*mi mujer* (i.e., a gendered, culturally accepted expression suggesting
possessiveness: "my woman") telling me what to do in public." This issue was
addressed in two contexts: culturally and contextually. As a successful male in
the business community, Luis was keen on maintaining his leadership position
in public. Carmen was able to reframe the conflict from a passive-aggressive
power and control issue to an understanding of how his leadership role was affected, especially in social situations involving his coworkers and community
supporters. The couple developed a plan to resolve similar incidents in the
future in that they were to remove themselves from the public eye to discuss
sensitive topics privately.

Issues of displacement were central to Carmen, who had lost her mother at
an early age and experienced racial discrimination and stigmatization in a predominantly Anglo American community, as well as in the African American
community because she was "Spanish." Moreover, she projected cultural biases into her own marriage by assuming that she was rejected because she was
a *Nuyorican,* and her marital difficulties related to the stereotypical assumptions that all Latino men are unfaithful to their wives. She also felt insecure
about her mothering because "I did not learn how to be a mother from my
mother and I worried that Luis and his family would not approve of me."
Therefore, any feedback or lack of feedback she received from Luis's family
she interpreted as disapproval with her performance as a mother or as a wife.

As therapy unfolded, the infidelity worries began to dissipate and more salient day-to-day marital and familial conflicts took priority. A central issue for Carmen was her feeling fatigued and overwhelmed with the demands of parenting two elementary school-age boys with many academic difficulties.

Luis praised his wife for the outstanding job she did as a mother and wife and described his family role as one of a provider and disciplinarian. Carmen recognized that she expected Luis to be more involved in parenting as her father had been. Luis's perception of Carmen as one who was imposing on him a more active parenting role was reframed from a power and control issue to one of life's experiences. Luis also recognized his public need for authority and the importance of being more attentive to Carmen in social gatherings.

This case is an example of how a Latino couple sharing similar heritage experienced cross-cultural conflicts. This case also exemplifies how a serious problem such as infidelity is intertwined with cultural, marital, gender, family of origin, and phenotype factors. In particular, addressing cultural variants allowed for the identification of themes that were partially hidden behind stereotypes; the case provides evidence that growing up with discrimination influences personal struggles. The counseling process also identified workable life problems embedded in cultural and contextual variables. The model proposed by Falicov (1986) to address cross-cultural relationship problems proved helpful in this case. In particular, Falicov identified three major areas of conflict found in couples of different cultural backgrounds. These are related to (a) knowledge of the cultural values or "cultural codes" of the partner (e.g., marital and family expectations, parenting roles), (b) early history of the couple and the family's permission to intermarry (e.g., extended family's acceptance of the relationship), and (c) heightened cultural stereotypes during periods of acute stress (e.g., using cultural stereotypes as a defense mechanism for underlying painful experiences).

Realities

Despite the role of biculturalism in adaptation, only two models are available that provide us with clinical direction. One is Padilla's (1994) bicultural development theory, and the other is Szapocznik et al.'s (1984) Bicultural Effectiveness Training Program. (See the discussion of this model in Chapter 8.). With this in mind, we address important concepts and clinical observations that can be incorporated into a framework for counseling bicultural families: (a) Latino ethnic identity, (b) bicultural development, (c) bicultural dissonance, and (d) bicultural parenting.

Latino Ethnic Identity

The development of a positive identity is central to optimum psychological well-being. One can extrapolate from research findings that Latino parents who are psychologically stable will provide the most balanced and positive family structure for their children (Johnston, 1996; Wasserstein, 1998). Consequently, to be psychologically adept in the United States, Latinos also need a solid and positive ethnic identity (Padilla, 1994; Romero, 2000). This refers to owning cultural and familial roots to embark on a journey of self-actualization, regardless of the challenges posed by discrimination, the language barrier, and in the case of recent immigrants, the process of adaptation. The development of ethnic identity has been found to serve as a buffer against the deleterious effects of discrimination and prejudice (Baptiste, 1990; Croker & Major, 1989; Padilla, 1994). Therefore, Latino children benefit when their parents hold a strong Latino identity because parents model and communicate ethnic traits of self-assurance and self-efficacy. In addition, heightened ethnic awareness in the family increases the children's ethnic knowledge and opportunities to learn about prejudice (Quintana & Vega, 1999). In contrast, parents who belittle the cultural values or characteristics of their partners may disrupt the development of a positive ethnic identity formation in the children.

The example of the couple discussed earlier addresses the process in which ethnic identity issues are carefully unveiled in counseling. Crohn (1998) recommends that bicultural parents introspect and identify the areas most important in their sense of identity: ethnicity, nationality, race, religion, language, family of origin, and so forth. In our case, Carmen's ethnic identity was primarily described as a combination of geographic location (i.e., *Nuyorican*) and race ("I'm Black and darker than him"), whereas Luis's ethnic identity was defined by his nationality (i.e., Puerto Rican) and his family of origin (i.e., being the "the accomplished good son"). Ethnic identity issues can be attended therapeutically without much denial and resistance when the disclosure of emotionally charged issues— in this case, racism, prejudice, abandonment, and displacement—is fully clarified. Three steps facilitate this process. First, allow for catharsis of emotionally charged content. Second, clarify perceptions, distortions, and generalizations based on cultural and familial variants, and finally, focus on the day-to-day, manageable problems that are changeable. When these three steps are followed, clients regain control, hope, and empowerment in their lives.

Bicultural Development

Amado M. Padilla (1994) theorized that Latino children and parents face different socialization paths leading to what he calls bicultural development. His framework focuses on a range of issues encountered by Latinos who are (a) recent immigrants, (b) children (offspring) of immigrants, (c) later generation children and adolescents, or (d) children of mixed heritage. According to Padilla, each of these types of Latinos experience a unique set of challenges, issues, and problems. For instance, the children of parents who immigrated to the United States may receive mixed messages from the parents who stress the importance of adopting the behaviors of the dominant culture (becoming "Americanized"), yet encourage their children to adhere to cultural traditions. Another example involves those who are of mixed ethnic heritage. These Latinos may struggle with identity issues because they are dealing with two or more different cultures.

It is important to note that Padilla's model incorporates clinical and empirical findings with a clear explanation of the primary challenges Latinos encounter, such as acculturation stress, reestablishment of a balance between the native and dominant culture, discrimination, and multicultural functioning. For instance, empirical findings have supported the impact of the language barrier in Padilla's model, linking language problems to depression, distress, and suicide (Roberts & Chen, 1995). Moreover, Zavala (2000) found bilingual adolescents who lacked institutional and systemic linguistic support to be living *entremundos* (between two worlds). These children were troubled by conflicting environmental demands and feelings of confusion and disengagement.

Bicultural Dissonance

McGoldrick and García-Preto (1984) suggest that the more similar the partners, the fewer conflicts are evident in the relationship. If true, one might conclude that bicultural families may experience greater dissonance when the parents have not achieved a resolution to their differences. This dynamic is a rule of thumb of a functioning family system, where parents are consistent with the implementation of rules, expectations, and actions. Different levels of acculturation in Latino families may indicate not only parent-child conflict, as is typically the case, but also parent-parent conflicts. In the case of cross-cultural families, the dissonance may primarily occur in adult-adult conflict with offspring becoming tangled in triangulation dynamics. Suro (1999) indicates that acculturation in cross-cultural couples is a reciprocal process. That is, Latinos in cross-cultural marriages adopt many of the European American values of their partners, while their partners adopt Latino worldviews. The acceptance and integration of different cultural worldviews become central to family and marital therapists who work with cross-cultural unions.

It is important not to lose sight of the quality of the familial relationships, regardless of the bicultural dissonance. A solid, positive parent-child and husband-wife relationship may attenuate the difficult tasks they encounter. Although problems may arise with external stressors and internal adaptation conflicts, well-established familial relationships tend to help members endure painful and traumatic events. In addition, adopting the clinical approach of accentuating dissonance or differences to identify strengths in coping styles appears to be an effective intervention (Ho, 1990).

Bicultural Parenting

The challenges of child rearing in bicultural families can easily be underestimated. Perel (2000) labeled children of cross-cultural couples "a time-bomb" as child-rearing practices are culturally embedded and most couples underestimate the potential for serious conflicts in this area. Negy and Snyder (2000) conducted a study where the stress and acculturation levels of two mono-ethnic couples groups were compared with a Mexican American and European American cross-cultural married couples group. The researchers found no differences in marriage satisfaction and general stress level among all three types of couples. However, significant differences were found in cross-cultural couples in the area of child rearing, especially among highly acculturated Mexican American wives married to Caucasian European American husbands.

Negy and Snyder (2000) also contend that although children from cross-cultural marriages have been described in the literature as suffering identity conflicts and poor self-esteem, their problems stem from parental role conflicts regarding child behavior expectations. The differences often motivate bicultural families to seek counseling when they fail to agree on *what* and *how* to parent.

Bicultural parents, more than any other parents, cannot afford to be ambivalent about their position on many areas affecting child development: religion practices, racial issues, social class issues, and the like. Differences in family rituals, rules, gender role socialization, religious practices, communication style, and many more factors may clash in these families.

Moreover, language barriers may interfere with the quantity and quality of support parents in cross-cultural unions receive. For this reason, preventive measures, such as psychoeducational intervention, should be provided to these families at risk (Negy & Snyder, 2000). Most scholars agree that bicultural parenting should include teaching children about methods to cope with prejudice (Crohn, 1998; Padilla, 1994; Quintana & Vega, 1999). Crohn (1998) urges parents not to impose their own culture on children, especially adolescents, and to provide children with a rich and positive exposure to each parent's culture. With time, bicultural children and multicultural children internalize different aspects of their experiences and beliefs. When this process crystallizes, these children are able to function successfully with multiple worldviews and demands (Ho, 1990; Padilla, 1994).

In general, three basic steps might facilitate the process of bicultural parenting: (a) identification of and consensus about what values and expectations are most important in child rearing, (b) selection of five or fewer basic rules that can cover many misbehaviors (e.g., treats others with love and respect), and (c) consensus development of three discipline actions that are commensurate with the severity of the child's transgression: mild, moderate, and severe. Because the best predictor of future behavior is past behavior, asking parents how they were raised, disciplined, and encouraged in their childhood facilitates the disentanglement or reduction of parenting polarization (Ellickson & McGuigan, 2000; Kunkel, 1997).

Counseling Implications

The following counseling implications are relevant based on the above discussions:

Determine the extent to which the problem lies in acculturation differences, cross-cultural differences, or both.

Incorporate ethnic identity constructs in the counseling process by identifying barriers and enhancers of ethnic identity development.

Apply Padilla's bicultural developmental model as a guideline to possible familial and individual processes.

Explore the extended family's attitude and acceptance with the bicultural characteristics of the family. Falicov (1986) and McGoldrick and García-Preto (1984) agree that a major obstacle in intermarriage is the extended family's approval of the relationship. These attitudes may weigh heavily on Latino families, who tend to be highly involved with the extended family.

Identify acculturative stressors. In bicultural families and families undergoing acculturation, conflicts need to be depersonalized and reframed as cultural differences (Sciarra, 1999). In therapy, metaphors can be used that normalize and incorporate bicultural processes, such as "cultural transition" (Falicov, 1986, 1998), "building a bridge" (Garcia-Preto, 1998), "a rebirth to a new life" (Hernández & McGoldrick, 1999), and assuming a "tourist or immigrant" perspective to the host culture (Perel, 2000).

Apply the Bicultural Effectiveness Training Program whenever family members are identified as experiencing intercultural disparities due to different acculturation levels.

Explore all possible areas of differences, failed expectations, cultural stereotypes, discrimination, and unresolved conflicts. Socioeconomic differences are often overlooked but are well camouflaged in Latino bicultural relationships. Explore how foreign-born and U.S.-born Latinos and their respective families of origin perceive and accept differences (e.g., *Mestizo* traits, use of Spanish and English languages, connection with the country of origin).

Identify and focus on coping strengths (Ho, 1987, 1990). Although it is important to identify the factors that polarize the family, healing takes place by the identification and nurturance of strengths in the family.

The Immigrant *familia*

Characteristics

The complexity of Latino immigration cannot be defined in general terms because each story is formulated by different incentives, enacted by different personalities, and experienced in different contexts. The decision to migrate may have been made voluntarily, involuntarily, or under pressure, and it is generally triggered by one or a combination of three motivating factors. First, the decision to migrate may involve the desire to improve one's economic situation and resources through employment or education or to have better access to medical or educational services for a particular family member, such as a disabled child. Another motive centers on being "pulled out" (Mock, 1998) from the native country due to national disasters, wars, or political unrest, or oppression. Many immigrants who leave their country due to these conditions may be given refugee status; however this can only be granted by the host culture (Espín, 1999). Finally, reuniting with family and friends, or what clients describe as *la sangre llama* (ancestry calls), is a strong motivating force that propels people to leave their homeland (Garvin, 2000).

The specific characteristics of Latino immigrants also vary. Latinos from all socioeconomic and educational levels immigrate, as well as entire families or members of families. In addition, there are gender differences in the immigration experience. Espín (1999) indicates that women make up the largest number of immigrants in the United States. Espín's scholarly work on the impact of migration on women is a valuable framework to understand the process of personal transformation with Latinas. For example, she contends that due to patriarchic family structures, immigrant women may not be involved in the decision-making process to migrate. Similarly, Espín postulates that acculturation allows women a sense of liberation not experienced prior to immigration, which in turn may block their interest in returning to the country of origin.

Age is a characteristic that notably influences the migration experience. For instance, it appears to be easier for young children to adapt than older children, adolescents, and adults. Mena, Padilla, and Maldonado (1987) found that the age of 12 seemed to be a decisive milestone that predicted stress level and coping skills of immigrants. If the migration occurred after the age of 12, immigrants experienced more acculturative stress and a more direct coping approach, as they seemed to lack the social support networks of later generation immigrants. Nonetheless, children and adolescents experience potentially more complications in family adjustment as intergenerational conflicts intensify with the clash of different levels of acculturation in the family. These conflicts may lead to familial distancing at a time when children need parental support the most.

In addition, Hernández and McGoldrick (1999) believe that the migration experience is such a long-lasting, powerful event in people's lives that it should be considered a new life-cycle stage for all families undergoing this experience. Migration disrupts the family's natural developmental process and may negatively affect the structure of the family (Inclán & Hernández, 1992). For example, *who* migrates and *with whom* has significance. Depending on the circumstances, men tend to migrate first while women stay behind raising the family. This separation usually lasts until men obtain economic stability in the host culture. Family separation of the immigrant family inevitably changes the structure of the family, the quality of the familial relationships, and the adjustment process of reunification. Salgado de Snyder (1999) described the difficulties Mexican women encounter when they are left behind to tend to raising children under difficult socioeconomic circumstances. Sciarra (1999) also observed the difficulties of reunification and unresolved emotions of two daughters who were left behind with relatives in Central America for many years until the parents found economic stability in the United States

As outlined in previous chapters, the context of migration also involves sociohistorical influences that modulate the degree of acceptance and support given by the host culture. Those labeled as refugees may experience more governmental support and resources than those classified as immigrants. In contrast, undocumented or illegal immigrants may encounter harsher experiences in their pre- and postmigration periods than immigrants who arrive as refugees. The vulnerability of undocumented immigrants cannot be overlooked because in their struggle to enter the country and to obtain validity, they are at risk of victimization, exploitation, oppression, and marginalization. These traumatic events may produce both acute and chronic anxiety.

Realities

To access necessary clinical information and develop culturally sensitive interventions, the culturally competent professional needs to have knowledge of various frameworks that help to understand the migratory experience and its impact on the psychological well-being of an individual and family. As outlined in Chapter 3, migration can be best understood as a three-stage process: premigration, migration, and postmigration. Each of these stages is characterized by different tasks and challenges. First, Arredondo-Dowd's (1981) model addresses three affective states that occur in the second and third stage of migration: (a) relief, the initial admission to the host culture; (b) disenchantment and disillusion, the unmet expectations with the host culture; and (c) acceptance, the integration of positive and negative components of the host culture. Arredondo-Dowd's model is useful in revealing emotional content, loss issues, and coping mechanisms.

A second framework by Lequerica (1993) conceptualizes Latino immigration from a "cultural shock" framework, indicating that the process of immigration involves internal and external factors. Internal factors or the "crisis of loss" represent negative affective and cognitive processes such as anxiety, fear, guilt, mourning, loss, marginalization, victimization, prejudice, and racism. External factors are defined as a "crisis of load" or the contextual demands immigrants encounter in daily life such as housing, employment, citizenship status, language barriers, and poor medical care. In essence, these models are useful in understanding two fundamental affects of immigration: acculturative stress and trauma.

Acculturative Stress

Stress has been conceptualized as a life change with potentially negative consequences leading to psychological and physical illness. A move to a new community is a significant stressor because there is a need to adjust to the demands of novel situations while dealing with loss of familiarity (Johnson, 1986). From this perspective, Latino immigration becomes a stressful event because it involves the uprooting of individuals and families (Padilla, Cervantes, Maldonado, & Garcia, 1988). These effects may range from mildly stressful experiences to post-traumatic stress disorder. Regardless of the degree of psychological burden experienced, the immigration process demands a constant state of cognitive negotiation between internal and external demands.

The general assumption is that acculturation is a psychosocial stressor of immense proportions because the problems faced in the new culture may be long-lived and unexpected (Jasinski, 1998; Lequerica, 1993). A growing body of empirical and clinical findings supports the notion that acculturative stress experienced by first-generation immigrants may be more aversive than commonly known psychological stress (Saldaña, 1998), and prolonged acculturative stress may produce significant negative psychological consequences. For example, a direct relationship has been found between the immigrant's acculturation level and substance abuse (Flores-Ortíz & Bernal, 1990), domestic violence (Jasinski, 1998), identity confusion (Birman, 1998),

and depression (Alderete, Vega, Kolody, & Aguilar-Gaxiola, 1999). Therefore, the powerful effects of migration transcend several generations
(Espín, 1999; Hernández & McGoldrick, 1999).

Trauma

Immigrants experience trauma in different areas, different periods, and
different intensities. Some Latino immigrants leave their country of origin to
avoid the negative effects of physical and psychological trauma. Other immigrants experience trauma during the actual process of migration, such as the
Cuban *balseros,* who faced extraordinary risks and losses while fleeing in
makeshift boats or floating devices, or Mexicans crossing the border. These
horrifying events may be long term and cumulative or acute and short lived.
Regardless of the duration, the mere experience of trauma is not usually
volunteered or easily resolved, and the counselor should assess symptoms
to rule out post-traumatic stress disorder.

Children, women, and elders are considered by some to be more vulnerable
to trauma (Espín, 1999; Zea, Diehl, & Porterfield, 1997). In the case of Central American children, Zea and associates (1997) argue that although little is
known about the effects of "low-intensity" war exposure, children living with
civil war have experienced "massive exposure to violence," such as witnessing morbid executions of family and friends. The authors also report that
these children have experienced the loss of parents through death and separation. Because these children do not have the protective function of family
support and are undergoing critical periods of development, these traumatic
experiences lead to a host of psychological problems ranging from acute distress to severe psychopathology. Among some Latina groups, in particular
Puerto Ricans, a history of victimization, trauma, and suppressed anger has
been associated with *ataques de nervios* or physical symptoms such as trem-
bling, pseudocardiac complaints, difficulty breathing, fainting, and the like
(Rivera-Arzola & Ramos-Grenier, 1997). In addition, Paniagua (2001) indicates that among Latinos, symptoms associated with acute stress disorder
may be commonly found as the culture sanctions moderate to severe reactions to difficult life event stressors.

The culturally skilled counselor should have the knowledge base to recognize
symptoms of stress-related disorders so that proper treatment can be sought.
For example, young children regress to earlier developmental stages when they
are traumatized (e.g., enuresis, clinging behaviors, sucking fingers). Separation anxiety may be a justifiable behavior as a result of traumatic experiences,
yet, these children need intervention to prevent further decompensation and
the development of secondary problems. Likewise, attention should be given
to symptoms such as insomnia, numbness, and inability to remember or re-
fusal to disclose premigration, migration, and postmigration experiences.

Trauma is also perpetuated in our society by exploitation, discrimination, and abuse during and after the migration phase. Furthermore, the lack of a supportive community exacerbates the adaptation process. Migrant workers, in particular, often reside in segregated communities that may provide them with substandard living and working conditions. The following two cases illustrate important cultural variables to consider when trauma is a critical issue.

THE CASE OF MARTA

Marta, a 35-year-old Cuban woman, was admitted to a psychiatric hospital after a serious suicide attempt. Six months earlier, she had emigrated from Cuba to join her mother and sister in the United States after waiting for a visa for 7 years. The hospital staff seemed perplexed by her suicide attempt. Marta would say over and over again, "I want to return to Cuba . . . and if I can't, why should I live?" The clinical staff concluded that her pathology was severe, not only because of the suicide attempt, but also because she wanted to return to Cuba even though her mother and sister were in the United States, and Marta preferred to return to the socioeconomic circumstances that had motivated her migration. The staff knew little about the Cuban migration experience, unfortunately; they could not help her translate into English some of her concerns. Marta was experiencing the loss of family and the community of friends who supported her in Cuba. She was also losing sight of the positive expectations she once had about the new host country.

THE CASE OF MIGUEL

Miguel, a 4-year-old, was the only child of a young Mexican couple who lived in a citrus migrant compound in Florida. His parents took him to the public health clinic because they were concerned that he had begun to soil his pants. Miguel had been successfully toilet trained for a year, but for the previous 2 months began to exhibit problems crying whenever he entered the bathroom and resisted sitting on the toilet. At the clinic, no one spoke Spanish. The health department physician referred Miguel to a bilingual mental health professional to rule out sexual abuse.

Miguel's parents took him to the evaluation and were cooperative with all the procedures; however, they were confused about Miguel's referral to the mental health agency. The professional explained to the parents that the physician had not found any medical basis for his condition and, therefore, referred Miguel to the clinic for psychological assessment. The individual evaluation revealed that he had a close and affectionate relationship with his parents. The evaluation also revealed that he was not sexually abused. Instead, it was found that his symptoms began after he saw a movie in English. Because he did not speak or understand English well, he was unable to understand the nature of the story; however, during a session, Miguel repeatedly mentioned in Spanish that there were "little animals" coming out of the toilet. Further exploration confirmed that Miguel had seen a movie (with his parents) that was not suitable for a pre-schooler, but neither parent knew beforehand anything about the content of the movie, let alone its R classification.

During the course of Miguel's treatment, his mother began having difficulties following through with recommendations because she was having frequent and severe headaches and dizziness. She was also having difficulty completing basic tasks. At one point during a session, she told the counselor that she had fallen from a ladder while at work. The father explained that she had been unconscious for about an hour, did not receive any medical attention that day, and was sent home sick.

Treatment shifted to referring Miguel's mother to the public health department for a medical evaluation of a head injury. The counselor spoke with the clinic's nurse to explain the referral. However, at the clinic, Miguel, not his mother, underwent a CAT scan to determine the extent of the head injury. On learning this, the counselor contacted the physician, explained the nature of the referral, and attempted to clarify the miscommunication. The CAT scan showed that Miguel's mother had suffered a significant closed head injury and needed to be referred to a neurologist for treatment.

Once the mother's medical condition was addressed, behavioral treatment resumed and Miguel again exhibited appropriate elimination behaviors. Both parents were eager to implement behavioral interventions to address Miguel's problems. They were educated on the nature of Miguel's symptoms and on behavioral strategies.

Counseling Implications

The above discussion leads to the following implications for counseling:

Identify the interaction of immigration with family life-cycle stage, and the characteristics of family members (e.g., age, gender, language mastery, education level). Also, explore the motives that lead to immigration and supportive networks of post-migration.

Build continuity between the old and new culture. This is accomplished through narratives of migration stories. Pay attention to pre- and postmigration events. Do not allow immigrants to disengage with their past, as this past is important in identity solidification and resolution of the grieving process. (See case study of David in Chapter 6.)

Incorporate the new and the old within a contextual framework. Suppressing the old culture in favor of the new culture to facilitate adaptation may deplete the family's internal resources and coping strategies. Similarly, being a "cultural militant" of the family's native culture may jeopardize adjustment in the new culture.

Explore the coping mechanisms used during the process of acculturation (both ineffective and effective). Because change can be stressful explore the coping strategies used to adapt.

Assume a flexible mental health professional role that expands beyond the 55-minute office session. Advocacy is particularly effective with immigrants because they lack information about the community and often lack the means to explore resources (Lequerica, 1993; Smart & Smart, 1994).

Use the self as a resource in helping to normalize the experience of immigration. For those professionals who have had personal experiences with immigration, scholars recommend sharing such experiences (Falicov, 1998; Hernández & McGoldrick, 1999; Mock, 1998; Sluzki, 1998; Smart & Smart, 1994).

Summary

Four Latino family types were discussed: the intact, the single-parent, the bicultural, and the immigrant family. The characteristics, realities, and counseling implications of these four Latino family types were presented. In additional, parenting and child development issues were discussed.

Correct Answers to Self-Assessment

1. True. Although the influence of Catholicism and strong family values contribute to overall marital satisfaction, the welfare of the children appears to be the central force in the family. (See pages 69-72.)
2. True. Traditional intact Latino families have a hierarchical structure. (See pages 73-74.)
3. True. A main objective of a traditional two-parent family is to teach children to respect authority, to adopt appropriate social graces and skills, and to maintain hierarchical relationships. (See pages 75-77.)
4. False. Latino parents do not typically adopt lenient approaches to child rearing. (See pages 77-78.)
5. True. The problems associated with poverty and the demands of single parenting may place single parents at higher risk of mental health problems. Similarly, immigrants are at risk because of the associated stress of pre- and post-migration (See pages 81-85.)

6. True. Although a Latino couple may share ethnic heritage, they may experience cultural conflicts involving other differences in experience, for example, being U.S. or foreign born. (See pages 87-90.)

7. False. Individuals within a single family may be of the same heritage but have different acculturation levels, whereas other bicultural families may consist of parents, each of a different ethnic/cultural background, and children who are of mixed heritage. (See pages 90-93.)

8. True. The migration experience may be considered a major life event affecting the majority of Latinos. As a result, researchers have proposed that it be considered a life-cycle stage of family development. (See pages 95-97.)

9. False. Acculturation stress can be both acute and chronic, manifested for years after migration. (See pages 97-98.)

10. True. Connections with family and friends provide important supports to immigrant families. (See pages 97-100.)

PART II

Counseling Issues and Intervention

6

Initial Stage of the Counseling Process

Issues and Alternative Strategies

Atrévete y vencerás.
Dare and you will win.
Rovira, 1984, p. 159

Objectives

- To examine specific processes (e.g., client-therapist match and interpersonal etiquette) that affect the establishment of the therapeutic relationship in the early stages when counseling Latino clients and their families.
- To review relevant Latino-centered cultural values that may play an important role in early stages of the counseling process.
- To examine the role of culture and language in assessment.
- To examine issues that affect treatment planning.

Competencies

As a result of studying this chapter, counselors will:
- Be knowledgeable about specific issues concerning client-therapist match and the role of language in assessment and counseling, as well as issues affecting treatment planning
- Be capable of identifying culturally sensitive interpersonal strategies when working with Latino clients.

Latino-Specific Competencies

AWARENESS

- Culturally skilled counselors can recognize some of the challenges non-Latino counselors face in counseling Latino clients.
- Culturally skilled counselors are aware of cultural influences that may impede or enhance a trusting and positive relationship between a client and a counselor.

KNOWLEDGE

- Culturally skilled counselors can identify specific Latino value orientations and interpersonal etiquette that facilitate rapport.
- Culturally skilled counselors can understand the role of language and culture in assessment and treatment.

SKILLS

- Culturally skilled counselors can apply a cultural-linguistic approach in the early stages of counseling.
- Culturally skilled counselors may also be bilingual and, if not, they ensure that the family is assisted by a competent clinician who speaks the family's preferred language.
- Culturally skilled counselors can develop a treatment plan that uses a multidimensional framework, incorporating aspects of the Culture Centered Clinical Interview (CCCI).

Self-Assessment

Directions: Answer True or False. The correct responses are at the end of the chapter.

T   F   1. Current models of counseling Latinos are derived from a variety of theoretical frameworks, such as bicultural development and empirical research on family therapy.

T   F   2. Client-counselor matching by culture, race, and language is preferred but not a necessity in counseling Latino clients.

T   F   3. Translators should never be used with Latino clients.

T   F   4. Despite claims that Latinos are people oriented, they tend to be formal and prefer not to engage in small talk.

T   F   5. *Confianza* refers to the development of trust and intimacy in relationships.

T   F   6. It is not necessary to consider sociopolitical contexts in the assessment of the Latino client's issues and concerns.

T   F   7. Bilingual clients should be evaluated by language specialists to assess their language history and fluency.

T   F   8. Bilingual Latinos can only express their emotions openly in one language.

T   F   9. Language preference is associated with generational status, education, and place of residence.

T   F   10. A culturally sensitive and effective treatment plan for a Latino client involves goal-oriented, one-hour counseling sessions.

Introduction

Reports on the failure to respond to the needs of Latinos in the areas of health (Ambrose, Flores, & Carey, 2000; Seijo, Gómez, & Freidenberg, 1991), education (Arbona, 1990; Gloria & Rodríguez, 2000), and mental health (Echeverry, 1997; Leong et al., 1995; Ramos-Sánchez, Atkinson, & Fraga, 1999) point to the need for a culturally sensitive paradigm of service delivery. Despite the growing endorsement of multicultural counseling, few approaches are Latino-centered.

Nonetheless, contributions by early pioneers cannot be overlooked. Amado M. Padilla at UCLA set the foundation for the development of Hispanic psychology, made important contributions to the field, and developed theoretical frameworks such as the bicultural development model. Likewise, José Szapocznik and associates at the University of Miami pioneered the first scientific studies on family therapy with Latinos, developed several models of intervention for bicultural Latinos, and contributed to the development of contextual and ecological approaches in family and child psychology. Furthermore, the team of Guiseppe Costantino, Robert Malgady, and Lloyd Rogler developed and studied the effectiveness of a Latino-centered treatment approach called *Cuento* therapy. Their scholarly work paved the way for the development of new culture-centered paradigms for treatment and outcome studies.

In recent years, culture-centered measures have been developed to study variance between- and within-Latino groups (Jasinski, 1998; La Roche, 1999; Zea, Diehl, & Porterfield, 1997). These new tools have increased our understanding of constructs such as acculturation, *simpatía, personalismo,* and *familismo* (Cuellar et al., 1980; Marín & Marín, 1991; Marín et al., 1987). It is also recognized that Latino mental health professionals, in particular, are providing new pathways of knowledge in therapeutic methods (e.g., Baptiste, 1987, 1990; Bracero, 1998; Carey & Manuppelli, 2000; Comas-Díaz, 1981, 1997; Espín, 1999; Falicov, 1998; Flores & Carey, 2000; García-Prieto, 1996a, 1996b; García & Zea, 1997; Paniagua, 1998, 2001; Zuñiga, 1992a).

With this in mind, the purpose of this chapter is to present a variety of issues and innovative strategies that may be useful during the initial stages of counseling. The strategies described in this section of the book are based on documented case studies, research findings, and clinical experience. However, they are not intended to be a technical panacea, nor should they be viewed as the only way to meet the counseling needs of all Latinos. This chapter begins with a discussion of two matching situations that are generally recommended in the literature: client-therapist match by ethnicity and match by language. These situations are summarized below.

The Client-Counselor Match

Multicultural researchers and scholars concur that matching client-counselor characteristics by race, culture, and language facilitates the therapeutic alliance, enhances modeling and identity development, and reduces treatment attrition (Malgady & Costantino, 1998; Martínez, 2000; Seijo et. al., 1991; Sue & Sue, 1999). Guided by efficacy and client satisfaction, behavioral health organizations also encourage Latino client-counselor match. Matching undoubtedly provides the first step toward strengthening a therapeutic relationship by bringing about commonality between client and counselor. However, client-counselor matching may be difficult to achieve because of the diversity among Latinos, including race, English and Spanish preferences, cultural practices, and country of origin. Furthermore, this problem is compounded by the shortage of Latino health professionals (Malgady & Costantino, 1998; Trevino & Sumaya, 1993).

It has been difficult to develop a set of guidelines concerning Latino client-counselor match because of the complexity of the issue. For instance, the available research has been guided by a similarity and difference paradigm that has generated much controversy in the scientific arena (Speight & Vera, 1997). Client-counselor match has been examined in the context of level of acculturation and generation status (Ramos-Sánchez et al., 1999), social desirability (Abreu & Gabarain, 2000; Coleman, Wampold, & Casali, 1995), language of the counselor (Malgady & Costantino, 1998), and language of the client (Ramos-Sánchez et al., 1999). Moreover, many of these studies have used college students, therefore limiting the generalizability of the findings to other Latino populations.

Match by Ethnicity

Some clinicians believe that matching by race may not be as important as matching by ethnic background (Carey & Manuppelli, 2000; Romero, 2000). Ethnic matching may be preferred as a means to reduce errors in assessment and diagnosis (Paniagua, 1998), as well as to ensure the inclusion of cultural variables in therapy (López et al., 1989). In particular, we need to attend to counselors' biases. Arroyo (1996), who was interested in Latino ethnic bias, conducted an analog videotape study where the same actress enacted the identical script in two first-interview vignettes, one as a White client and the second as a Latina client. In the latter scenario, the Latina client spoke with a Spanish accent and her skin was purposely darkened. Arroyo found that mental health professionals (a) rated the Latino client as having blunted affect with a poor prognosis and (b) rated the counselor in the vignette as having less empathy. Arroyo explained these findings as stemming from mental health professionals' cultural bias related to ethnicity and language. The following incident illustrates the denial of cultural variables by a national professional trainer.

THE CASE OF DR. M

A nationally recognized presenter in the field of family violence was conducting a workshop for licensed mental health professionals. She requested a volunteer from the more than 200 participants to demonstrate an interaction. To establish a dialogue for the demonstration, Dr. M selected the topic "mother . . . let's talk about your mother." Dr. M moved close to the volunteer, increasing the proximity between them. Her questions were also animated and somewhat louder than the usual tone she used during the conference. The volunteer, who was a licensed clinical social worker from California, eagerly and enthusiastically answered all inquiries, which seemed to increase in frequency without noticeable pauses. The volunteer talked about her 85-year-old Mexican-born mother, whom she missed but could only visit twice a year. During the demonstration, Dr. M. abruptly terminated the dialogue and asked the volunteer how she felt about the presenter's style of communication. The volunteer responded eagerly, "Oh, great!" Dr. M was momentarily silent and expressed openly to the audience her confusion because the example she wanted to demonstrate "was not working." Perplexed, Dr. M. asked to repeat the demonstration and engaged the volunteer on the same topic again. This time, Dr. M's style questioning was more emotive and "in your face." At the end of the demonstration, she asked the volunteer, "How did you feel about the way I spoke to you?" The volunteer answered, "Fine." Once more the presenter excused herself with the audience and asked to move to another subject, saying, "I don't know what is happening, but this has never happened to me before." The presenter explained that she wanted to demonstrate an example of an "aggressive" intimidating verbal interaction but that the volunteer failed to perceive her aggressive style. Dr. M moved to the next topic and never acknowledged the possible cultural factors that were influencing her communication style with a volunteer who was a Mexican American.

In the clinical setting, Latino clients who request Latino counselors do so because they believe Latino counselors share their experience of cultural clash, oppression, and marginalization. As a client once said, "they [Latino professionals] will understand me, they will understand what *Hispanos* have to deal with." When confronted with a difficult situation, Latinos may shift from a specific country of origin label, such as Mexican or Dominican, to a global label *Latino* or *Hispano* underscoring the concept of "us" as a member of a minority group and "them" as the dominant majority group.

Match by Language

For Latino clients, matching clients and therapists in language may be more critical than matching by ethnic background. The language barrier is often seen as the cause of limited access to health care (Preciado & Henry, 1997; Seijo et al., 1991), undertilization of mental health services (Echeverry, 1997; Ramos-Sánchez et al., 1999; Santiago-Rivera, 1995), diagnostic errors (Altarriba & Santiago-Rivera, 1994; Malgady & Costantino, 1998; Pérez Foster, 1998), and inappropriate interventions (Bamford, 1991; Gallardo-Cooper, 2000; Santiago-Rivera, 1995; Sciarra & Ponterotto, 1991).

Although the body of work on the importance of considering language in treatment has made important contributions to the literature, it has focused on the language proficiency of the client and not on the language proficiency of the provider (Gallardo-Cooper, 2000). A counselor's bilingual skills may not be proficient enough to meet the demands of a session with a monolingual or bilingual Spanish-dominant client. Thus, it may be necessary to match these clients with a counselor who can speak Spanish fluently.

A bilingual counselor with a strong grasp of both Spanish and English is able to adapt to the speed of the conversation and is aware of subtle yet powerful variations in meaning when the client communicates with metaphors, regionalisms, proverbs, sayings, and semantic differences. For example, Puerto Ricans use *coraje* to express the emotion of anger; Bolivians use *coraje* or *valentia* to denote courage. The goal is to match the counselor's fluency level with that of the client as closely as possible.

Although this recommendation represents the ideal, it is often the case that a counselor-client match on language is not an option. In such instances, the Latino client may appreciate the monolingual English-speaking counselor who says a few words in Spanish. The value orientations of *personalismo* and *dignidad* often interplay in these interactions. For example, Carey and Manuppelli (2000) found that applying humor to clarify a translation of a word or phrase not only facilitated rapport with the client but also enhanced communication. Thus, joining with Latino clients, even with simple Spanish words, demonstrates the value placed on *personalismo* and helps to communicate to the client that the counselor appreciates their *dignidad*.

The Use of Translators

The need to match language has led to the use of translators in both psychological testing and counseling. However, this is far from ideal as errors occur in the translator's interpretation. In counseling, translators also change the counseling structure and dynamics (Bamford, 1991; Bradford & Muñoz, 1993; Seijo et al., 1991). This is often the case when a Latino child serves as the translator for a family member. In fact, allowing a Latino child to translate in family therapy is highly discouraged because the hierarchical balance of the family is inverted (García-Preto, 1996a).

Even though translators create specific problems, risk management issues and the lack of Spanish-speaking professionals may require their use. However, anecdotal stories about practice—for example, bringing a client's sister to translate in individual therapy when other bilingual therapists are available or bringing a physically abusive spouse to translate for his wife—raise serious ethical issues.

Because the use of a translator in counseling may be inevitable, several recommendations may prove helpful, particularly if the translator is not well-trained. Bradford and Muñoz (1993) recommend the following counseling strategies: (a) direct translators to repeat verbatim what the client says; (b) direct the client to speak slowly, taking pauses to facilitate the translator's recall; (c) maintain eye contact with the client not the translator; and (d) position the translator behind the client. Specific and detailed recommendations on the use of translators can be found in Paniagua (1998, pp. 12-13).

Many factors contribute to the consumers' selection of, preference for, and perception of health service providers (Speight & Vera, 1997). Because clear answers cannot be obtained from empirical formulations, there is a need to examine all practice possibilities. In conclusion, the following guidelines are useful to consider with respect to client-therapist match:

Latino clients should be asked for their preference of provider. In particular, gender and type of problem may influence the preference for a particular provider. For example, a Latino female with sexual trauma or sexual dysfunction may experience *vergüenza,* or shame disclosing intimate events. If a Latino female professional is not available, gender commonality may be preferred over ethnic matching. Cultural matching in these cases is not relevant, as cultural variants such as gender role socialization and traditional value orientation generalizations influence consumer preferences.

The referral source may be a determinant of the best choice in client-therapist match. Carey and Manuppelli (2000) interviewed therapists who provided services to Latinos and found matching was more important in the early stages of counseling. A court-ordered therapy referral may require a strict client-therapist match to increase the client's motivation. In contrast, not responding to the request for a Latino provider by a self-referred or motivated individual may hinder the initiation of counseling.

Client-therapist match will need to consider socioeconomic status, educational level, immigration history, residence status, and generational status. In cases where the prospective client is poor, uneducated, and first-generation immigrant with problematic residence status, making a strict client-match by ethnicity and language may create the only hope to access this often overlooked, at-risk population. Furthermore, not all Latinos in need of counseling have a choice (Gallardo-Cooper, 2000), the financial resources (Leong et al., 1995), or the knowledge to access preferred services (Leslie & Leitch, 1989).

Interpersonal Etiquette

The Rogerian core elements of the therapeutic alliance are fundamental to counseling practice regardless of cultural differences. However, these methods are enhanced when cultural sensitivity is incorporated in verbal and nonverbal communication. For example, knowledge of Latino-centered cultural value orientations and social etiquette is important to consider and must be applied with sound clinical judgment. Taking a normative view and keeping in mind that there are always individual differences, these value orientations are most prominent in Latino interpersonal relationships: *personalismo, respeto, dignidad, simpatía, confianza,* and *cariño.* These values correlate with each other and often are difficult to identify separately. A brief description of each follows.

Personalismo *represents an orientation where the person is always more important than the task at hand, including the time factor.* In other words, the patient is more important than the 5- or 10-minute time frame allocated for a medical visit. Included is the practice of personal warmth and genuineness in interpersonal relationships. A word of caution must be added here: Counselors need to obtain confirmation of clinical impressions to determine what may be cultural influences and what constitutes maladaptive behaviors. In other words, it is important to clarify what is and what is not personalismo. The following case illustrates this point.

THE CASE OF MERCEDES

Mercedes was a 65-year-old South American woman who came to therapy regularly for anxiety and depression. She was married, but her husband worked overseas. Even though she worried excessively about her health, she did not present with any medical conditions except for common colds and sinus infections. She was an attractive woman, proud of her youthful appearance. Whenever she experienced a mild and temporary illness, she would complain and worry about her fragile state. However, although she would visit many specialists, she refused all prescriptions and medical recommendations. In therapy, progress was slow, as Mercedes justified her problematic behaviors. The day of her therapy session, the secretary called Mercedes to cancel and reschedule her appointment because her therapist was ill. Mercedes asked the secretary what condition the therapist had, but the secretary refused to say, as was customary. Instead, she politely said, "Mrs. R., she is very ill and cannot come to the office today." Mercedes became enraged with the secretary, arguing that she needed to know what the therapist's illness was. Still, the secretary politely refused and changed the topic to setting the next appointment. Curiously, Mercedes left a message in the therapist's voice mail: "How do you dare to be sick—you know what I am going through. Call me *por la bondad de Dios*" (in God's name). When the therapist addressed this message, Mercedes denied leaving it. In exploring the issue, it was revealed that Mercedes was angry with the secretary because the secretary refused to inform her about the therapist's medical condition. When asked what made this information so important to her, she replied, "I would have liked to know so that I could pray for you to get better."

Respeto *(respect) represents sensitivity to the individual's position and creates a boundary within which conversations should be contained to avoid conflict.* The Spanish language has both formal and informal systems of communication (i.e., use of *usted* for formal and *tú* for informal pronouns). The structure of language reinforces the hierarchical position among individuals (e.g., authority figures, parents, elders) and relational boundaries.

Typically, the titles Don and Doña are used before the first name in a respectful and semiformal manner to address the elderly or older adult (Paniagua, 1998). Children are taught to address all adult nonfamily members with the *Don* and *Doña* titles. Similarly, in-laws or family members through marriage or association are expected to use them as well. A counselor may want to use these titles to underscore a more established relationship with a geriatric client. The following case illustrates the importance of *respeto*:

THE CASE OF CYNTHIA

Cynthia, a Latina counselor, was asked to conduct an intake with Mr. and Mrs. Garcia. She was assigned the case because of her Spanish-speaking ability and because her supervisor believed that the cultural similarity would benefit the clients. Following the initial session, Mr. Garcia contacted Cynthia's supervisor and asked for another counselor. He complained that they were treated *sin respeto* (with disrespect) because the counselor called them by their first

names, she was too young, and she asked too many personal questions that did
not relate to their visit.

Dignidad *(dignity) is linked to the first two values: Latinos believe in actions
that enhance a sense of pride, regardless of the individual's position.* In interpersonal relationships the *dignidad del hombre* (man's sense of dignity) is
reflected by the belief that a person is worthy and respected.

Simpatía *relates to what many call* buena gente *(the plural form of a nice person).* Latinos are attracted to those who are easy-going, friendly, and fun to be
with and like to represent themselves as such (Triandis, Marín, Lisansky, &
Betancourt, 1984). Szapocznik, Scopetta, Aranalde, and Kurtines (1978)
found that Cubans, for example, seek approval in interpersonal relationships.
Being perceived as *simpático* may be associated with this style of communication. Furthermore, *personalismo, dignidad,* and *simpatía* may relate to the
tendency to avoid direct interactions and confrontations.

Confianza *refers to the development of trust, intimacy, and familiarity in a
relationship* (Bracero, 1998). The term implies informality, *familismo,* and
ease of interpersonal comfort. For example, an individual may be allowed
to witness an act or the stating of a personal comment because he or she *es de
confianza* (can be trusted). The safety net that *confianza* brings may allow
Latinos to be more direct in conversations and will help in the establishment
of a therapeutic alliance.

Cariño *represents a demonstration of endearment in verbal and nonverbal
communication.* The personal characteristic of *cariñoso* is highly esteemed. In
relation to this term, the Spanish language allows for a suffix to be added to
nouns (i.e., *ito* or *ita*), changing the meaning of the word to a diminutive or
childlike meaning. Children's names reflect this language concept: *Miguel*
changes to *Miguelito.* Consequently, when used in adult conversation *cariño*
communicates an endearing message by adding the suffix *ito.* For example,
the phrase *mi amor* (my love) is an affectionate phrase toward an individual,
child or adult. When the suffix *ito* is added, it changes to *mi amorcito,* and it
represents a deeper more intimate form of expressed affection. In practice,
Latino clients and patients may address their provider as *doctorsito* instead of
the more formal and distant *doctor.* This expression will communicate a
closer relationship with the provider. A person that is *cariñoso* (i.e., male
reference) or *cariñosa* (i.e., female reference) also expresses affection nonverbally, for example, by kissing on the cheek in greeting, touching the person while talking (e.g., on the shoulder), and hugging. However, variations
exist in the manner in which Latinos conduct themselves interpersonally. For
example, Latinos from the Caribbean and coastal areas of Latin America and

Central America are often more expressive and uninhibited in communication style than Latinos from the inland areas of the region.

It is important to note also that Latinos use nouns depicting family roles in their expressions of affection toward adults and children, such as mother, father, and son. *Mi'jo* is a shortened word deriving from *mi hijo* or my son. This word is used between adults who have a loving relationship and may also be expressed with the diminutive form as mi'jito. A wife may address her husband or son as *papito* (i.e., little papa), and the husband may address his wife or daughter as *mamita* (i.e., little mama).

Non-Latino counselors have asked Latino clients in dismay: "You call your husband 'little papa'?" A counselor ignorant of Latino interpersonal style may find this observation a gender role problem in need of counseling attention. This is an example of a value difference among Anglos and Latinos. Labels linked to family are powerful words that can express intense emotions both positive and negative. Reacting negatively to this issue may create undue discomfort, and worst of all, trying to change this behavior and perceiving it as a sexist or feminist issue may lead to treatment attrition.

Many scholars (Paniagua, 1998; Sue & Sue, 1999; Zuñiga, 1992b) agree on the application of Latino interpersonal etiquette to facilitate rapport. The following are the most salient recommendations:

1. Begin counseling in a formal style, then move into more informal verbal and nonverbal interactions.

2. Address adults with formal titles: Mr. and Mrs.

3. Allow proximity in seating arrangements and personal communication.

4. Follow a hierarchical approach to greetings, starting with males or elders and adults before children.

5. Recognize differences in last names and possible differences in a client's recorded name. It is important to note that in Spanish-speaking countries, individuals keep both parents surnames, but in the United States, only the father's surname is typically used.

6. Maintain a flexible time frame without rushing the visit or conducting time-pressured sessions.

7. Start with *platicar* (personable small talk), a necessary prerequisite before engaging in serious conversation.

In addition, following the preferred language of the client, at least initially, facilitates rapport (Martínez, 2000; Santiago-Rivera, 1995; Sciarra & Ponterotto, 1991). We would like to expand on some other strategies that are useful when working with Latinos.

Telephone contact prior to the appointment has been used as a way to increase attendance at the first visit. With Latinos, a call can serve as a way to assess the language preference and fluency of the client. It also decreases a client's anxieties regarding client-therapist match and encourages *personalismo* and rapport. Furthermore, it helps to clarify the logistics of the appointment (e.g. time, place, transportation) and to educate about the counseling process.

Counselors should know that some Latinos may speak louder and may be more expressive with their hands when talking.

Latinos enjoy platicar, *a form of "personable small talk."* This communication style is linked to the *personalismo* value orientation. *Platicar* often occurs when the counselor walks with the client to the office. Talking about the weather may not be as personable as talking about the difficulty of finding the address or asking questions about the client's hometown. Also, the client may engage in a more personal dialogue, focusing on the counselor's background or how long he or she has lived in the area. This type of disclosure is considered culturally sensitive and is not necessarily a violation of the parameters of the client-counselor relationship. As Sue and Sue (1999) explained, the apparently intrusive style of *personalismo* should not be misinterpreted as a boundary problem. More than anything, this form of talk eases and engages clients in conversation they can relate to from a perspective of familiarity.

Educate Latino clients about the counseling process and structure. Some individuals may perceive counseling as going to a medical visit, having a one-time visit, or making a visit whenever needed.

Latinos may find direct communication methods rude or insensitive. To ensure rapport, present sensitive issues with an apology or recognition that the message could be interpreted as strong or offensive (e.g., "Please excuse me but I need to address an issue that may be difficult. . . . " or "With all due respect, I need to let you know. . . . "). Some examples for the bilingual professional to use in these circumstances are (a) *Ustedes perdonen, pero necesito hacerles ciertas preguntas que pueden ser difíciles de contestar pero necesarias para el tratamiento* (Please excuse me but I need to ask you certain questions that may be difficult to answer, but it is important for the treatment), (b) Con todo respeto le tengo que informar que. . . . (With all due respect, I have to inform you that. . . .), and (c) *Por favor excúseme pero necesitamos enfocar en temas que usualmente no se discuten* (Please excuse me but I need to focus on some issues that are usually not discussed).

Practice methods and procedures must accommodate the linguistically different. Some Latino clients may encounter difficulties completing agency forms, test protocols, and consent documents. Although as a society, we have become more bilingual, as evidenced by the availability of bilingual instructions with consumer products, poor language proficiency or illiteracy may be a barrier. Some may not be able to complete routine forms properly while they wait in the waiting room. Even bilingual clients experience difficulty understanding consent issues. Because of *respeto,* many Latinos may readily comply and sign consent forms they do not understand. The therapist needs to complete and review the initial paperwork with the client. To ensure and protect clients' rights, it may be necessary to conduct informed consent procedures in the clients' dominant language.

Informing the Latino client of the parameters of confidentiality, mandates of abuse reporting and informed consent, and the role of the counselor are fundamental responsibilities that should be addressed early in treatment to ensure high standards of ethical mental health practice. The process, however, can be time-consuming.

Assessment Issues and Approaches

Mental health professionals traditionally initiate counseling with the assessment of the client's presenting problem, functioning level (behavior, cognition, affect, and socialization), client's outcome expectations, history (medical, family, developmental, educational, vocational, relationships), risk factors, strengths and weaknesses, and barriers to change. Depending on the setting and expertise of the professional, the client most likely will receive a diagnosis or some other form of classification (i.e., educational placement), and the professional may need to respond to the concerns of a referring source. Counselors may also intentionally tailor the assessment process based on their theoretical orientation or expertise. For example, a behavioral analyst may seek specificity of contingencies, a family therapist may look for patterns of coalitions, or a vocational counselor may focus on employability skills.

However, these methods, although clinically sound, fail to understand some Latino clients and fail to assess divergent processes central to successful intervention. For example, culture-bound psychiatric diagnoses are well documented, raising questions about the validity and cultural sensitivity of diagnostic guidelines (Malgaldy & Costantino, 1999; Marsella & Yamada, 2000; Paniagua, 1998, 2001; Rivera-Arzola & Ramos-Grenier, 1997) and assessment methods (Altarriba & Santiago-Rivera, 1994; Rogler, 2000).

A solution to these limitations is the incorporation of a multidimensional framework in which culture, context, and social domains are addressed in assessment and treatment (Arredondo et al., 1996). A discussion follows on the application of this framework in counseling assessment where culturally relevant domains are integrated into sound clinical practice: the culture-centered interview and language evaluation. Assessment, we must stress, is an ongoing process in counseling, but for purposes of organization, it is included in this chapter on the initial stages of the counseling process.

Culture-Centered Clinical Interview

Santiago-Rivera and Esterman (1999) demonstrated the powerful impact of a culture-centered interview with a Latino family. Specifically, they showed how resistance to treatment was overcome when the interviewer shifted to a culturally relevant domain: the family's migration history. As they narrated their stories about the experience, at times painful, they were able to talk about their feelings of loss and despair. The opportunity to talk about these experiences propelled the family to recognize and address some of the underlying tension between family members. The family would have continued in a state of resistance had the counselor not asked the family to talk about this important life event.

The above example shows the importance of considering the client's cultural background in the assessment process. The Culture-Centered Clinical Interview (CCCI) format responds to this need by expanding the clinical interview to include psychocultural domains (Gallardo-Cooper, 2001a). The end result is a blueprint for treatment planning and clinical action that can be easily applied to individual, marital or couples, and family counseling.

The CCCI has several advantages: comprehensiveness, linkage to treatment planning, and flexibility (see Appendix C). In addition, its semistructured format provides the flexibility to conduct the interview with ease. Another benefit is that the CCCI allows for a smooth connection between assessment and intervention, a preferred practice in applied psychology (Kratochwill & Sheridan, 1990).

In addition to the CCCI, we recommend the use of the three-dimension model of personal identity developed by Arredondo and Glauner (1992), outlined in Chapter 1. This model can easily be incorporated into an interview format.

Regardless of the format used, the clinician needs to carefully navigate the rough waters of the interview to obtain information that is sometimes difficult for people to disclose. Fear of government regulations and changes, institutional distrust, and lack of information about confidentiality may block some Latinos from openly disclosing in therapy (Echeverry, 1997; Leslie & Leitch, 1989). The trauma of immigration, the loss of dear ones, separation from family, shame over nontraditional behaviors, disillusion with unmet expectations after immigration, and discrimination are but a few of the many areas Latinos may not readily discuss. In addition, Latinos' formality in the initial stages of counseling may also require a greater need for the development of *confianza* or trust with the counselor, a nonfamily member.

For this reason, the models presented are not formatted as structured interviews. Instead, a flexible format, where the clinician carefully attends to cultural cues without following regimented questions and sequence, is best suited to Latino clients. Maintaining ease in conversation, such as in *platicar,* will enhance disclosure. Depending on the client, culture-centered interviews may not be completed in one session. The client must tell his or her story. The counselor should carefully listen to the client's narratives and explore culturally related elements without flooding the client with direct questions. Cultural cues provide windows of opportunity in need of exploration. Interviewing skills and knowledge about culturally relevant Latino domains are necessary prerequisites to facilitating disclosure. The following interview with a Salvadoran father and son illustrates the process of a culturally sensitive perspective.

THE CASE OF DAVID

David was a 15-year-old *mestizo,* straight-A student without behavioral problems. One day, he engaged in a verbal altercation with two teachers over a minor incident involving another classmate. David became highly agitated when one of his friends, a Mexican American boy, was sent to the principal's office. David kept telling his friend to disobey the teacher because he was innocent and "you do not need to take it." The school called David's family and expressed serious concerns about David's atypical defiance, he was suspended for one day, and he was referred to outpatient counseling.

David was the oldest of three children. His parents left El Salvador during the peak of the civil war. They moved to the Northeast, where David's father, who was 18 years old at the time, worked several construction jobs to help purchase the family's first house. David and his family moved to this deteriorating two-story house when he was just starting school. By the time David was 10 years old, the house was completely renovated and used as a rental unit. At the time of the interview, David's father was self-employed doing a series of skilled home remodeling jobs as well as managing his four rental properties. David's mother, who spoke limited English, was a full-time homemaker and cared for the children.

David was seen with his father for the first interview because his mother was ill. During the interview, both father and son showed a close, affectionate relationship. The session was conducted in both Spanish and English; the father often used more Spanish, and David used more English. David was taller than his father and presented with a serious mood, a not too *simpático* demeanor. He did not feel counseling was necessary, and since the school incident, he had become irritable, withdrawn, and uncooperative at home. David's father began by describing how proud he was of his son: "David is a 4.0 student, and he is in the honor society at school . . . he is a great kid and soccer player." His father was proud that his son knew almost as much as he did about home remodeling and would help him on weekends or during school vacations. However, he added that he was getting increasingly concerned about his son's temper. "I just do not want him to get in trouble, but sometimes if he thinks that there is some-thing *unfair,* he loses it." His father expected David, as the oldest, to be more responsible and to set an example for the other children. This was the first time David ever got in trouble at school and the first time they met with a counselor. The father stressed that getting in trouble at school was simply not acceptable. David responded in anger—"You and *Mami* are always on my case"—and di-rected to his father, "but you are a pushover." His father quickly corrected him: "You do not talk to me like that, remember *soy tu papá, con respeto.* (I am your father, keep the respect").

The counselor explored the area of unfairness and the context in which these episodes occurred. At one point during counseling, David said that he wanted to go to college and become a lawyer because he wanted to help people who suffer injustice. The counselor explored this comment by asking him, "David, if you had been a lawyer, how could you have helped your family?" David took a moment to answer, trying to hold back tears, and related the memories of his early childhood living in a non-Latino neighborhood where he and his family were unwelcome. "Children in the street used to make fun of our house, and neighbors did not even say hello to us because we were poor and *Hispanos.* I used to be scared and felt bad for my dad who worked so hard." David added that after his father fixed the house and got it ready for rental, they left the neighborhood. The neighbors were sad when they moved. David proudly stated, "Dad had the best house on the street, and he always helped the neighbors. He would shovel the snow off their sidewalks and driveways." His father inter-rupted while holding David's shoulder: "Remember son, we need to take care of each other; if I was already working with the snow-plowing machine, one or two more houses more was no problem. We needed to survive and teach people who we are."

Even though David's narrative had a happy ending, it was observed that his and the father's mood were becoming more dysphoric. The counselor concluded that significant issues were at the surface. The counselor asked, "And what else happened?" David began to sob, and his father expressed discomfort witnessing his crying: "David, what is happening? *¿Qué te pasa?*" David responded, "It just does not stop, remember what happened at the store?" Still, David's father was confused. David said to the counselor, "You know my dad bought my com-puter with cash, . . . he knew I needed it for school and well, he worked real hard to get it, and he did, just like that."

David went on to explain that the clerk at the store would not accept his father's application to use the store's no-interest promotion to purchase the computer, even though he had no debts and a good credit history. David recounted that the clerk acted rude and disrespectful and abruptly told them to move away from the line so the clerk could attend to other customers. Eventually, David's dad wrote a check and bought the computer.

It became evident that other similar situations of a discriminatory nature had occurred. David told about a recent soccer match with his brother's team. The father was the coach, and the other team was cheating and telling players to keep playing during a foul. David's father stopped the game and told his play-ers if they were not going to play by the rules, then they would leave. David said that he overhead some parents from the other team saying, "Why don't you go back from where you came from!" David's anger began to escalate. David became agitated and wanted to retaliate. His father had to direct him to stay in the car. In contrast, David's father kept his head down. The more emotive David became, the more silent the father became.

The counselor struggled over the contrasting reactions of father and son. Significant information was shared, and there was a need to manage the session as she noticed that David was becoming increasingly agitated. The counselor concluded that she did not want to let David relate more incidents because the intensity of his anger was escalating. She wanted to avoid a situation where the father would be correcting his son. She wanted to reduce the tension between David and his father. She asked David, "David, what is going on right now in the session?" David was quiet for a second and said, "This is what upsets me . . . he does not do anything, he just takes it. . . . I don't know why. . . "

The counselor turned to the father, who did not respond to his son, and said, "Please help me understand, what is happening?" She suspected something had happened to the father in the past and wanted to check the migration history and the circumstances surrounding his adolescence in El Salvador but chose to be silent waiting for a cue. David's father began to cry and said, "With all that I have gone through, I do not want to deal with these petty incidents." David responded in dismay, "But Dad this is not a little thing. You've always taught me to be proud. How can you say this is nothing!" The counselor took an opportunity to explore the migration history.

The father related for the first time the circumstances that led to his leaving his country, the family members who died in the war, and the few family members he left behind. "There were bodies everywhere in El Salvador . . . my grandmother raised me and when she died, I decided to leave and make a new life." The father added that he had empathy for his son's experiences of discrimination, but he would not take a fighting posture. He added, "Working harder and succeeding . . . that's how we earn respect and that's how we fight back."

The emotional content expressed and the affirmation of the troubling issues experienced in the family history reduced the tension between parent and son. David was somber and not argumentative; he expressed surprise with his father's disclosure. The session shifted to addressing oppression and moved toward an understanding of other relevant issues in need of attention, such as different and similar life experiences of the father and son, loss and trauma, the connection between these issues and the presenting problem, and coping strengths.

Language Issues

Considering that 90% of Latinos in the United States continue to use the Spanish language (Dana, 1993), counselors need to know that there is a growing population of bilingual Latinos who have varying degrees of language proficiencies in English and Spanish. Some Spanish-dominant Latinos who enter counseling will require language accommodations, whereas others may be fluent English language speakers. If the therapist is monolingual, it will be important to identify which of the two languages contains the expressive structure of affection (Rozensky & Gómez, 1983). If the therapist is bilingual, careful consideration should be given to the strategic use of the two languages in therapy (Sciarra & Ponterrotto, 1991).

Because of the complexity of the bilingual individual's representation of language and the expression of emotion, as well as access to experiences, we strongly recommend an assessment of language history. Pérez-Foster (1998) and Santiago-Rivera and Altarriba (2001) offer language assessment protocols that mental health professionals can use to gather important information about first- and second-language acquisition, including developmental, psychosocial, and cultural dimensions of language.

For this reason, all Latino clients should be assessed for language history and fluency. Despite the importance of language, there is a relatively little published research on bilingual counseling practice. The reader is referred to Pérez-Foster's (1998) noteworthy endeavor to publish the first book on language and psychological practice. Likewise, Santiago-Rivera (1995) offers a promising theoretical and practice model that incorporates cultural factors and language.

Second-Language Acquisition

Neurolinguists differentiate between automatic language and acquired language learning. The first is our mother tongue, which is automatically learned during early development and through experience. The second refers to language learned after our first language has been introduced (Fabbro, 1999). Both the automatically learned and acquired languages are stored and organized in separate neurological language systems (Pérez-Foster, 1998; Pernani et al., 1998), and both languages access different cultural cues (Hong, Morris, Chiu, & Benet-Martínez, 2000).

Learning a second language has different implications for adults and children. Adults learn a second language in a more formal manner, for example, in a class (Fabbro, 1999), whereas children may learn a second language through exposure to the environment (López & Gopaul-McNicol, 1997). The younger the child, the easier it will be for the child to acquire the second language. However, López and Gopaul-McNicol (1997) contend that older children may acquire a second language with less confusion because they have developed higher cognitive functions that facilitate the understanding of the mechanics of language.

In clinical practice, age of second-language acquisition will have an impact on the ability of a Latino client to access the emotional content of certain experiences. For example, a client who learned a second language as a child and grew up in a bilingual language environment will have an easier time accessing certain emotions in either language (e.g., English or Spanish). In contrast, an individual who learns a second language as an adult may be unable to use that language to access certain childhood experiences that were "lived" in the client's first language learned. These experiences are encoded in memory in the language in which they occurred and are not easily retrievable in another language (Santiago-Rivera & Altarriba, 2001).

Language Preference

Language choice among Latinos appears to be affected by contextual (Hakuta & García, 1989) factors. For example, Zuñiga (1992b) reports that many second- and third-generation Latinos prefer Spanish for social and informal interactions and prefer English for work and formal interactions. Also, language preference is associated with generational status, education, and place of residence in the United States. Many of these contextual variables are directly related to acculturation.

Other factors that affect language preference center on psychological barriers such as (a) anxiety, (b) fears, and (c) defense mechanisms. Spanish-dominant bilinguals may exhibit anxiety because they are communicating in a language they have not mastered. Thus, not all observed hesitation, guardedness, and tension reflect underlying psychological barriers or resistance to treatment (Malgady & Costantino, 1998; Sue & Sue, 1999). Communication in a nondominant language may indicate problems with word retrieval, which lead to client frustration. Seijo and her associates (1991) recommend that monolingual physicians who care for bilingual Latinos should take time with their patients to establish a "formal friendliness." This approach could help minimize the apparent social distance that may be demonstrated in health care visits when using their nondominant language. Their findings support Poma's (1983) contention that Latino patients express somatic complaints and related problems in their native tongue.

On the other hand, Latino clients may prefer to speak English rather than Spanish because they fear discrimination. Individuals who struggle with discrimination may project their own insecurities on to others, interjecting inadvertently a defeated sense of Latino identity and denial of Latino self. For example, parents may express protective "good intentions," directing their children to dispose of their Spanish language *para que no tengan problemas* (so that they will not have problems).

In addition, bilinguals may also deliberately choose a particular language as a form of psychological defense (Clauss, 1998; Marcos, 1976; Martínez, 2000; Pérez-Foster, 1998; Rozensky & Gómez, 1983; Sciarra & Ponterotto, 1991). As stated earlier, bilinguals have been shown to have two different language systems, and they may process the emotional content of an event in a particular language, which is not easily transferable to the other language. For example, if a trauma occurred in a Spanish-speaking environment, disclosing the event in English may not contain the corresponding emotions because the emotional content was encoded and stored in the Spanish language system. This phenomenon has been called the detachment effect, whereby the individual is split off from emotions related to the experience (Marcos, 1994; Marcos & Alpert, 1976; Marcos & Urcuyo, 1979).

Language Literacy

Toppelberg (1997) reports that almost 50% of adults and children from language minorities do not speak English adequately. Yet, this area is often overlooked in clinical practice. Latinos as a group have the lowest levels of educational attainment of any group in the United States, and some immigrants are illiterate (Arbona, 1990; Gloria & Rodríguez, 2000). In addition, having conversational skills in English may not indicate reading and writing skills in that language.

The forms required in clinical practice, such as the application for services, historical forms, and treatment plan contracts, may need to be explained and sometimes completed for some Latinos. When Spanish forms are used in practice, literate Latinos may have difficulties understanding what they read. Also, forms are often poorly translated with improper syntax and verb use, which then creates confusion and elicits unreliable information. Spanish translations, although a sensitive solution, cannot be applied across the board with all Latinos because there are different dialects. Many variations are found in the choice of words, regionalisms, and so forth. Therefore, what appears at times as noncompliance with form completion may be related to poorly written forms, lack of understanding, and poor reading and/or writing skills. The following case illustrates this point.

THE CASE OF VIRGINIA

One of the authors was consulted by a colleague about the "resistance" of a 60-year-old Mexican American woman who was hospitalized for a suicide attempt. The client, Virginia, came with her family to the United States when she was 16 years old, married at 18, and stayed home raising her now adult children. However, she had a long history of dysthymia since adolescence. Her husband was also Mexican American and had a successful career as a union leader. He was very supportive of counseling and active in his role as husband and father. Of Virginia's three children, two had completed several years of college, and the other was a successful physician. Virginia was described as often speaking Spanish and English at home, and was fluent in conversational English. The counselor did not speak Spanish.

Concerns were raised about Virginia's lack of progress and her recent suicide attempt. Although Virginia was taking psychotropic medications and her depression symptoms had subsided, she was not compliant with counseling "homework" tasks and she continued to express negative attributions. The counselor found herself to be at an impasse by focusing her counseling strategy on Virginia's noncompliance with diary writing, or "forgetting" to bring her written tasks. Sensitive to her Spanish language heritage, the counselor told Virginia that she could do all writing tasks in Spanish, if preferred; then, the work could be addressed in English in the session.

The only sample provided by Virginia was incomplete work in Spanish that revealed significant writing difficulties. Her penmanship was childlike, the words were misspelled, and the sentence construction was incomplete. The counselor was directed to check on Virginia's educational level. A review of her records revealed that the agency forms had been completed by the husband and the educational level item was left blank. At this point, it was suspected that Virginia's educational level was limited.

Because of the apparent difficulties Virginia had in openly disclosing her limitations with writing and her educational level, the counselor was directed to address the issue not as a confrontation but instead as a clinical error. The counselor apologized about asking her to do so much homework and said that she was learning that journal writing was not effective with many clients. It was then that Virginia said, "You know it was really hard for me to do, I only had 3 years of schooling and I have always felt insecure about myself because of that."

Language Style

The qualitative nature of language is important to assess because it will direct the clinician to explore the impact of language on areas of self-perception and will also, as will be discussed later, expand possibilities for therapeutic strategies. The following styles are evident in Latino Americans.

Language switching or code switching: This process is found in bilinguals, who mix words or phrases in two languages during a conversation.

Spanglish: This term refers to individuals who shift between Spanish and English when they speak or modify English words with Spanish sounds or apply the Spanish phonetic sounds to vowels (e.g., *foorneetoora* is pronounced for furniture, *marketa* for market).

Semantics: Words can be interpreted differently and create misunderstandings. Certain words depicting a tangible object may not be easily misinterpreted, but others may have different meanings, such as *fat* and *skinny,* which may be measured by different standards. In addition, the same word may represent different meanings to different Latino ethnic subgroups. For example, *banqueta* in Mexico refers to sidewalk, whereas it designates a stool for other Latino groups.

Development of a Treatment Plan

Regardless of the setting, all counselors develop a plan of action. For example, school counselors implement guidance and treatment programs with the goal of meeting a need. Counselors in the private sector, agencies, or institutions also develop a treatment map. Many in the field must comply with required written treatment plans, imposed by organizations, agencies, and third-party payers.

Mental health professionals typically use two treatment plan models, (a) problem driven or (b) diagnosis driven. The problem-driven treatment plan is based on the "chief complaint" clients describe as the reason for initiating counseling (e.g., "failing school," "our family is fighting too much," "I am not doing well at work," etc.). This type of treatment plan is developed through a collaborative contract between the counselor and client. Brief therapy models, especially collaborative empowering models, rely on problem-oriented counseling where the client defines the problem.

The second type of treatment plan follows the medical model of diagnosis whereby the counselor takes the lead in developing and explaining the treatment goals to the client. An example would be the preferred treatment guidelines developed by professional organizations such the American Psychiatric Association for specific diagnoses such as major depression and attention deficit disorder. This type of treatment plan is popular among managed care companies, risk managers, and medically based practices.

Although these models are popular among mental health professional and managed care companies, they may not be the best approaches with Latinos. Perhaps Latinos expect the counselor to take charge in the counseling process because they perceive him or her to be an authority figure as suggested by Szapocznik, Scopetta, Aranalde, & Kurtines (1978). If this is the case, then what type of treatment planning will be culturally sensitive with Latinos? Limited empirical and clinical data are available on the most suitable treatment planning approaches for this population. Both methods are based on salient clinical parameters; however, Latinos fall between the two approaches because they tend to be problem oriented and expect the counselor to take charge in the counseling process. A collaboration may be a difficult treatment planning approach for some Latinos to grasp, especially recent immigrants in the early stages of the counseling process.

From this perspective, the treatment planning approach should address the client's level of acculturation and educational level. Collaboration is the democratic mainstream mode of problem solving. However, Rogler (2000) indicates that a problem-solving approach is not a recognized method of coping among some Latino populations. Latinos prefer a hierarchical style in interpersonal relationships, and the perception of professionals as authority figures may contribute to a different perception and expectation of the treatment and counseling process (Szapocznik, Scopetta, Aranalde, & Kurtines, 1978; Szapocznick, Kurtines, Santisteban, & Rio, 1990). Thus, Latinos generally approach counseling with the expectation that the professional will be direct, give advice, and know what is best (Bean, Perry, & Bedell, 2001; Paniagua, 1998), as with a medical visit. In other words, a passive counselor who focuses on reflection and expects Latino clients to take the lead may not be successful in engaging and motivating them in therapy. In addition, research findings suggest that Latinos, particularly those not experienced with counseling, benefit from treatment goals that address immediate and concrete concerns (Rosado & Elias, 1993; Szapocznik et al., 1990). The present-time orientation often contributes to seeking mental health services when in crisis, thus underscoring a client-defined problem-oriented approach.

Outcome research findings suggest that what seems to work for Latinos also works for the mainstream population. For example, the development of clear and specific treatment goals increases clients' treatment compliance (Beyebach, Rodríguez Morejón, Palenzuela, & Rodríguez-Arias, 1996), and the maintenance of a focused treatment plan predicts successful outcomes (Murphy & Duncan, 1997).

Based on clinical observations, Latinos quite often are not focused on the task of developing managed care- or agency-required treatment plan contracts, but rather they just want to talk. More than anything, signing contracts and specific documents may appear to be intimidating and anxiety provoking, and some may approach it with suspicion, particularly those who are not legal residents (Echeverry, 1997). Likewise, Latino clients may not be concerned with treatment plan development or collaborative methods of clinical problem solving because such plans are based on an individualistic, goal-setting orientation. As previously noted, the values of *personalismo, familismo,* and *platicar* clash with a procedure that may seem to some Latinos as culturally impersonal and not person-centered.

The challenge of developing an adequate treatment plan requires an understanding of what the client wants to gain from the counseling experience. It is the responsibility of the counselor to understand the realities of the Latino client. It is also important to note that not all problems can be resolved in traditional one-hour weekly office visits. Counselors must broaden their role to include case management, community outreach, and advocacy work.

In many respects, Latino clients do not differ from non-Latino clients in what they want to obtain from counseling. What seems to differ is the road taken to achieve the goal: the cultural path. For this reason, several prerequisites need to be met before a treatment plan is developed with Latinos; these are (a) an understanding of the counseling process, (b) a clear understanding of the role of the counselor, (c) the development of rapport, (d) realistic expectations about the benefits of the counseling experience, and (e) goals set within a culturally sensitive framework.

Summary

This chapter presented a variety of important issues to consider during early stages of counseling, such as client-therapist match, interpersonal etiquette, and assessment of language proficiency (both English and Spanish). A culture-centered interview framework was presented, including suggestions for developing an effective treatment plan.

Correct Answers to Self-Assessment

1. True. Pioneers such as Padilla and Szapocznik have paved the way for the development of new paradigms. (See pages 107-108.)
2. True. Although highly effective, it may be difficult to achieve client-counselor matching on race, language, and culture. (See pages 108-111.)
3. False. Translators are sometimes necessary and can be used successfully following certain guidelines. (See pages 111-112.)
4. False. Latinos value interpersonal relationships, as evident in such values as *personalismo, simpatía,* and *platicar.* (See pages 112-114.)
5. True. *Confianza* refers to trust and familiarity in relationships. (See page 114.)
6. False. A multidimensional framework in a clinical interview is recommended. (See pages 118-121.)
7. False. The age at which the bilingual Latino learned the second language and the frequency of its use will determine the degree to which emotions can be expressed in that language. (See pages 121-123.)
8. True. Generation, education, and residence affect language preference. (See pages 123-124.)
9. False. Culturally competent counselors can initially assess the client's language history and preference through the application of several counseling relevant language assessment guidelines or protocols. (See page 121.)
10. False. A goal-oriented approach that does not take into consideration the values of *personalismo, la plática,* and *familismo* may be ineffective. (See pages 126-127.)

7

─────────
─────────
───

The Middle and Last
Stages of Counseling

A más riesgo, más provecho.
The greater the risk, the greater the gain.
Rovira, 1984, p. 159

Objectives

- To review specific strategies that can be used during the middle and last phases of the counseling process, such as language switching, storytelling, and metaphors.
- To examine the above Latino-centered counseling strategies through case illustration.
- To review practice accommodations that are Latino-client centered.
- To examine a variety of termination issues and ethical dilemmas.

Competencies

As a result of studying this chapter, counselors will:
- Have knowledge of specific strategies that can be used across theoretical orientations during the middle and end phases of counseling.
- Have a better understanding of ethical dilemmas and the need to develop specific standards.

Latino-Specific Competencies

AWARENESS

- Culturally skilled counselors are aware of the importance of Latino-centered strategies such as accepting with ease the client's use of Spanish words in the counseling process.
- Culturally skilled counselors are aware of the expectations they place on Latino clients when traditional practice methods and procedures are employed.

KNOWLEDGE

- Culturally skilled counselors have knowledge of different counseling theories and models that are appropriate to use with Latino individuals and families.
- Culturally skilled counselors are able to describe ways in which specific strategies such as language switching, culture-centered storytelling, and Spanish proverbs can be used effectively in counseling.
- Culturally skilled counselors are knowledgeable of the clients' personal and cultural history and are able to develop motivating interventions that are tailored to the specific characteristics of the client.

SKILLS

- Culturally skilled counselors can adapt and develop Latino-sensitive counseling methods and treatment programs.
- Culturally skilled counselors can interject a wide range of Latino-centered interventions including key images, Spanish words, metaphors, and storytelling techniques in counseling.
- Culturally skilled counselors can effectively use TEMAS as a therapeutic intervention in counseling individuals, groups, and families.

Self-Assessment

Directions: Answer True or False. The correct answers are at the end of the chapter.

T   F   1. Because multicultural counseling supports a multi-dimensional approach, a variety of counseling theoretical orientations can be incorporated in a treatment program.

T   F   2. Because Latino clients tend to be more formal interpersonally and often lack proper expectations of and preparation for the counseling process, expressive methods involving imagery may be too intrusive.

T	F	3. Allowing a bilingual client to freely speak in his or her language of choice may help identify certain themes.

T	F	4. Culture-specific folktales are appropriate mental health prevention strategies and counseling interventions with Latino youth.

T	F	5. *Cuento* therapy has been shown to be less effective than art/play therapy for Puerto Rican children.

T	F	6. *Dichos* may increase client resistance.

T	F	7. Culture-specific metaphors in counseling may be powerful tools in all modes of treatment.

T	F	8. TEMAS is an apperception test for ethnically and culturally diverse children, adolescents and adults.

T	F	9. Outreach programs, crisis intervention, and group therapy may be congruent with Latino-centered value orientations.

T	F	10. When working with Latino clients, an ethical dilemma involves the referral of clients to another counselor when there is no other mental health professional available.

Introduction

Culture-centered counseling incorporates the unique experiences of diverse individuals associated with acculturation, migration, gender role socialization, identity development, language background, and value orientation. When these cultural factors are taken into consideration, several traditional counseling approaches provide sound guidelines for the development of effective interventions. The following perspectives are particularly noteworthy when working with Latinos: (a) the multiple realities of postmodern constructivism, (b) the rejection of deficit thinking, (c) the focus on individual's strengths and resources, (d) the empowering methods of social justice, (e) the narrative approach to counseling process, (f) the constant self-evaluation of the counselor, (g) the developmental understanding of trauma, (h) the client-centered methods of relationship building, and (i) the ecosystemic or contextual view of the individual.

The above supports a judicious and eclectic integration of counseling methods. For example, Ponterotto (1987) recommends a multimodal counseling approach with Mexican Americans. Multicultural counseling theory supports a multidimensional framework, allowing for the integration and complementary interaction of many theoretical orientations. Moreover, application of different treatment frameworks such as feminist therapy and behavioral and cognitive methods with Latinas has proven effective, as long as the interventions allow for sensitivity to cultural conflicts and adaptations of culturally endorsed values (Comas-Díaz, 1985; Comas-Díaz & Duncan, 1985; Lijtmaer, 1998).

At the core of culture-centered counseling is the notion of different world-views, a parallel orientation with postmodern constructivism. Therefore, the art of eclecticism is based on a client-centered approach where the client, not the therapist, directs the selection of the counseling method and where the competent professional practices constant self-evaluation. This latter process is what Martínez (2000) calls the "stepping back" of the counselor to recon-struct without biases the realities of the client. This process can be labeled differently, but it is rooted in the psychodynamic principles of transference and countertransference.

A variety of approaches can meet the therapeutic needs of Latinos. Those experiencing oppression and victimization will benefit from a feminist ap-proach (Comas-Dìaz, 1987; Lijtmaer, 1998) because an underlying function of all counseling is social justice (Flores-Ortíz, 2000; Sue & Sue, 1999). The application of an ecological perspective can address sociopolitical and insti-tutional changes. Stories of survival and success attest to the resiliency of im-migrants (Falicov, 1998; Quintana, 1995; Sluzki, 1998) and by focusing on solution-oriented models, troubled Latinos restore effective coping strategies. Methods that use metaphors and narratives are extremely useful because Latinos want to share their stories, and culture-based metaphors enhance progress. Through their stories, clients gain awareness, affirmation, and reso-lution (Bracero, 1998). Furthermore, the familial orientations reinforce a systemic approach to intervention that includes structural, intergenerational, strategic, and narrative perspectives. Table 7.1 summarizes a selection of coun-seling strategies with Latinos that are derived from traditional and culture-based approaches. Furthermore, various models can be applied to the follow-ing case illustration.

THE CASE OF LYDIA

Lydia was a 40-year-old woman who was raised in a small town in Puerto Rico. She came to the United States with her husband, who worked for a large corpo-ration as an electrical engineer. Lydia and her husband had lived in the United States for the previous 15 years. Due to an unusual condition, she underwent extensive surgery. Her doctor recommended therapy to address multiple stressors and psychogenic headaches.

Her husband was working extra hours at his new job and had minimal time to spend with Lydia and the family. However, further exploration of the dy-namics in Lydia's marriage revealed that since her mother-in-law died 5 years prior to her surgery, her husband had become detached from the family and

(text continued on page 135)

Table 7.1 Selected Counseling Strategies With Latinos

Author	Technique	Problem	Population	Description/Recommendation
Barón & Constantine, 1997	Interactive culture strain	All types	All	Assessment of acculturation level, ethnic identity, and gender role are integrated to seek biculturalism.
Bracero, 1998	Storytelling, narratives, metaphors, and images	Gender issues, oppression, abuse	Women	Group or individual therapy: Incorporates value orientation, short stories, and religious icons to address Latina issues. Provides insights on gender issues of male Latino therapists.
Clauss, 1998	Guidelines for monolingual therapists	All types	Bilinguals	Free association and allow client to translate; Explore client's self-perception in two languages or dual self.
Comas-Díaz, 1997	Release of ethnoracial anger	Racism, prejudice, oppression	Latinos in the workforce	Psychoeducational methods to channel ethnoracial anger via conflict resolution, culturally assertive techniques, and increased support systems.
Gómez, 1999	Grandmother/ *abuelita*	Child abuse/ poor parenting	Children and families	Grandmother as protector of child and mediator of positive parenting style of parent.
Gutiérrez, 1990	Empowerment and problem-solving skills	Consciousness raising	Women	Group therapy: recommends small groups as ideal setup to address empowering strategies; focuses on client's analysis of the problem or intervention vignette to introduce social justice issues (e.g., power distribution) and self-awareness of power of each problem or situation.
Lijtmaer, 1998	Feminist approach	All	Women	Adapts and incorporates feminist therapy within a cultural and linguistic framework
Costantino, Malgady, & Rogler, 1986	*Cuento* therapy	Adjustment issues	Children	*Cuento* therapy: Storytelling technique using native culture stories and characters.
Malgady & Costantino, 1998	Guidelines for monolingual therapists	All types	Bilinguals	Observe nonverbal behaviors; match client-therapist by ethnicity, race, and language; check context of interview and observed anxiety; symptoms minimize in second language.
Martínez, 2000	"Stepping-back," self-awareness	All types	Ethnic minority	During interview "stepping-back," detach from client to assess own biases; allows client to give own explanation of illness and treatment goals before disclosing psychiatric evaluation findings.
Inclán & Herron, 1998	Bridge building: (a) siblings	Acculturation and gender role conflicts	Adolescents	(a) Family therapy: Siblings facilitate intercultural bridge between patient and parents.
	(b) therapist		Adults/ Couples	(b) Therapist's role used to build a bridge to host culture.
	(c) prevention and intervention	Developmental tasks	Adolescents	(c) Psychoeducational groups facilitate adolescent disclosure of issues not raised in individual therapy. Structured, time-limited, direct approach covers 10 important areas for psychological well-being.
Pérez-Foster, 1998	Psycholinguistic history interview	All types	Bilinguals	Provides guidelines to conduct a language evaluation for bilingual clients. Two major areas of assessment are time and context of first- and second-language acquisition and use.

Table 7.1   (continued)

Author	Technique	Problem	Population	Description/Recommendation
Poma, 1983	Medical visits	All types	Bilinguals	Recommends physicians spend more time with Spanish-dominant patients to allow for better communication as medical complaints are disclosed in native tongue.
Ponterotto, 1987	Multimodal therapy	All types	All	Recommends a behavioral, comprehensive, active approach where client chooses goals and the counselor applies the BASIC ID acronym.
Ramos-McKay, Comas-Díaz, & Rivera, 1988	Storytelling; Latino plays, music, and poetry	All types	Women	Group therapy: reenactment of plays, music, poetry. Therapists read dramas that represent client's issues. Discussion among group members follows the presentation.
Santiago-Rivera & Altarriba, 2001	Language assessment	All types	All	Protocol developed to assess language issues relevant to counseling.
Sciarra, 1999	Reframing	Separated immigrants	Immigrants	Family therapy: Reframes conflicts related to separation with intercultural conflict. Uses acculturation and cultural variants in intervention.
Sciarra & Ponterotto, 1991	Language switching	Family therapy	Bilinguals	Initiates family therapy by following language changes of the client. Later chooses language as strategy to change roles and family structure.
Szapocznik et al., 1988	Strategic structural family therapy	Substance abuse	Resistant adolescents and families	Therapist is responsible for engaging family by using joining and restructuring. Identify power in family system to engage adolescent and family in treatment; initial focus of treatment is not drug abuse (or identified patient) but resistance and family dynamics.
Szapocznik & Kurtines, 1993	Reframing	Inter-generational conflict	All	Reframes intergenerational conflict with different cultural views.
Szapocznik et al., 1984	Bicultural effectiveness training (BET)	Inter-generational conflict	Parents and children	Family therapy: Communication between parents and children where native and host cultures are affirmed. Parents talk freely about how problems were handled in native country, and children can do the same. Goal is biculturalism.
Szapocznik, Scopetta, Aranalde, Kurtinez, 1978	Value orientation treatment planning	Cuban immigrants	All types	Incorporates value orientation assessment findings into treatment planning: family involvement, present/crisis orientation, therapist in need to take charge, restore lineal-hierarchy family relationships, action-oriented, concrete objectives, addresses environmental pressures.
Trostle, 1988	Child-centered group play	Social-emotional development	Preschoolers (3 to 5 years old)	Educational and preventive strategy to enhance self-control and social and adaptive skills. Group structure: same four members per group for 10 weeks; member selection aims for balance of temperament and gender.
Zuñiga, 1992a	Dichos or metaphors	All types	Bilinguals and mono-linguals	Spanish proverbs, sayings, words interjected to convey client's behavior, thoughts, conflicts, and so on in a storytelling/ self-disclosure style.

worked a minimum of 12 hours a day, including weekends. Because Lydia required extensive care and support, especially with two school-age children, Lydia's retired parents left Puerto Rico and moved close to her. Lydia loved her parents but explained that she felt closer to her mother since childhood due to her father's long history of alcoholism. Lydia, a soft-spoken woman, described her father as demeaning and controlling, often making irrational demands on the mother, who then pulled away from Lydia. Although hers was not a violent household, Lydia described her mother as handling marital conflicts by avoiding altercations, not confronting, and never refusing her husband's requests. Lydia's father refused to seek counseling. The counselor observed Lydia's ineffective interpersonal skills, which often paralleled her mother's passivity and avoidance. The counselor asked, "What keeps you from letting those you love know your needs and feelings?" Lydia quickly answered, "I can't. . . . I cannot do it because of *respeto.*"

Therapeutically, the professional counselor can use several models to understand and strategize Lydia's treatment plan. For example, the addiction model may focus on breaking the adult children of alcoholics syndrome and target Lydia's enabling behaviors. The feminist model would seek to empower Lydia from an abusive father, a withdrawn husband, and a defeated and passive mother. A behavioral therapist would focus on "learned helplessness" to address Lydia's interpersonal ineffectiveness and perhaps include assertiveness training in treatment. Although these examples provide reasonable tools for intervention, the lack of cultural accommodation may result in an impoverished counseling process or even in premature termination (Malgady, Rogler, & Costantino, 1990b).

In Lydia's case, the family of origin clearly shows a history of dysfunction, but her distress could be intensified if the approach selected ignores her worldview, gender socialization, and value orientations. Thus, a multidimensional approach may be considered. Also, by addressing her belief system, the schemata that organizes her worldview, one can facilitate the process of change by engaging with the client's worldview.

The counselor should explore Lydia's cultural coping patterns to gain insights into areas in need of counseling focus and cultural modification of methods. Helpful questions that could address cultural variants are: How do women in your family cope with family problems? How can Puerto Rican women address difficult topics with *respeto?* What worked well for you when you were in this predicament?

With this in mind, the chapter explores counseling strategies and specific interventions to consider during the middle and later phases of counseling. Language-based strategies and the use of narratives and metaphors are discussed. In addition, this chapter covers outreach and ecological strategies, practice accommodations, counseling termination, and a variety of ethical issues.

Language-Based Strategies

Language Switching

Among bilinguals, language switching can be used as a counseling intervention. As previously outlined in Chapter 6, many factors contribute to this form of communication, such as language preference, affect, resistance, and diversion. For this reason, the bilingual counselor may be able to incorporate language choice as a strategic intervention (Pérez-Foster, 1998; Santiago--Rivera, 1995; Santiago-Rivera & Altarriba, 2001; Sciarra & Ponterotto, 1991). Several suggestions are proposed. First, language switching can be used strategically with the client to facilitate the therapeutic relationship. A shift to the native tongue may assist in the exploration of medical and somatic complaints, as clients express physical symptoms and related problems in their native language (Poma, 1983). By following the client's lead in language choice, the counselor may be able to identify certain themes. Second, language switching may assist in the resolution of problematic issues and effects of traumatic events.

Related to the latter, Gallardo-Cooper (2000) describes a case where language was essential to the resolution of a presenting problem. Specifically, she described a 35-year-old woman raised in Central America who moved to the United States as an adolescent. At the time of counseling, she was a college-educated woman, married with two young children. Problems with frigidity led her to seek counseling with a well-respected English-speaking professional specializing in post-traumatic stress disorder. The client was fluent in English and very motivated to address her sexual abuse trauma, which occurred in a school auditorium when she was 8 years of age. After 6 to 8 months of outpatient therapy, progress was observed, and both the client and therapist agreed to terminate treatment. Several months later when the client went to one of her children's preschool functions, she had a relapse. The client recognized that her traumatic memories and flashbacks were in Spanish. Soon after, she made an appointment with her therapist. During the session, the client reported, "I think that now I have to work on this in Spanish," and the therapist recognized that her English translations filtered the emotional and troubling cognitions of her childhood. Both agreed that she needed to resolve her trauma in Spanish, as the trauma's underlying emotions were processed and retained in the Spanish language. The client was then referred to a Spanish-speaking therapist, with whom she worked successfully and resolved her difficulties.

Language switching also represents different contexts of the self. A client's self-perceptions may vary depending on the language setting. The following case illustrates this notion of duality in the individual.

THE CASE OF SUSANA

A 29-year-old nurse sought counseling with her husband for marital discord. After the birth of her first child, she and her husband immigrated to the United States. Her husband, a Latino accountant, described her as often lazy, withdrawn, and irritable. She had been in the workforce for the previous 5 years and was fully bilingual in both Spanish and English. At home, she spoke Spanish with her spouse and "Spanglish" with her children; at work, she spoke English. During the course of marital counseling, it became apparent that Susana's marital conflict followed a "bad day at work." Susana preferred to stay home with the children, especially after the birth of her 2-year-old, but due to financial concerns, she felt "forced" to work full-time. As the counselor explored the sequence of events further, Susana broke into tears and began to disclose the excessive tension she experienced at work, due to what she termed *porque soy Latina* (because I am Latina). When she described the unfair and discriminatory attitude of her supervisor, she used English, but when she addressed the conflicts with her husband, she spoke in Spanish.

The case of Susana reflects how a bilingual client compartmentalizes different life experiences by language. Although she narrated the work problem in English, she used Spanish to narrate her marital problems and emotional dimensions. Susana described her new experiences with oppression and prejudice in English but used Spanish to express core emotional content, thus using both languages to answer the counselor's inquiries.

Narratives and Metaphors

Storytelling

One of the most important contributions to multicultural counseling is the work of Costantino, Malgady, and Rogler, who developed and empirically tested a culture-specific therapeutic modality using folktales and storytelling. The premise for designing this approach is based on empirical evidence that folktales can (a) educate individuals about cultural values and standards of behavior, (b) enhance the development of ethnic identity and pride, (c) communicate a complex message with simplicity, (d) adapt easily to the elements of the existing realities of the culture, and (e) reinforce achievement and motivation. Furthermore, storytelling is an effective medium that promotes moral development (Costantino & Rivera, 1994).

Costantino and his associates developed several innovative clinical approaches based on Puerto Rican cultural folklore and history. For example, they developed a storytelling technique with a moral message rooted in folktales, created for children, called *cuento* therapy. In a landmark study, Costantino, Malgady, and Rogler (1986) compared the impact of three therapeutic modalities: (a) *cuentos* from Puerto Rican culture that modeled adaptive behaviors, (b)art/play therapy considered traditional, and (c) no therapy. These investigators identified 210 first- to third-grade children who were assessed as having maladaptive behaviors, along with their mothers. These dyads were randomly assigned to one of the three groups, each of which lasted 20 weeks. In the *cuento* therapy group, the therapist and the mothers read the stories to the children, and then there was a discussion about the characters' behaviors, as well as the moral of each story. Interestingly, the results showed that the *cuento* therapy approach was superior and significantly reduced trait anxiety in the children, even 1 year after the study, compared with the play/art therapy and control groups.

In more recent studies, Malgady, Rogler, and Costantino (1990a, 1990b) applied this culture-centered approach to high-risk adolescents, using in treatment the stories of Puerto Rican heroes or heroines (i.e., hero/heroine therapy) who demonstrated courage, achievement, and triumph. With the exception of some mixed results based on grade level, gender, and family composition factors, the authors found significant overall benefits in reduction of anxiety symptoms, improvement in self-esteem, heightened ethnic identity awareness, and increased effective coping skills.[1] In addition, the gains observed in positive self-concept and ethnic identity support this approach as a culturally based preventive mental health intervention.

In addition to using selected therapeutic stories with children and adolescents, the literary works of Latino writers can also be employed to enhance change in the therapeutic process. Depending on the presenting problems and characteristics of the client, some readings from Latino authors are recommended for bibliotherapy or as a therapy exercise during the session (e.g. poem, short story). Although incorporating such readings in bibliotherapy may prove beneficial, it is recommended that the counselor assess the client's reading level, cognitive abilities, emotional state, and motivation before implementing this strategy. See Appendix D for a selection of some helpful books. Nevertheless, non-Latino and Latino mental health professionals alike should read these selections to best understand Latino-specific processes and to recommend selections that have clinical relevance.

Dichos

Popular wisdom is richly captured in short phrases, sentences, or rhymes that depict Spanish proverbs or sayings, called *dichos*. Because *dichos* are automatically learned through language and used in daily communication, they are readily available to clients to express themselves, assess a situation, summarize a process, or describe a coping strategy. Spanish-speaking individuals quite often use metaphors, similes, and regionalisms in conversation. Moreover, an extensive number of *dichos* are applicable to all types of life events and experiences and can be used in individual, marital, family, and group counseling. One of the powerful elements of *dichos* is the rich imagery of the metaphor, because the use of indirect and covert messages is a common form of communication among Latinos.

Although *dichos* have been used for centuries, Zuñiga (1992a) was one of the first practitioners to examine their effectiveness in treatment. In clinical settings, she has used the power of *dichos* to reduce client resistance, reframe problems, and increase motivation (Zuñiga, 1992a). Some of these proverbs are common across many Spanish-speaking countries, whereas others are more specific to a country or region. If the counselor lacks knowledge of them, a simple strategy might be to ask the client for a common *dicho* used by his or her family or friends that helped them cope. For example, one of the authors worked with a Bolivian woman who suffered discrimination and oppression. When asked what dicho helped her cope, the client said, "*El oro brilla hasta en el basurero*" (Gold shines even in the garbage can).

In addition, the client may use a metaphor to explain coping with a difficult situation, as in the case of Caridad, which follows.

THE CASE OF CARIDAD

Caridad was a 75-year-old Cuban who had been married for 55 years. She lived with her husband, whom she described as controlling and demanding. During their married life, Caridad's husband had been a successful businessman, but for unknown reasons, the family made abrupt moves. Ten years ago, she realized that her husband had a serious gambling *vicio* (vice), and the many moves were due to his gambling losses.

Caridad immigrated to the United States in the mid 1960s. Her family was religious and stayed very close during their residence in the United States. She complained of never having any money because her husband cashed her Social Security check and would give her only $40 a month. Caridad did not drive and depended on her husband or relatives for all transportation needs. Caridad had three children: the only daughter, who had died of cancer several years earlier; a son who was a minister; and the youngest son, who was very ill and dependent on dialysis treatments. Caridad experienced severe back pain and often had to stay in bed for days. It was observed that she often had significant difficulties walking and sitting down during the sessions. Caridad had several herniated discs and arthritis, but she was pessimistic about medical treatment, especially the back surgery recommended by her physicians.

When she initiated counseling, a concern was raised about her lack of response to psychotropic medication. She could not sleep and continued to report depressive symptoms. She used to complain about her husband but refused to bring him to counseling, because as she said, "I deserve some time without him."

At one point during counseling, the counselor asked what Caridad did to cope with the hurdles she had in her life. She responded, "*Camina la milla*" (Walk the mile). She also expressed this *dicho* with an intonation that prolonged the message: *Camiiiiina la miiiilla.* Whenever she would mention a problem, such as her youngest son's deteriorating health, she would repeat this phrase spontaneously.

The counselor also asked Caridad what she wanted to gain from counseling, and she said: "I don't know, but coming here, I can let it all out and feel better." The counselor explored further, and Caridad said, "When I come here, I remember what I have gone through and the 'many miles' I have walked, and that makes me feel better." In other words, Caridad felt empowered by affirming her own past coping experiences. In every session, the counselor interjected, at appropriate times, that Caridad was "walking the mile." At other times, she asked Caridad, "How are you walking the mile with that one?" The metaphor became the driving force in the counseling process and revealed the lighter side of Caridad, who displayed increasing wit and feistiness as therapy unfolded.

After several sessions, Caridad reported that she did not feel she needed to come as often because she was feeling better. She acknowledged that she did not want to "walk the mile" with the recommended back surgery. Counseling then addressed her fears about surgery and hospitalization. By her last appointment, Caridad had discontinued psychotropic medication, undergone successful back surgery, and begun attending regular religious services with her niece.

Caridad's metaphor was her safety net throughout her life. By assessing her internal dialogue, an inner resource was discovered. She was able to focus on what her family and culture had given her as a way to cope. By keeping the metaphor alive in every session, the counselor reminded Caridad of her previous successful experiences, thus reducing her fears and increasing her confidence to take risks.

Images

Culture-specific images refer to visual stimuli in the form of pictures, art, or photographs that trigger a cognitive and affective response in the form of a story. A story about a picture is essentially a projection of the individual's psychological structure. Miller-Jones (1989) argued that if the visual stimulus does not represent some aspect of the client's realities, the image fails to trigger the necessary mental abstraction and emotional domains, which it is purposely trying to assess.

Based on this idea, Costantino and colleagues (Costantino, Colón-Malgady, Malgady, & Pérez, 1991; Costantino, Flanagan, & Malgady, 2001) developed the projective assessment tool called TEMAS (Tell Me A Story), consisting of card illustrations that depict different scenarios and situations. Although TEMAS was primarily developed for urban minority youth, it is currently used with adult inpatient and outpatient clients in individual and group therapy. *Temas* is also a Spanish word, which literary translates to *themes.* Because the cards depict culturally relevant scenes in urban settings as well as daily activities, Latino children, adolescents, and adults can identify with the pictures and can readily produce stories, more easily than with traditional projective cards (Malgady, Costantino, & Rogler, 1984).

Once used primarily as a personality assessment tool, TEMAS is now used as a viable therapeutic intervention. For instance, Costantino and Rivera (1994) found that the use of TEMAS decreased anxiety, improved self-esteem, enhanced ethnic identity and pride, and increased positive behavioral changes among a group of adolescents. More recent work is centered on using it in psychoeducational group therapy (Ranson, 2000) and with inpatient psychiatric patients (Hernández, 2000), indicating positive outcomes in adult treatment.

Other images have been used to elicit therapeutic disclosure, such as religious icons (Bracero, 1998) and the artwork of Frida Kahlo (Sesin, 2000). For example, Bracero has used the picture of Anima Sola, a naked woman in chains rising from the flames of hell, with Latinas who have been victimized. This icon is commonly found on altars of *espiritistas* and can be readily identified by many Latina women, especially Puerto Ricans.

The surrealist art of Frida Kahlo has been a powerful therapeutic tool, as well. Frida Kahlo, a Mexican artist, painted primarily self-portraits depicting sensitive issues such as physical pain, suffering, death, despair, isolation, domestic violence, miscarriages, immigration, duality, and identity. Sesin (2000) describes how the artwork triggered intense emotional reactions, especially among recently immigrated women in group therapy. Sesin postulated that Kahlo's paintings revealed gender- and culture-related conflicts, which were transformed into narratives and later processed within the group.

Another powerful visual strategy is the use of photographs in individual, group, and family therapy. For instance, childhood and family photographs taken in the native country can be powerful in linking pre- and postmigration experiences, identifying losses and identity issues, and identifying cultural practices and traditions, particularly when used with recent immigrants. In addition, images can be triggered with the use of music pieces during expressive therapy or guided imagery. Indigenous instrumental music has been very effective in unveiling significant emotional content in individual and group therapy sessions. For example, one of the authors successfully used native music in flute and harp with a Latin American client who was not progressing while hospitalized for severe depression.

Alternative Strategies

Given these various perspectives, we offer the following guidelines to enhance the therapeutic narratives that result from these alternative strategies, especially for those providers who may have limited English language skills and work with bilingual clients.

Allow the client complete freedom of expression. During the course of treatment, ask in what language the client is processing events (e.g., self-talk, metaphors, etc.) and what language is preferred. If communicating a difficult issue in English becomes an issue, allow the client to express it in his or her native language. Allow self-expression, no matter which language is chosen, and observe nonverbal behaviors. Similarly, allow any journal writing to be done in Spanish or in both languages (Gallardo-Cooper, 2000).

Be cautious with diagnostic impressions after a client narrates his or her story. This is particularly important when working with a Spanish-dominant individual, who may present distorted affect due to communicating in a second language (Marcos, 1994).

Follow with open-ended questions such as, What did you experience? What was learned about yourself in the Spanish narrative? Let the client lead the way in the process.

*Learn some Spanish proverbs (*dichos*) and their meaning.* When applicable, these proverbs can be used to support therapeutic issues. Also, ask the client for a *dicho* that summarizes or symbolizes the past, current situation, or coping strategies. As in Caridad's case, find a creative metaphor in either English or Spanish that captures a powerful message. As stated earlier, the use of metaphors in counseling is another form of communicating meaning without didactics (Barker, 1985).

Learn from the client's cultural traditions, music, geography, and the like to incorporate images that will motivate the client to explore relevant clinical issues.

Practice Accommodations

Practice accommodations refer to clinical and service adjustments made to respond Latino clients. Two useful models are available to guide the clinician. Both models have overlapping concepts, but each provides valuable recommendations that facilitate Latino cultural adaptations and thus ensure treatment receptiveness and adherence. A brief description of both models follows.

First, Rogler, Malgady, Costantino, and Blumenthal (1987) recommend accommodations in three broad areas: (a) accessibility of services (e.g., logistics that interfere with accessibility of services such as bilingual and bicultural clinicians), (b) traditional clinical methods that are congruent with the culture (e.g., adjusting traditional methods to decrease cultural barriers and applying methods that support cultural values), and (c) clinical methods specifically developed for the Latino population (e.g., *cuento* therapy, TEMAS, *dichos*, religious beliefs accommodations such as *espiritismo*). The reader is directed to Costantino and Rivera (1994) for an example of how a traditional psychoeducation program was adapted to Latino families of chronically ill psychiatric patients.

Second, Bernal, Bonillo, and Bellido (1995) provide eight concepts necessary to implement a Latino-centered approach: (a) understanding of language (i.e., as a representation of culture, affective expression, style, etc.), (b) sensitivity to client-counselor issues (i.e., therapeutic relationship, counselor's self-awareness, client-counselor match), (c) application of metaphors (i.e., *dichos*, images, stories), (d) inclusion of cultural content (i.e., gather and integrate relevant cultural dimensions about the client), (e) knowledge about cultural concepts (i.e., cultural dimensions that are imbedded in the problem, (f) implementation of culturally defined and empowering goals, (g) application of interventions congruent with the culture (i.e., structural family therapy, genograms), and (h) incorporation of all contexts relevant to clients (i.e., sociopolitical and historical contexts, immigration phase, acculturation process and possible effects).

From a utilization perspective, logistics such as transportation, geographic distance, payment source, and the waiting period before the first appointment also influence access and use of mental health services. Some Latino clients may benefit from on-site services, advocacy, or home visits; school mental health programs; and case management, especially those with multiple psychosocial problems. Zayas, Kaplan, Turner, Romano, and González-Ramos (2000) staunchly refute the myth of resistance by emphasizing that it may be the issue of access that drives the underutilization of services among Latinos.

Last, agency procedures need to accommodate Latino clients. Records may need to be completed in two languages (Gallardo-Cooper, 2000). For example, correspondence for Spanish-speaking Latinos should be written in Spanish, but the letters also need to be translated into English for the official records. Similarly, counseling notes should have the client's verbatim remarks in Spanish to avoid misinterpretations, but they also need to be written in English to comply with agency and audit requirements.

Termination Issues

The pattern of mental health services utilization has been discussed as brief and usually crisis oriented. However, Latinos also participate in long-term counseling. Clients who are of higher socioeconomic backgrounds and are highly acculturated approach the counseling experience differently than the poor with lower levels of education. When comparing Latino and Anglo American service utilization by socioeconomic status, a similar pattern is evident; however, the language barrier experienced by Latinos clearly places them at a disadvantage.

When clients disclose that they are ready to stop attending, and there are clearly no risk factors, it may be best to respect their decision and terminate counseling. Although the counselor may disagree with the client, accepting the decision to terminate may be an empowering intervention in and of itself. Failure to do so will communicate disapproval and lack of *respeto* for their *dignidad* and inner resources.

Ethical Considerations

Several ethical issues need to be revisited when working with Latinos. First is the issue of accepting personal gifts. It is not unusual for a Latino client to give a gift that expresses appreciation, represents a special holiday or occasion, or marks termination. This creates a dilemma for professionals, as our ethical standards direct us not to accept gifts from clients. Among Latinos, it may be rude not to accept a gift. (Paniagua, 1998).

A second issue needing further exploration is when to refer a client. The lack of bilingual mental health professionals often creates ethical dilemmas if no other referral can be made (Gallardo-Cooper, 2000). What is the obligation of the professional if no referral is feasible or possible? Depending on clinical and legal ramifications, in some cases, it could be unethical to refuse counseling to a family member of a client previously or presently receiving services. Specific guidelines—for example, how should the clinician structure counseling and address confidentiality issues?—need to be developed to assist the mental health professional in these situations. Third, culturally competent counselors apply clinical judgment regarding the use of translators—professionals, paraprofessionals, and client relatives—in the assessment and counseling process. A fourth ethical issue, also raised earlier, is that practice procedures and accommodations must ensure that Latino clients thoroughly understand the parameters of the counseling process, such as informed consent, confidentiality, and the therapeutic relationship.

Fifth, the issue of dual relationships also needs specific guidelines. As discussed earlier, Latino family boundaries are more permeable than the boundaries of European American families. Therefore, a particular counselor may be preferred by a Latino client because he or she is a friend or a social acquaintance. In many cases, Latino clients will refuse necessary services when referred to professionals whom they do not perceive as trustworthy because there is no previous social association.

Last, professionals who consider themselves bilingual should communicate the limits of their language fluency and competence to their bilingual and Spanish monolingual clients (Gallardo-Cooper, 2000).

It is important to note that mental health professionals in general and bilingual professionals in particular who work with Latino clients have extraordinary ethical responsibilities (Gallardo-Cooper, 2000). The limited English skills of many Latino clients and their particular circumstances may require professional advocacy beyond the 50-minute hour. One colleague once said to a Latino counselor: "You know, you are doing too much for her [referring to a client]. That's not good, you are creating dependency." What appears to be "too much" by traditional counseling parameters may not be enough to respond to the needs of some clients who do not speak the language, have limited resources, and experience multiple problems.

It is well recognized by the profession that ethical dilemmas need to be considered in the context of multiple factors. This approach becomes even more salient when working with Latino clients. As more attention is given to these complex issues from a multicultural competency perspective, it is hoped that ethical standards will be sensitive to the realities of different ethnic populations.

Summary

This chapter addressed methods and processes relevant during the middle and last stages of counseling Latinos. Traditional counseling models and culture specific strategies were discussed as viable and effective frameworks. In particular, the practice of a prudent, eclectic approach that incorporates cultural dimensions to traditional methods was recommended. Several Latino specific strategies covered were language based strategies, storytelling, *dichos,* and images. In addition, this chapter included models and recommendations for practice accomodations as well as a discussion on termination issues, and ethical considerations.

Correct Answers to Self-Assessment

1. True. A variety of counseling orientations are used in multicultural counseling. (See pages 131-135.)

2. True. Latino clients may switch from one language to another (e.g., English to Spanish) when discussing childhood experiences, to express certain emotions that are more meaningful, or to avoid discussing certain emotional experiences. (See pages 136-137.)

3. True. Research studies have shown that folktales as a therapeutic approach reduce trait anxiety and increase self-esteem, identity formation, social judg-

ment, and coping skills in children. Culture-based hero and heroine intervention with high-risk adolescents also has proven successful in reducing anxiety
and enhancing personality development, thus supporting its mental health
preventive value. (See pages 137-138.)

4. False. *Cuento* therapy is more effective. (See pages 137-138.)

5. False. *Dichos* have been used to decrease client resistance and increase client
comfort. (See pages 138-140.)

6. False. Latino clients respond well to culture-centered imagery used in counseling. (See pages 140-141.)

7. True. Culture-specific metaphors can be powerful treatment tools. (See pages
140-141.)

8. True. TEMAS is an assessment tool based on storytelling and used with Latino
clients. (See pages 140-141.)

9. True. Latinos clients benefit from a variety of mental health interventions, and
counselors may need to take on an advocacy role connecting Latino clients to
a wide range of services. (See pages 141-144.)

10. True. The issue of when to refer a Latino client for mental health services can
result in ethical dilemmas. (See page144.)

NOTE

1. A more detailed description of *cuento* therapy for children, and hero/heroine therapy for
adolescents can be found in the cited works by Costantino and colleagues.

8

Latino Family Counseling

Models of Helping

Palabras sin obras, guitarras sin cuerdas.
Words without deeds are like guitars without strings.
Rovira, 1984, p. 103

Objectives

- To examine family therapy theories and their application to Latino families.
- To review four specific Latino-centered frameworks: Bicultural Effectiveness Training; Multidimensional Ecosystemic Comparative Approach; Rules, Roles, and Rituals; and Latino Transactional Model.
- To review culture-centered approaches in constructing genograms in family assessment.
- To examine special issues and guidelines in working with Latino families, such as language issues, structuring sessions, and decision making.

Competencies

As a result of studying this chapter, counselors will:
- Be knowledgeable about different family therapy theories and culture-centered family counseling frameworks.

- Be knowledgeable about how to assess the family from a culture-centered perspective.
- Be knowledgeable about how to structure and conduct family therapy with Latino clients.

Latino-Specific Competencies

AWARENESS
- Culturally skilled counselors can identify the cultural and idiosyncratic characteristics of their own family of origin.
- Culturally skilled counselors are aware of the importance of adapting different kinds of family therapy models with Latino families.

KNOWLEDGE
- Culturally skilled counselors have broad knowledge of family systems theories as well as culture-centered family therapy models.
- Culturally skilled counselors can identify possible barriers to family interventions with Latino families.

SKILLS
- Culturally skilled counselors can differentiate between what is culturally driven and what is idiosyncratic in the Latino family's functioning.
- Culturally skilled counselors can effectively integrate multiple frameworks and interventions in counseling Latino families.

Self-Assessment

Directions: Answer True or False. The correct answers are at the end of the chapter.

T   F   1. Latinos readily seek professional help and, in particular, family therapy.

T   F   2. There is no consensus on the best family therapy approach for Latinos.

T   F   3. The self-differentiation or individuation construct as defined by Bowen is a universal process applicable to all individuals, regardless of cultural background and age.

T   F   4. The Bicultural Effectiveness Training is a psycho-educational intervention to increase multicultural tolerance.

T   F   5. The Multidimensional Ecosystemic Comparative Approach supports the multicultural competencies framework.

T   F   6. Exploring the rules, roles, and rituals of the family helps to identify idiosyncratic family dynamics and general cultural characteristics.

T	F	7.	*Respeto* is a value orientation only prevalent in parenting issues.
T	F	8.	Latinos use a vertical communication style.
T	F	9.	Traditional genograms are culturally biased and, therefore, not suitable for Latinos.
T	F	10.	Children and parents should not be seen separately because it will diminish the authority of the parents.

Introduction

Scholars concur that *la familia* plays a central role in the psychological well-being of all Latinos, regardless of place of birth (Comas-Díaz, 1988; Falicov, 1998; Ho, 1987; Inclán, 1990; Sue & Sue, 1999). Latinos typically continue a close bond with their families of origin throughout their life span, making *la familia* a major source of growth, support, conflict, and problem solving. Inevitably, counseling Latinos requires systemic expertise as well as sensitivity and understanding of the cultural variants embedded in *la familia*. However, the successful implementation of family counseling with Latinos is complex and may be jeopardized when four basic practice errors occur. The first centers on the difficulty experienced in deciphering the dynamics of what is culture driven and what is idiosyncratic to the family. Too much emphasis on cultural characteristics may normalize pathogenic features. Like other families, Latino families experience a wide range of social, psychological, and systemic problems.

The second error occurs when culture-related factors are denied, or realities experienced by Latino families in the United States are overlooked. Family treatment needs to address how the family system is adjusting to the specific psychosocial stressors experienced by Latinos in education, the workplace, and the community. Without an understanding of the additive effects of the language barrier, acculturation, immigration, generational dynamics, socio-political history, discrimination, and prejudice on *la familia,* practitioners may fail to respond in otherwise effective interventions. When Latinos are compared to other populations, problematic family dynamics may stem from different causes. For example, Flores-Ortíz and Bernal (1995) found similarities in symptomatology among families of Latino and Anglo American addicts, but both groups differed in the precipitating events and underlying reasons that led to the addictive behavior. The researchers discovered that addiction among Latinos in their sample was preceded by the negative effects of migration, manifested by unresolved grief, intergenerational conflicts, and family communication problems due to the language barrier.

A third type of practice error results when Latino family values are misunderstood. The importance given to family loyalty, closeness, and ethnocentrism has been viewed pathologically as enmeshment, overdependency, and even oppression. Cooperation and interdependence are highly intertwined in Latino standards of family problem solving. This value orientation can clash with dominant culture values of individualism, independence, and competition. Practice errors occur when the family counselor's focus is on separating adult children from their parents or when the focus of treatment is on the individual rather than on the well-being of the family.

The fourth type of error involves the misguided perception that all Latino families readily want to engage in family therapy. This problem may stem from confusing family involvement with family therapy. The boundaries of *la familia* are large and permeable. Involvement by kin and extended family in economic, social, psychological, and health-related affairs is a natural occurrence among Latinos. It is not uncommon to find an adult sister, a brother-in-law, or a *compadre* accompanying a relative to doctors' appointments, medical procedures, or mental health visits. These individuals may be asked to serve as advocates, translators, supportive companions, or transportation providers, and they often are permitted or feel entitled to ask questions about the patient, medication, diagnosis, and/or treatment. In this instance, the focus of the family involvement is on the identified patient, not the family. In contrast, traditional family counseling emphasizes the consensual participation of all significant family members in problem solving a shared complaint. Despite this distinction, innovative, new paradigms in clinical methods should be developed to maximize systemic intervention with Latino family involvement situations.

Counselors must be aware that the degree of involvement in counseling may be dictated by culturally defined gender roles. For instance, Latino men may be discouraged from showing emotions and complaining about illness, because these expressions may be interpreted as a sign of weakness (Romero, Cuéllar, & Roberts, 2000). Thus, their involvement may be difficult in family therapy (Ho, 1987). Furthermore, Latino men have been described as guarded in making disclosures about personal problems (Arcaya, 1996; Torres-Rivera, 1999; Zambrana, 1995); they are expected to *controlar o aguantar* (control or withstand) emotionally laden conflicts (Dana, 1993). For this reason, the counselor may need to strategize on how to motivate male family members to participate in traditional therapy (Szapocznik et al., 1988) or may need to explore ecologically based family interventions. Similarly, there is a belief that family honor is protected when problems are suppressed from the public eye (Falicov, 1998; Inclán & Hernández, 1992). Latino families may be distrustful of mental health services. Openness and engagement in family counseling with an outsider may be a difficult experience. Instead, the trend is to initiate help seeking in their natural support system of la familia and to postpone professional help (Flores-Ortíz & Bernal, 1995; Inclán & Hernández, 1992; McMiller & Weisz, 1996).

Beyond the family, both nuclear and extended systems, informal sources of help are often sought with clergy, folk healers, and other community resources (Hoberman, 1992; McMiller & Weisz, 1996). Thus, careful attention must be given early in family treatment to (a) joining strategies, (b) identifying intrafamily resources, and (c) integrating informal types of help seeking in the therapeutic process.

With these considerations in mind, this chapter will address strategies for helping Latino families change. It is not intended to be a thorough review of family therapy theories and methods but a discussion of integrated Latino-centered approaches in clinical practice. This chapter will cover three areas of family counseling: (a) a review of traditional and alternative models and their application, (b) a review of systemic and ecological perspectives in the use of genograms, and (c) a discussion of special issues in counseling Latino families.

Family Counseling Models

The integration of theories enriches the therapeutic process by providing the culturally competent counselor with a multitude of lenses through which to examine and intervene with diverse families. Hardy (1990) defends the need to respond to diversity by creating new theoretical conceptualizations to eliminate the effects of sameness in family therapy, as well as the "fix it all" mentality of one single process theory.[1] Hardy's contention is well taken in that there is no family therapy theory that is applicable to all Latinos and their problems. Moreover, any traditional family therapy approach can be helpful when adapted to the cultural worldview of the family.

Clinicians and researchers support the application of traditional family therapy models with Latinos, for example, structural (e.g., Szapocznik, Rio, et al., 1989; Szapocznik, Kurtinez et al., 1997), Bowenian (Ho, 1987), strategic (Ho, 1987; Szapocznik et al., 1988), contextual (Bernal & Flores-Ortíz, 1982; Szapocznik & Kurtines, 1993), family life cycle (Falicov, 1998; Lyle & Faure, 2000; McGoldrick & Carter, 1998), narrative (Gallardo-Cooper, 2000), and ecological models (e.g., Falicov, 1998; Inclán, 1990). Borrowing from these broad theoretical perspectives, culture-centered family therapy models have also been developed for Latinos. The following section outlines several of these models, including the description of two family therapy approaches: the Bicultural Effectiveness Training model (Szapocznik & Kurtines, 1993; Szapocznik, Santisteban, Kurtines et al., 1984; Szapocznik, Santisteban et al., 1986) and the Multidimensional Ecosystemic Comparative Approach (Falicov, 1998). It is important to note that although they were developed for Latino families, these models can be applied to other ethnic/cultural groups.

In addition, we present two frameworks that have facilitated our work with Latino families. One is based on rules, roles, and rituals of the family, and the other is a proposed model based on transactional dynamics.

Traditional Family Therapy Models

The cultural adaptation of traditional models, or a "pick and choose" approach to concepts and theorems, has been the key to successful Latino family therapy practice. Several examples are discussed to clarify this position. First, structural family therapy is highly recommended with ethnic minorities because it incorporates a generational view, focuses on balancing the structure of the family, and uses a direct, concrete, here and now approach to problem solving (Wilson, Kohn, & Lee, 2000). The model's hierarchical parent-child relational position parallels Latinos' vertical communication style and reinforces the expected boundaries within the family. Similarly, the broad family framework, with a direct, no-nonsense, problem-solving approach, agrees with the preferred style of intervention among Latinos (Ho, 1987; Sue & Sue, 1999; Wilson et al., 2000).

José Szapocznik, a pioneer in family therapy outcome research with Latinos, and his associates (e.g., Szapocznik & Kurtines, 1993; Szapocznik et al., 1986, 1988, 1997) have applied the combination of structural and strategic family therapy methods within a culturally sensitive framework. For example, they found positive outcomes with families who were experiencing significant distress with the substance abuse of their children by using a structural approach. Moreover, by using a strategic approach, they were able to increase participation of family members considered difficult to motivate (Szapocznik et al., 1990; Szapocznik, Kurtines, et al., 1986; Szapocznik, et al., 1988).

Bowenian models can also be adapted to Latino families (Ho, 1987; Inclán & Hernández, 1992). This approach incorporates important intergenerational processes, allowing the counselor to explore paramount historical events and intergenerational patterns affecting current functioning. Titelman (1998a), a follower of Bowen's applications, writes, "The best prognosis for basic change is when there is potential for open communication and relatedness to the family of origin" (p. 63). Titelman further explains that Bowen's theory conceptualizes family changes in a nonpathological framework as the family adapts to a stage in the life cycle such as marriage, birth of a child, departure of each child, retirement, aging, and death.

The self-individuation process as theorized by Bowen, however, was developed for the dominant culture and is not applicable to Latinos (Ho, 1987; Inclán & Hernández, 1992). Bowen theorized that the goals of therapy were to strengthen each parent's individual sense of self to enhance the functioning level of the entire family (Titelman, 1998b). Instead of self-differentiation, the general rule among Latino families is not to separate but to maintain connectedness; the "we" takes precedence over the "I." For example, adolescent children are not expected to move out of their parents' home when they reach 18 years of age and are encouraged to live close by when they are adults. The relational and interdependent nature among Latinos corresponds with an understanding of the self-construct as a collective developmental process instead of a differentiated individualistic self. Terms generated to replace the dominant culture construct of the *differentiated self* among Latinos are the *familial self* (Falicov, 1998) and the *cultural self* (Romero, 2000).

Another framework is an ecological perspective, which originated from the contributions of Brofenbrenner's (1979) developmental theory. The framework explains behavior as stemming from the ripple effects caused by the interaction of environmental factors as defined by culture and context (Bernal & Flores-Ortíz, 1982; Falicov, 1998; Inclán, 1990; Marsella & Yamada, 2000; Szapocznik & Kurtines, 1993; Szapocznik et al., 1997). The family is understood as a system molded by differences in experiences, contexts of time, nationality, historical events, and sociopolitical factors. Outside forces are considered in the assessment process and in the development of intervention strategies. Thus, the model focuses on a cultural and ecological process of change rather than a self-oriented perspective. In addition to the applications of ecological family therapy, indirect service delivery in the form of consultation and advocacy are examples of ecological interventions. Increasing the support network, improving health care, offering educational interventions, and advocating social justice are all ecological interventions that go beyond helping the family, as treatment gains may be long-lasting and may benefit a larger community.

Bicultural Effectiveness Training

Landmark studies conducted by Szapocznik and colleagues in areas such as the role of Cuban value orientations in therapy (Szapocznik, Scopetta, & King, 1978; Szapocznik, Scopetta, Aranalde, & Kurtines, 1978), the differential rates of acculturation among family members (Szapocznik, Scopetta, Kurtines, & Aranalde, 1978), and treatment methods to resolve intergenerational and acculturation conflicts (Szapocznik et al., 1984; Szapocznik, Santisteban, Rio et al., 1986) provided the basis for the development of several family treatment models.

Specifically, the three models of family treatment developed by Szapocznik and his group are (a) Brief Strategic Family Therapy, (b) Family Effectiveness Training, and (c) Bicultural Effectiveness Training (Szapocznik et al., 1997). The Family Effectiveness Training is a prevention program for children at risk of developing substance abuse problems based on addressing inadequate coping patterns and intergenerational and intercultural factors (Szapocznik et al., 1989). Of the three models, Bicultural Effectiveness Training has received the most attention because it focuses on specific family interventions to address intergenerational and intercultural conflict. The premise of BET is that family members may experience difficulties due to differences in the acculturation process.

Bicultural Effectiveness Training is a 12-session structured psychoeducational intervention based on a contextual theoretical framework in which the individual is viewed as embedded in two contexts: the culture and the family (Szapocznik & Kurtines, 1993; Szapocznik et al., 1984; Szapocznik et al., 1986). Four basic concepts borrowed from structural and systemic frameworks are used: (a) detour, (b) identified patient role, (c) reframing, and (d) boundaries. Systemic theory indicates that family problems are not confronted directly but are detoured through a third party or transmitted covertly, through what Minuchin (1974) called the identified patient or the party on which the systemic problem is projected. During early stages of treatment, the counselor carefully assesses the problem as defined by the family with the presenting complaint. The process of change begins by detouring the problem away from the family or individuals. This is accomplished through the reframing of the presenting problem as a cultural problem. As a result of redefining the problem in this manner, the tension in the family is markedly reduced, allowing the family to become receptive to change. In addition, reframing heightens awareness about things that are common among family members and deemphasizes intergenerational differences. Accordingly, this strategy leads to establishing boundaries around the family and promotes positive interaction patterns between parents and their children. The goal of this approach is to increase acceptance of different values by parents and youth. The power of the Bicultural Effectiveness Training model is based on its cultural adaptation to traditional, well-established therapeutic concepts. Of even greater importance is that the model has evolved into a Multicultural Effectiveness Training Program (Szapocznik et al., 1997) and can be applied to families of different ethnic/cultural backgrounds.

A number of benefits are derived from the application of this model. First, the model takes the pathology out of intercultural conflict by conducting a psychoeducational based intervention. Second, the training program is clear, well developed, and easy to implement through the application of exercises that parents and children follow to increase cultural understanding. Third, the here and now, concrete quality of the training program fits with the preference for a direct style and "in the present" value orientation. Last, the model fits well with the common problems found in families with adolescents, where a delicate balance between autonomy and family connectedness is necessary.

Multidimensional Ecological Comparative Approach

Falicov's (1998) Multidimensional Ecological Comparative Approach model is derived from her extensive clinical experience with Latino families but is also applicable to different cultural groups. The model incorporates a comprehensive framework that responds to the complexity of individuals and the need to approach therapy from three major perspectives: (a) multidimensional, (b) ecosystemic, and (c) comparative. The first one addresses a variety of factors (e.g., nationality, language, political affiliation, gender, age, etc.) within a culture that shapes the worldview, coping style, and affective reactions of individuals. The second perspective, the ecosystemic, incorporates the contexts in which families interact in the environment. And last, the comparative perspective refers to the family therapy task of searching for "differences that make a difference" (Falicov, 1998, p. 16). The first two perspectives are representative of what Falicov considers culture, and the last one defines the role of the counselor and the therapeutic process through the use of comparisons.

The comparative process of the model is applied to four domains: (a) the impact of migration and cultural change (i.e., stories of migration and the dynamics of adaptation), (b) family organization (i.e., parent-child and husband-wife relationships, communication style, etc.), (c) the current ecological environment of the family (e.g., social network, health and coping beliefs, spiritual views, and support, and (d) the family life cycle or transitions (e.g., the cultural blueprint of natural developmental stages that families undergo throughout the life span). These four areas of comparison constitute the most important aspects of her model.

The first task for counselors who are following Falicov's principles is to become aware of their own cultural map or background. This self-awareness process reveals the similarities and differences, connectedness and dissonance, between two cultural maps, the family's and the counselor's. This constant process of reciprocal insight is necessary to conduct the comparisons of her model. Engagement occurs through empathy, observation, curiosity, and collaboration. By redefining the role of the counselor as one who can explore different realities through "sociological imagination," stereotypes, preconceptions, and prejudices are minimized. Within the first two sessions, Falicov contends that the counselor should engage in an open dialogue about similarities and differences that will provide necessary assessment information and, at the same time, develop rapport with the family.

Rules, Roles, and Rituals

Another useful approach in generating salient family data is the examination of rules, roles, and rituals (Anderson, Anderson, & Hovestadt, 1988). Individuals acquire strong, imprinted cultural values from the exposure over time to rules, roles, and rituals that reinforce specific standards of behavior. These internalized standards and value orientations become so pervasive in the belief system of individuals that they become automatic, unconscious, and very difficult to change (Comas-Díaz, 1988). Because all families, regardless of ethnicity, function under a set of rules, expected roles, and predictable rituals, the counselor can use this approach to differentiate between cultural and clinical characteristics manifested by the family. This approach can be adapted to generational and bicultural conflicts manifested in distressful relationships (Gallardo-Cooper, 1998). At the same time, the three concepts maintain a dynamic relationship and are associated with different developmental tasks occurring across the life span (see Figure 8.1). How Latinos approach marriage, death, and caring for the elderly are some examples of life events that require adaptation to different rules, roles, and rituals.

Rules are defined as direct and indirect instructions used throughout our lives. Some rules are direct and clear whereas others are not. In relationships, we also indirectly learn what is right and wrong through the communication of covert, unspoken, yet powerful rules. Latinos use *indirectas* (indirect comments) and other forms of metaphorical communication (García-Prieto, 1996a, 1996b). An example among Latino parents is when daughters reach adolescence. Latino parents stress supervision at this age. They also may use covert messages that reinforce sexual abstinence by openly discussing with the children the "tragedy" and "dishonor" to a family when a daughter has an unwed pregnancy. Although this is the cultural standard, Latina teenagers have a high incidence of unplanned pregnancies. Likely contributing factors are acculturation and socioeconomic background.

Roles in this framework are related to gender role socialization. For example, Latinas learn gender-specific roles first from their mothers, aunts, sisters, and grandmothers and also through directives about standards of proper behavior. The emulation of significant others in one's life is not new in psychological functioning, but when these roles contrast with role expectations of a parent or spouse, conflict inevitably occurs. For instance, role confusion and role conflict can happen in bicultural marriages or in families whose members are at different acculturation levels.

Rituals are very important in human development and in intervention, particularly for children, because they provide a sense of predictability and control of the environment, resulting in a sense of security. Wolin and Bennett (1988) defined three types of family rituals: celebrations (e.g., holidays, weddings, baptisms), traditions (e.g., birthdays, vacations, anniversaries, Sunday dinners, visits to relatives, dating), and interactions (e.g., greetings, eating together, discipline practices, affective expressions, bedtime routines). All three types of rituals are important to address in identifying culture-specific behaviors and distinct aspects of the family's dynamics.

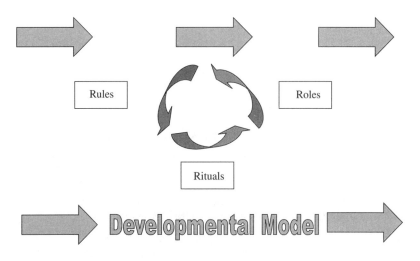

Figure 8.1. Rules, Roles, and Rituals Model
SOURCE: Anderson, Anderson, & Hovestadt, 1988; Gallardo-Cooper, 1998.

From a macro perspective, celebration rituals are based on cultural norms and thus are heavily defined by culture. They also provide information on the extent to which the family adheres to the culture of origin. In contrast, family tradition rituals are influenced by the choices and habitual patterns of each family. Wolin and Bennett (1984) explain that birthdays, which are family tradition rituals, may be influenced by cultural expectations, but how the family chooses to celebrate birthdays becomes more idiosyncratic or characteristic of the family. In addition, interaction rituals assist in the understanding of more fluid and concealed interpersonal dynamics that structure daily life. Interaction rituals are also influenced by integenerational and cultural factors and may more clearly reveal unique characteristics of the family, which are presented in the therapy session. The frequency in which these interaction rituals occur makes them more susceptible to daily pressures and conflict. The counselor can address a here and now, behavior-specific approach by focusing on these daily interactions, which often accumulate and have the potential to hinder family functioning.

In addition to the identification of specific conflicts generated by the above rituals, attention is given to the interaction among the three Rs (Gallardo-Cooper, 1998). The interdependence of rules, roles, and rituals is found in many presenting complaints of families. An example would be when parents complain that their children do not have a closer relationship with the extended family. A close look at the complaint may reveal that the parents grew up living close to extended family and engaged in daily or weekly family activities together. These rituals inevitably reinforced the family bond, loyalty, and solidarity. However, because of frequent geographical moves and the children's acculturation process, the rituals were not consistently carried out; thus, the role expectation could not be met, and the rule or standard was not followed.

In the application of the three Rs, the primary task is to identify and openly discuss the nature of the emotions associated with the conflict. The family as a system needs to understand the dissonance that causes conflicts and the illogical nature of the conflict. Circular questions can uncover the family dynamics of the three Rs, such as who in the family is the least interested in keeping the family dinners and who is the most enthusiastic in having family dinners. Without diminishing the authority of parents, the family counselor then directs the family to negotiate a more realistic and congruent interaction between the three constructs through the identification of rules, the adaptation to multiple roles, or the implementation of supportive rituals.

Latino Transactional Model

The emphasis on social relations as a cultural script of Latinos has implications for transactions in different settings and situations. For instance, Latinos may stay with the same employer throughout their lives, regardless of difficulties encountered, reflecting a sense of loyalty to the work family. In her analysis of Latinos in the workplace, Comas-Díaz (1997) describes the tendency to avoid conflict with coworkers and keep a "team member" attitude. In friendships, *personalismo* may also lead to avoiding displeasure and presenting a pleasing, noncontroversial attitude (Arcaya, 1996). Latinas in particular may be guided by *marianismo* (self-sacrifice) and may suppress outward expressions of interpersonal discomfort. Therefore, it is speculated that Latinos, in general, may approach relationship problems from different perspectives. Depending on the context, there will be a tendency to use other methods of resolution, such as maintaining consensus, accommodating others, or providing lengthy explanations justifying decisions made (Gallardo-Cooper, 2000). This latter observation is based on the tendency among Latinos to maintain the dignity of the receiver instead of communicating the personal justification. For example, if a Latino declines an invitation, there is a higher probability that a lengthy excuse will be used instead of giving a "something came up" response. In addition, learning successful communication skills among Latino clients requires modifications to assertive interactions by adapting a more deferent and respectful approach to requests, confrontations, and directives (Arcaya, 1996; Comas-Díaz & Duncan, 1985). Compared to African American and Anglo American women, Latinas tend to perceive as aggressive what others might view as assertive and persistent interactions, thus showing a lower tolerance to direct interactions (Yoshioka, 2000).

These patterns of interactions are vital to address when conducting relationship therapy, but there is no model that addresses how Latinos "typically" communicate, how they resolve conflicts, and what guidelines can be used to assess these interpersonal processes. For this reason, a transactional model for counseling Latinos is necessary (Gallardo-Cooper, 2000). Transactions are defined as a contextual construct in which individuals interact to communicate, develop relationships, and problem solve. The model incorporates five major components believed to emerge in Latino communication: (a) value orientation, (b) message modes, (c) directional level, (d) problem solving style, and (e) language mechanics. These components are examined for different systems or dyads: child-child, adult-adult, husband-wife, and parent-child. (See Figure 8.2.)

The first component of this model refers to the values of *personalismo, familismo, dignidad,* and *respeto,* which are embedded in the family standards of acceptable interpersonal behavior. As stated earlier, the dynamics of interdependence and loyalty found in many Latino families do not correspond to clinical constructs such as individuation. Moreover, Inclán and Hernández (1992) argue that codependent tendencies are found in Latino families with and without addiction, thus disputing the application of this well-established clinical construct with Latino families.

For example, *respeto,* as stated in previous chapters, has many functions in Latino transactions, such as maintaining the hierarchical family structure (Inclán & Hernández, 1992), defining boundaries in relationships, and providing a standard to respond to interpersonal discord. *No faltarle el respeto* (not disrespecting) is a golden rule that children and adults abide by with peers, parents, elders, and authority figures. This implies not raising one's voice, not talking back, not asserting oneself, using the proper formal Spanish pronoun of *usted,* and not breaking a set rule (e.g., curfew). Thus, the broad application of *respeto* implies that compliance and obedience are components of this important value orientation.

Falta de respeto (lack of respect), for example, is a pervasive cause assigned for failures in relationships or communication problems between adults, parent-child dyads, and families. A significant number of negative interactions or failed relationships are measured against the standard of *respeto.* Moreover, the attribution implied with *falta de respeto* reflects a personalized offense, and it contrasts with its equivalent, "how rude" or "she is so rude" response commonly used in our society today. The English equivalent represents an externalized observation and not a personal attack on the individual's *dignidad,* as implied in the attribution of *falta de respeto* in Spanish.

The second component represents the message mode used in interactions: verbal or nonverbal communication modes. Latinos use covert methods of

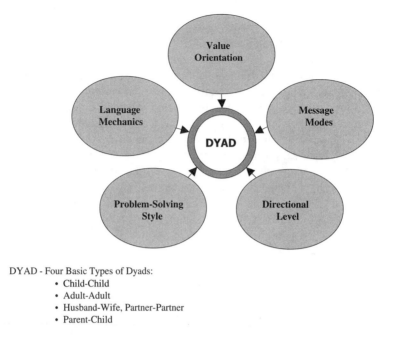

DYAD - Four Basic Types of Dyads:
  • Child-Child
  • Adult-Adult
  • Husband-Wife, Partner-Partner
  • Parent-Child

Figure 8.2. Latino Transactional Model

SOURCE: Developed by Maritza Gallardo-Cooper, Ph.D. (not to be reproduced without written permission); Gallardo-Cooper, 2000, 2001(b).

communication in the form of metaphorical messages in *dichos* and *indirectas* (García-Preto, 1996a, 1996b; Zuñiga, 1992a). The tendency to communicate covertly through metaphors and *indirectas* is important, as the underlying treatment goal of family and relational therapy is to improve communication. In addition, nonverbal methods of communication such as tone of voice, intonation, and body language are used to convey messages as well. For example, *respeto* is projected nonverbally by staring downward and avoiding eye contact when interacting with an authority figure or when being scolded.

The third component, labeled language mechanics, refers to language choice and style. As outlined in Chapter 7, a significant number of Latinos continue to speak primarily Spanish, but a growing population of bilingual individuals have varying degrees of language proficiency in both Spanish and English. Therefore, it is the responsibility of the culturally competent counselor to explore the transactional patterns among Latinos as they relate to language background.

The fourth component explains the directional style of the transaction: vertical or horizontal communication style. Latinos hold a hierarchical or vertical communication style (Inclán & Hernández, 1992; Szapocznik, Scopetta,

Aranalde, & Kurtines, 1978), not only in parent-child relationships but also to a lesser degree between partners (Gallardo-Cooper, 2000), young adults and elders, and superiors and coworkers (Comas-Díaz, 1997). This hierarchical style clearly defines the boundaries between adults and children and between authority figures and others. For instance, acculturated children may expect to communicate with their parents as equals, adapting the dominant culture style, which encourages egalitarian relationships and assertiveness (saying what you think and feel). However, parents who are less acculturated may adhere to a less democratic system, in which the boundaries between parents and children are clear. In these cases, an attempt by the children to be assertive would be seen as a *falta de respeto*. Consequently, most Latino children are not expected to volunteer an opinion or engage in the problem-solving process of family conflict unless requested by a parent. However, it is important to note that a Latino family without a well-defined hierarchical system may reflect a high level of acculturation, whereas a low acculturated family with no hierarchical boundaries defined may present with significant dysfunctional dynamics. When viewing the Latino family as a micro system, the culturally competent counselor should be able to work with the preferred parental style. If the family prefers a hierarchical style to solving a problem within the family, the intervention should be adapted to fit this dynamic.

The fifth component is described as the transactions used to resolve conflicts. Rogler (2000) found that low socioeconomic status Puerto Rican families use different kinds of problem-solving strategies than non-Latino Whites in the United States. These Puerto Rican parents rely on role specificity to solve problems instead of openly discussing the problem and arriving at a mutually agreed on plan of action with family members. Also, older siblings are given quasi-parental duties demanding the obedience and respect of the younger children and assume a decision-making role.

In sum, it is important to explore conflict resolution patterns based on interactions, hierarchical patterns, role specificity, and indirect methods of problem resolution (Gallardo-Cooper, 2000). The latter refers to the pattern used to resolve certain problems. For example, a circular pattern may be observed when the father says no to a child, the child appeals to the mother for clemency, the mother separately advocates for the child with the father, and finally the father changes his mind in favor of the child's request.

Culture-Centered Genograms:
A Systemic and Ecological Assessment Tool

The genogram is a valuable data-gathering tool introduced by family therapists who practice a Bowenian, intergenerational, family of origin approach (Guerin, 1976). Since their introduction, genograms continue to be a popular assessment procedure regardless of counseling orientation. The genogram provides a visual summary of the structure, organization, history, and family dynamics of clients. The method is simple to use, encourages narratives in a nonthreatening way, has no cultural bias, and produces rich and valuable clinical information. It is a useful tool for understanding family struggles and triumphs, especially migration narratives and coping patterns.

The genogram can be introduced at any time during the counseling process and can be revisited throughout counseling. Depending on the clients' stability, the genogram can be most helpful if used in early treatment. Because the process of constructing a genogram engages individual family members in discussion, it may require extended sessions. Once completed, both the family and therapist can consult the family map to clarify or add information and to guide the development and implementation of interventions. An individual often gains spontaneous and powerful insights by "seeing my family on paper."

In addition, the genogram has been adapted successfully as a training tool (Hardy & Laszloffy, 1995) as well as a clinical procedure across therapeutic approaches (Kuehl, 1995) and presenting problems (McGoldrick, Gerson, & Schellenberger et al., 1999). Although not specifically labeled a culture-centered genogram, several family therapists have reported the usefulness of the genogram with bicultural marriages (Ho, 1990), families of addicts (Flores-Ortíz & Bernal, 1995), and Puerto Rican families (García-Preto, 1996a, 1996b). Hardy and Laszloffy (1995) used the term *cultural genogram* as a didactic method to train family therapists in the areas of cultural awareness and sensitivity, which fits well with the multicultural competencies model. They contended that by constructing and analyzing in detail the family genogram, counselors in training gain insights into the subtle but powerful effects cultural and familial patterns have on their sense of identity and worldview.

The reader is referred to the classic work of McGoldrick and her colleagues (1999) to learn the mechanics and applications of genograms in family therapy. Although in practice, there is consistency in the use of basic symbols (e.g., square for males, circle for females), counselors can use different symbols and shades of a color to identify levels of acculturation. In addition, information is documented on immigration, language preference, gender role socialization, frequency of contacts with the native country, and bicultural characteristics. The genogram of the Rosales family illustrates the application of a culture-centered approach (see Figure 8.3).

THE CASE OF THE ROSALES FAMILY

Mr. Rosales, a talented engineer, received an offer by an American investor to underwrite the development of a large corporation in the United States. Mr. Rosales convinced his reluctant wife, Mrs. Rosales, and three children to migrate to the United States. He promised his wife that the family would return to their homeland after the business was developed.

After 10 years in the United States, Mr. Rosales had built a reputable business and showed no signs of returning to Mexico. He worked long hours and experienced a great deal of stress due to the demands of the business. He was often exhausted and irritable. Consequently, marital discord intensified. Mrs. Rosales sought help from the family doctor, who referred the family to counseling.

Mrs. Rosales, a friendly and engaging woman, was a dedicated mother and homemaker, was active in local church activities, and managed to develop a supportive network of Latino friends. Likewise, Mrs. Rosales continued to maintain ties with her country of origin by traveling at least annually to visit family and friends.

All young adult children adapted well to the move to the United States. They had successful academic histories, were currently enrolled in college, and lived with their parents. They were considered bilingual: They spoke Spanish with their parents and primarily English among themselves and with their friends. However, during the initial stages of family counseling, it was noted that the children would, at times, talk to their parents in English. Although they gave no signs of rejecting their heritage, they were well integrated into their community and preferred to remain in the United States.

The daughter was the father's confidante, was the most vocal about family problems of the three siblings, and had the most argumentative relationship with the mother. The oldest son expressed the most conflict; he tried to please his parents by accommodating the native cultural values reinforced by his mother and the American cultural values held by his peers.

The more the children became "Americanized," the more Mrs. Rosales talked about returning to the homeland. Mr. Rosales complained of his wife's constant reminders about returning to Mexico, which seemed to have intensified since the children graduated from high school. Mr. Rosales disclosed that his preference was to remain in the United States.

Mrs. Rosales disagreed with the dating practices in the United States and let her children know about her negative views on the subject. She engaged in arguments with the daughter over dating and independence, especially because the daughter was dating a Latino who was raised in the United States and who was perceived by Mrs. Rosales as "very Americanized." Mrs. Rosales also disapproved of her children's non-Latino friends because they did not have appropriate social graces. For example, she considered it a *falta de respeto* (lack of respect) when the friends of the children did not "visit" (spend time) with the parents. In contrast, Mr. Rosales, who was overly involved with his business, had no complaints about the children's rapid acculturation or choice of friends, boyfriends and girlfriends. Mrs. Rosales felt that she was fighting family issues by herself, and she received considerable heat from her daughter about her prejudice against Americans and the "American way."

Other issues concerning family of origin were apparent in this family. For instance, Mr. Rosales claimed that his mother was not a supportive woman, especially toward his father, who experienced episodes of severe depression. During times of marital discord, Mr. Rosales would compare Mrs. Rosales with

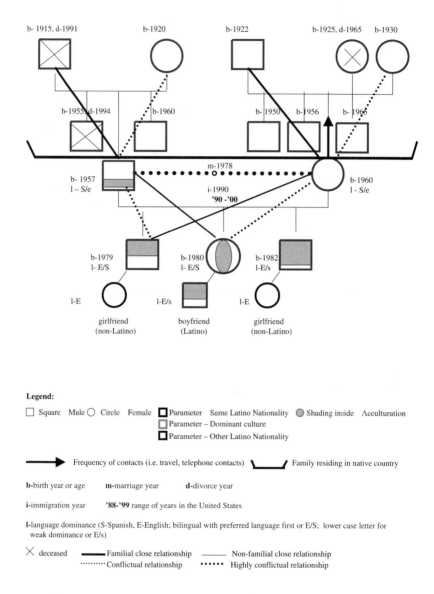

Figure 8.3. Culture-Centered Genogram: The Rosales Family

SOURCE: Developed by Maritza Gallardo-Cooper, Ph.D.; (not to be reproduced without written permission) Gallardo-Cooper, 2001(b).

his mother, saying that she was not supporting him and was contributing to his distress and dysphoria. Also, Mrs. Rosales disclosed that she had a good relationship with both of her parents until her mother passed away and the father remarried. She reported not getting along with her father's second wife.

In this case, many family dynamics are at play and in need of clinical attention. To name a few, there is evidence of (a) the different levels of acculturation in the family, with Mrs. Rosales being the most resistant; (b) the natural process of "individuation" in all three children within a Latino framework; (c) the changing role of Mrs. Rosales and her search for definition; (d) the expectations of Mr. Rosales that his needs and decisions take precedence over others in the family and that his wife should support these decisions; (e) the triangulation of the daughter as the new confidante of her father; (f) the unresolved issues between the couple regarding unmet promises to return to the homeland; (g) Mr. Rosales's history of overinvolvement with his work and his tendency to overlook family problems; (h) the lack of affirmation for the wife's contribution to the family and to adjustment related to postmigration; (i) the couple's family of origin issues affecting the couple's relationship; (j) the couple's differences in premigration history and motivation to relocate to another country; (k) Mrs. Rosales's loss and grief issues; (l) the polarization between the couple; and (m) the siblings' coalition by their use of the English language in the sessions.

Clearly, the natural process of the family's development, the responsibilities of a demanding business, the migration history, and the unresolved conflicts between the couple are contributing to the situation. In addition, cultural variants must be considered. For instance, the polarization between Mr. and Mrs. Rosales is expressed through a tug of war of loyalties between two countries. The threat of family severance is represented by the deflation of the native culture and the support of the host culture. Although the children are bilingual, they use English as an instrument to argue with their mother during counseling sessions. During these sessions, the father never commented on their use of English, although he would say to the counselor that he did not understand them at times. Also, it was evident that the acculturation process of the children contributed to different gender role expectations. For example, the acculturated children wanted to have a more egalitarian relationship when they marry, but they joined their father in expecting Mrs. Rosales to be self-sacrificing and to agree with the father's expectation of permanent residence in the United States. Mrs. Rosales expects her husband to be financially responsible for the family's expenses but struggles with her own vocational definition and her husband's limited time with the family.

The genogram in Figure 8.3 illustrates three generations of the Rosales family. The graphic impact of this genogram helps the mental health professional understand the family and develop a treatment strategy. Year of immigration is coded to address loss issues and developmental issues. Age of migration is important, as it relates to significant psychological disruption when migration occurs during early adolescence (Padilla et al. 1988; Szapocznik et al., 1997). Language preference is also coded. At first glance, the color-shaded symbols quickly reveal the division between two cultures. For example, the youngest son of the family migrated at 7 years of age, is the most acculturated, and does not have the same Spanish dominance as his siblings (i.e., represented as E/s). Mrs. Rosales is closely attached to her native culture and is rejecting of the host culture. In contrast, Mr. Rosales has undergone some acculturation and adaptation (as defined by Marín et al., 1987) and wants to remain in the United States. He visits his home country sporadically and endorses the family's full acculturation with the host culture. For this reason, his square is only partially shaded. All three of the children are highly acculturated but still participate in some of their Mexican customs. It is important to note that although dating relationships or ethnic background of partners are not routinely included in genograms, in this case, they are included because they highlight how the siblings are moving toward acculturation and multiculturalism.

Hardy and Laszloffy (1995) recommend addressing issues of shame and pride during the genogram assessment process. Both areas are important to explore. We have found that questions about pride (e.g., What events occurred in your family that produce pride?) are powerful in the assessment of family values and the identification of strengths. In contrast, if the family is fragile, explosive, or in crisis, the focus on shame issues early in treatment may lead to decompensation. The counselor needs to use sound clinical judgment to decide when to address these issues. Nonetheless, the focus on family pride, strengths, and resourcefulness accelerates rapport, treatment adherence, and progress. There is a sense of being accepted, understood, and respected when positive aspects of their system are affirmed.

Culture-Centered Ecological Genogram

A variation of the cultural genogram is one that uses an ecological perspective. The ecological genogram visually organizes the social and institutional world of the client or the family. This tool is also called an *eco-map* (Hartman, 1995) and can help to maintain a broad perspective in the assessment process and to expand intervention options. The culture-centered ecological genogram is modeled after Brofrenbrenner's (1979) ecosystemic approach. Specifically, Brofenbrenner hypothesized that an individual's development is influenced by multiple systems or ecosystems: (a) microsystems (e.g., the individual and the family), (b) mesosystems (e.g., the relationship between two systems, such as the family and the school), (c) exosystems (e.g., systems not directly connected with the individual, such as parent's employment or government programs), and (d) macrosystems (e.g., cultural and sociopolitical influences in a particular environment, such as a city). The ecosystemic approach to assessment can help identify outside forces that encroach on the individual and help the counselor understand the complexity of human behavior. With respect to its application, the ecology of Latino individuals may include extended family (*comadre* and *compadre*), church, and community resources such as religious folk healers and spiritual guides.

Special Issues in Family Counseling

The culturally competent counselor should attend to the following issues that affect the way in which the therapy is conducted with Latinos: (a) the role of language, (b) the structure of counseling and who should participate, and (c) the importance of keeping a balance between cultural and clinical factors.

Language Issues in Family Counseling

Earlier in the book, we discussed at length language issues that have an impact on the counseling process. In this section, we will address only language issues as they relate to family therapy. Latino families may be bilingual or monolingual in Spanish or English, or they may display a mixture of different preferences for Spanish or English among its members. Bilingual counselors may be able to manage a variety of language forms used during the session as well as redefine their role as a language broker. However, monolingual counselors may encounter additional challenges when family members speak more than one language during sessions. A brief discussion of specific guidelines to address these issues follows.

Rules of Engagement

Because the process of family therapy relies on communication, Gallardo-Cooper (2000) recommends assessing the preferred language of all family members. After assessing this aspect, she recommends setting treatment rules of communication early in treatment. For example, the family therapist should openly acknowledge that, often, it is easier to speak or share a difficult issue in the native tongue and that these remarks should be expressed regardless of the fluency of the therapist but that these remarks should be made openly to the entire family during the session and not to individual family members.

Language Brokering

Language brokering with children mostly refers to immigrant children who quickly learn English and become the translators for the parents. The situation occurs in all aspects of the family's daily life. For example, children may have to translate for parents to interpret bills, to address a school meeting with a teacher, to request a favor of a neighbor, to answer the telephone, or to respond to immigration officials. Language brokers who are children quite often may be "parentified" and may experience undue stress due to their sense of responsibility for their parents' and family's well-being. Moreover, parents often become highly dependent on these children and rather ineffectual in their parenting. Thus, it is recommended not to use children as translators in family sessions. In these cases, the counselor should be a bilingual who can address family issues without sabotaging the authority of the parents. If a bilingual therapist is not available to work with the family, a trained mental health translator may be used (Pérez-Foster, 1998) to maintain the status of the parents, empower them, and allow children to be children during the counseling process.

Structure and Participation of Family Members

The counselor needs to embrace a flexible position regarding how the family session will be structured, including making decisions about who should participate. When working with Latino families, the counselor may use a systemic approach by seeing siblings together as a unit and parents together as a unit. If the session is volatile, it is best to respect the parents' ineffectual handling of the situation and to divide the session, meeting with the parents and the siblings separately.

An important consideration is the involvement of extended family members in treatment. The decision to involve them should be based on whether or not extended family networks can contribute to attaining the desired goals. A common mistake is to not include extended family members in the counseling process because the perception might be that the family is enmeshed. We use the following guidelines to help clinicians decide on who to include and when to engage extended family in the therapeutic process.

Consider the family living arrangements and frequency of contact with the extended family member(s). If the member lives with the family, he or she should be considered as part of the family. For example, *hijos de crianza* (children raised by a nonbiological parent) should always, as a general rule, participate in family therapy if they continue to live with the family. If they reside close to and have daily contact with the family (e.g., he or she lives two doors down), consider the appropriateness of the involvement as it relates to the family's treatment plan.

Consider the extended family member's role in the family. Careful attention should be given to the power exerted by this extended family member on the family. Power may be defined by the frequency of contacts with the family, by the perceived esteem given by the family, or by dysfunctional dynamics.

In child-centered family therapy, it is important to involve grandparents who have frequent contact with the children or who provide any type of child care. For example, a grandmother living in the household may play a central role in the family and is part of the interactive patterns in problem resolution. Grandparents often advocate for the children and support the adult parents with their parental responsibilities (Gómez, 1999). From an ecological and culture-centered perspective, the involvement of grandparents is often a successful strategic intervention. Initially, elders should be seen by themselves to further assess the family dynamics. Subsequently, counselors can clinically judge whether or not the grandparents can be included in sessions with parents or the entire family. The culturally competent counselor needs to exercise sound clinical judgement on how to structure and strategize treatment when the family presents with dysfunctional patterns. For example, unresolved parent-child issues may be reenacted when an overly controlling and critical grandfather becomes involved with the parenting of the grandchildren, thus perpetuating the inadequacy of the father and sabotaging the discipline practices of the parents.

Clinical and Cultural Factors: Keeping a Balance

As stated earlier, a variety of theoretical guidelines suitable for Latino families have been presented. Having a solid background in family therapy theories is vital; however, in practice, the challenge is to develop the best plan of action based on the characteristics of the family and the magnitude of the presenting problems. Keeping a balance between clinical and cultural factors may be one of the most challenging issues faced by experienced and novice counselors alike. Counselors must consider the complexity in terms of family composition (i.e., single-parent family, intact family with young children, family with grandparents), acculturation level, socioeconomic status, education level, mental illness and substance abuse history, language, time of immigration, and nationalities. Language preference and style may easily reflect the family's overall level of acculturation. Likewise, the magnitude of the problems behavior, and symptoms; the results of the risk assessment of the problem; and the family's expressed needs must be considered.

The following case exemplifies the necessity of a solid balance between clinical and cultural lenses.

THE CASE OF THE MORALES FAMILY

Family therapy was requested to address the increasing acting out of the 15-year-old daughter, Verónica, who was described as being defiant and non-compliant, leaving the house without permission, and having "unacceptable" friends for the past year. In particular, acting out behaviors had escalated within the previous few months. Veronica was becoming increasingly irritable and having arguments with her other sisters.

The parents were born and raised in Puerto Rico, but their three daughters, ages 19, 15, and 13, were born in the United States. Mrs. Morales was a home-maker and did volunteer work. Two years earlier, she had been diagnosed with cancer. Mr. Morales was a successful retail manager who took a leave from his job to care for the family and his wife, who was undergoing chemotherapy treatment for the cancer. Consequently, Maria, the oldest child, lived at home and discontinued college to work full-time to help the family.

In the first interview, Mr. and Mrs. Morales described their family as close-knit. They said they were trying to raise their daughters as they were raised, holding strict and protective standards of discipline that Veronica constantly rejected. During the session, Mr. Morales took the lead and responded to all inquiries. Both parents spoke to each other in Spanish. The daughters were English dominant. The father spoke to them in English but spoke Spanish to Mrs. Morales.

The two oldest daughters joined together, complaining about the parents' strict ways and their discrimination against the girls' friends, who were primar-ily African American. In two incidents, both older daughters had clashed with the father over their African American boyfriends. The parents became defen-sive, explaining that they were not racists because, for them, race was not an issue as long as people were Puerto Rican. The nature of the volatile communi-cation led to having the parents and siblings interviewed separately. Interest-ingly, the mother became the primary reporter when she was seen alone with her husband. She explained in detail her disapproval of her daughters' boy-friends, whom she described as disrespectful whenever they visited the Morales home.

On two occasions, Verónica had climbed out her bedroom window in the middle of the night to be with her friends. Mrs. Morales also disclosed that her husband ignored the fact that Verónica had been in several fights in school and refused to change into gym clothes for her physical education class. He also ignored that recently, Lydia, her youngest daughter, had nightmares, was not eating, and had become more withdrawn. When the daughters were seen to-gether, they all concurred that their father was controlling and their mother was very strict. Maria, the 19-year-old, confronted Verónica about drinking and her poor choice of friends, who were described as school dropouts with criminal records. Maria also disclosed that she was having a relationship with a young Caribbean Black but kept it from her parents because they would object. Lydia, who was shy, denied serious problems with her parents, and did not volunteer information.

Verónica's combative behavior needed further attention. The next step taken
was to meet individually with her for additional assessment. Likewise, Lydia,
who was quiet and took a guarded stance during joint sessions, needed to be
seen individually. During the individual appointment, Verónica reported in
tears that she got drunk with her friends about 3 months prior and was raped by
an acquaintance. No one in her family knew. A week after the incident,
Verónica began the escalation of acting out behaviors by increasing her defiance and fighting at school and at home. Lydia, who was also seen individually,
reported feeling overwhelmed by the heated arguments and by her concerns
with the fate of her mother.

This family in crisis presented with a variety of clinical concerns, such as
trauma, depression, fear of loss, chronic illness, conduct problems, and dysfunctional family coping. Even though the Morales family could benefit from
Bicultural Effectiveness Training to address the intercultural, racial, and
intergenerational conflict, the family therapist needs first to attend to the
severity of the problems disclosed in the first few sessions to ensure family
stability. In this case, for example, an immediate treatment action is for the
family therapist to facilitate Verónica's disclosure of the rape to her parents,
comply with mandatory reporting, and stabilize the victim and her family.
The trauma of Verónica exacerbated her acting out trends and the family's
fragile organizational state since Mrs. Morales' illness was diagnosed. Long
before Verónica's rape, family functioning was deteriorating with the life-
changing events of severe multiple stressors. Maladaptive coping was manifested by the mother's intensification of somatic complaints and the father's
anxiety and rigidity. The daughters, in turn, responded with (a) Verónica's
overt acting out, (b) Maria's covert acting out by maintenance of a clandes-
tine relationship, and (c) Lydia's withdrawal and related behaviors. Thus, the
professional needs to walk a tightrope, quickly joining with the family's cultural worldview (e.g., structure separate sessions with parents and children to
divert the impasse of a power struggle related to strict discipline without minimizing the authority of the parents, especially the father) and promptly implementing direct interventions to address the issues that motivate acting
out and despair.

Guidelines in Latino Family Counseling

Given the preceding discussions, the following guidelines are offered.
These guidelines are based on empirical research and clinical observations.

Prepare the family. Preparing the client for the counseling process ensures
treatment adherence, especially with populations that have high probabilities

of attrition. As previously discussed, the lower the level of acculturation in families, the greater the need to spend more time in educating the family about what to expect in family therapy.

Define your role as a padrino *or* madrina. Ho (1987) recommends that counselors assume many roles with Latino families, such as educator, advocate, helper, culture broker, and *padrino*. As noted earlier, a *padrino* or *madrina* is selected because parents respect, admire, and trust these individuals. For Latinos, this role implies a mediator who has familiar authority and is invested in the well-being of the family or a specific child, sometimes formally entrusted through the process of godparenting (i.e., *ahijado* or *ahijada*). Some examples of how to define the therapist role in this fashion are: If I were your *padrino/madrina,* what would I be doing to help the family? If I were your *padrino/madrina,* what would your parents be asking me?

Assume a "humble expert" approach with the family. Falicov (1998) stresses the importance of approaching the family with curiosity. Similarly, Smart and Smart (1994) recommend assuming a position of "not knowing" to prevent stereotyping. Although this approach may be helpful, a balance must be maintained between approaching the family with humility and openness and being an expert. Therefore, careful attention must be given to the choice of questions and the manner in which these questions are asked. Being direct but humble is interpreted as awareness of the limitations of the counselor's knowledge but with a genuine respect for the family.

Focus on developing a therapeutic alliance. The naive counselor may assume that the family is committed to therapy sessions because the members are cordial during the first visit. The people/relationship orientation of Latinos may mislead the naive professional initially because typically, Latinos may be affected by the social desirability factor or a tendency to "look good." Family discontent may be concealed due to *dignidad, simpatía, respeto,* or *personalismo* issues. Only through the development of a trusting relationship will the family be able to openly disclose perceptions of the counseling process and the counselor, as well as any discontent with the treatment process.

Use the family narrative to define the problem. Latino families often seek professional help during periods of crisis or when parents are concerned about their children (Baptiste, 1987). Because sensitivity to the family is paramount to prevent attrition, the mental health professional needs to assess the problem as defined by the parents and begin the intervention from that perspective.

Determine the family's style of help seeking early in counseling. Following the mental health utilization research of McMiller and Weisz (1996), the counselor should assess parental history of help seeking. Learning *la familia's* style of help seeking will facilitate treatment compliance, therapeutic rapport, and treatment planning.

Learn critical cultural-familial themes. Stories of triumph and defeat are important to assess the family's value orientations and adaptive and resiliency patterns.

Check for themes of loss and grief. As noted throughout this book, migration is a life-changing experience associated with mixed and intense emotional reactions (Arredondo-Dowd, 1981; Falicov, 1998; Sciarra, 1999). This grieving process can range from severe and pervasive to mild and not clinically relevant to the treatment plan. However, the influx of Latinos to the United States within the past 50 years underscores that migration issues are relevant in counseling with most first-generation Latinos. As we noted in previous chapters, addressing the emotions linked to migration with the family can be a powerful turning point in counseling. At times, the rigidity observed in parents regarding their children may be an indication of a sense of unresolved loss that is manifested in power and control struggles.

Assess levels of acculturation of family members, including stress associated with this process. As stated throughout this book, acculturation is often overlooked in the clinical setting. Drastic differences in levels of acculturation between parents and children may underlie family's complaints because different worldviews collide with each other. In addition, this process of adaptation can be stressful for both the individual and the family system (Smart & Smart, 1994, 1995a, 1995b) and may be projected in conflictual relationships.

Pursue assessing the family's presenting problems and symptoms from a functional framework rather than the identification of diagnoses and systemic dysfunctions. Latinos in general have different ways to express distress, and many of these patterns are culturally defined (Koss-Chioino & Vargas, 1999; Paniagua, 2000).

Reframe intergenerational and acculturation problems as a "culture-conflict" problem and not as a family problem. Intergenerational conflicts between parents and children are more than doubled in intensity by acculturation factors (Sciarra & Ponterotto, 1991; Szapocznik & Kurtines, 1993).

Integrate extremes. Achieving biculturalism is a fundamental counseling goal with Latinos. Biculturalism resolves intergenerational and intercultural power struggles. The strategy to change the "either/or" into a "both/and" is useful because it joins opposing views by creating a win-win situation. For instance, Sciarra (1999) allows families to disagree and uses these differences to reframe the strengths of two different views. We also have used biculturalism as an alternative with acting out adolescents. Parents may experience distress with their acting out, acculturated adolescents who they find behaving in a way that is very "anti-Latino," and they may attempt to control the teenagers' behavior through traditional methods of Latino discipline. As a result, parents and children find themselves locked into opposing positions with intercultural conflicts. If the adolescent is not following the curfew or is refusing to follow the family rules, Latino bicultural parents can be asked how they want to handle the acting out problem: the Latino way or the American way. Helpful questions may be: How did your parents handle a similar situation? How do American parents handle similar situations? Which methods do you think will be most effective with your child? In this example, if parents choose the American way, then they set limits similar to the common concept of "tough love." If the situation is severe, it is possible that the Latino way of handling the acting out child may be through the use of extended family members or family kinship networks. This perspective expands the alternatives available to parents and frees them to consider a wider range of coping options.

Incorporate the family belief system into the intervention. Use *respeto* to apologize for misunderstandings, as well as to confront difficult questions and issues. Latinos label many social indiscretions, power and control conflicts, shame, lack of dignity, and other interpersonal discomforts as stemming from a *falta de respeto.*

Maximize the available resources in the family. The inclusion of the extended family and the Latino kinship system has proven beneficial during interventions with a wide range of presenting problems (Moncher, Holden, Schinke, & Palleja, 1990).

Avoid gender stereotypes. From a multicultural perspective, men and women manifest a wide range of roles and personality traits. Sometimes, the quietest, most submissive mother may hold the power in the family. However, respecting and affirming the authority of the father in family therapy is a must (Bean et al., 2001; Bernal & Flores-Ortiz, 1982; Paniagua, 1996). By the mere fact of being a professional, the family therapist is seen as an authority and an intrusion. With *respeto* of all family members, male or female, it is important to elicit congruence between the family's perception of keeping face with their projections of proper hierarchical structure.

Avoid stereotypes of *machismo*. Although many scholars define the term in a variety of ways, these definitions do not include violence toward others. Power conflicts do not justify violence in the family.

Incorporate spirituality and folk healers when applicable. Most Latinos value a supernatural aspect to health and behavior (Comas-Díaz, 1988; Zea et al., 1997, 2000). As part of a counseling intervention, including a spiritual framework may enhance the family's coping with adversity. However, counselors are urged to be careful that doing so does not interfere with the need to seek appropriate mental health services.

Summary

This chapter reviewed theoretical and practical aspects of Latino family counseling. A variety of family therapy models applied to Latinos were discussed, such as structural, intergenerational, and ecological models. Four Latino-sensitive frameworks also discussed were Bicultural Effectiveness Training, Multidimensional Ecosystemic Comparative Approach, rules, roles, and rituals, and a Latino transactional model. The second section of the chapter provided examples of the use of culture-centered genograms as a method of systemic and ecological assessment. The last section of this chapter covered special issues in counseling, which included a discussion on the role of language, the balance between cultural and clinical factors, and a presentation of guidelines. The last three sections provide a practical framework on how to implement a culturally sensitive family therapy approach with Latino families.

Correct Answers to Self-Assessment

1. False. Latino families can be distrustful of mental health service providers and tend to seek help through an extended family support network instead. (See pages 149-151.)
2. True. Many therapy approaches are useful for Latinos. (See pages 151-152.)
3. False. Individuation is a developmental concept that may not be applicable to most Latinos, especially those who are recent immigrants and low on acculturation. (See pages 152-153.)
4. True. Bicultural Effectiveness Training is a multicultural counseling tool. (See pages 153-154.)
5. True. The Multidimensional Ecosystemic Comparative Approach uses multicultural competencies. (See page 155.)
6. True. Examining rules, roles, and rituals helps achieve an understanding of family dynamics. (See pages 155-158.)

7. False. *Respeto* is a rule that has many functions in Latino culture. (See pages 159-160.)

8. True. Vertical communication is common among Latinos. (See pages 160-161.)

9. False. A genogram is an effective and simple culture-centered method of obtaining information about individual family members. (See pages 161-167.)

10. Answer: False. Meeting with different subgroups of the family support the authority of the parents and in some instances may enhance family assessment and intervention. (See pages 168-169.)

NOTE

1. Although the preference is to use the term *counseling* throughout the text, most of the literature on family treatment models uses the term *therapy*. Thus, the terms are used interchangeably throughout this chapter.

9

Future Directions

Objectives

- To set forth an overall agenda addressing Latino issues and considerations in mental health counseling, education, research, and practice.
- To articulate Latino-specific competencies.

Introduction

The preceding chapters have provided extensive information about Latino individuals and families residing in the United States. The historical accounting of the different Latino ethnic groups and their varied and shared historical experiences, from the original point of contact with the dominant U.S. culture to the more recent immigrants from the 1980s forward, has pointed to demographic diversity at different levels of identity: socioeconomic status, gender, religion, sexual orientation, and so forth. Throughout the text, we have underscored how important these factors are in the counseling process. The individuality of the person who comes from a collectivist cultural worldview is often difficult to reconcile, yet this is critical for culturally effective counseling to occur. Existing models and theories offer guidelines in classifying and categorizing behaviors, and culture-specific literature, discussed in this text, introduces useful generalizations. The challenge, therefore, is for therapists to have the adaptability to move from the macro to the micro levels, fully aware of the multiple contexts that influence themselves and the clients they intend to serve.

The timing of the release of U.S. Census 2000 data is extraordinary. In findings that are already controversial, the Latino population is estimated to be 35 million or 12% of the total U.S. population, exceeding predictions. In California, Latinos are the largest ethnic group other than Whites (U.S. Bureau of the Census, 2001a). This reality in California and other Southwest states, such as Arizona and Texas, has implications for how Latinos will redefine their minority identity status. In Florida, home to many Cuban immigrants and now second- and third-generation families, it has been reported that Latinos are now the state's largest ethnic minority group, sharply increasing their presence in all 67 counties in the state (Driscoll & Henderson, March 31, 2001).

Even before this "unexpected" census occurrence, there have been ongoing discussions about using the terms *Latino/a* and *Hispanic* in addition to specific ethnic identity, be it Mexican American or Puerto Rican. To this dialogue, we have also introduced the biracial/bicultural constant for most Latinos. The legacy of intermarriage among Europeans, primarily Spaniards, the indigenous peoples of the New World, and African slaves has created the *Mestizo* or *criollo* identity as well. With differences in acculturation and sociopolitical awareness within families, we have explored the delicacy of differences in self-identity within the same family unit and how this may affect communication and other Latino-centered values and norms. Is a person Chicano, Mexican American, *Nuyorican,* or Puerto Rican? Case examples have served to illustrate not only cultural conflicts but also breakdowns in family functioning due to other interpersonal strains and societal stressors, for example, employment. We have endeavored to underscore that acculturation is relevant, not only for immigrants, but also for Latinos born in the United States, to whom ethnic identity minority status is still attributed. Concomitantly, for those who have assimilated into the dominant culture, the continuous experience of culture-based cognitive dissonance is likely to be different.

Awareness and knowledge-building competencies have been addressed in multiple ways throughout the text, and the skill-building component was the subject of three chapters. The specific emphasis on family counseling has allowed us to discuss various family therapy models and interventions and their modification for application with different presenting problems by Latino families. Moreover, with the sample cases, there is also evidence of the eclecticism required and the necessity for therapists to be thorough and flexible in their approach with different family members, significant individuals from the extended family or kinship system, and the family unit as a whole.

In the next paragraphs, implications for counselor training and supervision, culture-specific competency development, and new challenges based on the newly redefined minority status of Latinos are discussed.

Teaching and Curriculum Considerations

Since the early 1980s, courses in cross-cultural or multicultural counseling have been the primary source of information about Latinos. As they do with the other cultural/ethnic groups in the United States, textbooks devote one chapter to Latinos, invariably providing general knowledge about this very heterogeneous population. In university environments, the most likely department to offer courses about Latinos might be in a Chicano/a Studies program; a Latin American, Latino, or Caribbean Studies program, bilingual education, or other similar programs. Otherwise, the burden falls on trainees to learn on their own or by experience. Unfortunately, even in teacher training with bilingual and multicultural education components, the emphasis on whole group descriptions and deficit thinking often leaves educators with even more negatively biased information about Latinos. Because so few people are prepared in Latino-centered counseling, educators, therapists, and supervisors far more often rely on their clients for guidance, on the one chapter in a textbook, or, if they are motivated, on continuing education experiences.

More recently, there have been various formal learning opportunities. Different institutions in the Southwest offer summer institutes preparing bilingual therapists; a new course entitled *Counseling Latinos* (at a major Hispanic-serving university), and learning institutes at national and regional conferences. There seems to be an increased consciousness about the presence of Latinos throughout the United States, and issues such as the disproportionately high school dropout rate and inaccessibility to quality health care now seem to have the public's attention. Latino-centered counseling courses are likely to become more prevalent simply based on need. When teachers and counselors admit they do not know how to intervene, then the continuing education process with a focus on Latinos must ensue.

This text has outlined the rationale for teaching Latino-centered counseling and for infusing relevant multidimensional models about identity, immigration, and acculturation with varying versions of Latino worldviews encompassing different belief systems and value orientations and research-based findings. But what exactly should a course or different learning experiences include? These are but a few of the topics:

- Historical contexts and immigration experiences for different Latino ethnic groups in the United States.
- Sections devoted to the dominant Latino ethnic group in a specific part of the country, for example, in New York, for Puerto Ricans and Dominicans.
- Belief systems and value orientations as influences on normative behavior for the different genders and how this may interact with other variables such as education, developmental level, religion, sexual orientation, and personality.
- The engagement in counseling of Latinos from different socioeconomic backgrounds.

- The engagement in counseling of Latinos based on presenting needs, as they parallel Maslow's hierarchy of needs.
- The interface between ethnic identity development and acculturation, whether one is a recent immigrant or first-, second-, or third-generation native of the United States, and how life experiences, whether one is surrounded by those of one's reference group or not, also affect worldview.
- The use of genograms and other methods that may more readily engage the Latino family and its kinship system.
- Historical and contemporary work and career patterns for Latino men and women.
- The use of Western versus alternative health care practices, religious and/or spiritual beliefs, and the role of prevention.
- Standardized and nonstandardized assessment procedures in clinical practice.
- The preparation of bilingual counselors who are not of Latino heritage and, for those who are bilingual, training on bilingual applications in counseling.
- The use of culture-centered personal interviews as a primary means for trainees to appreciate the uniqueness of Latinos/as.
- The application of ethical standards and guidelines in consideration of cultural and linguistic orientations and preferences.
- Application of cultural perspectives in clinical decision making.
- Educational sessions specifically for supervisors of trainees and clinicians working with Latino/a clients.
- Latino-specific competencies to guide clinical practice.

Culture-Specific Competency Development

In each chapter, we have set forth competency statements based on the Multicultural Counseling Competencies (Arredondo et al., 1996; Sue et al., 1992). As the field of multiculturalism and culture-specific counseling continues to evolve, the articulation of Latino-specific guidelines for preparation, research, and practice increases. Rather than repeat what has already been put forth in the previous chapters, we will offer new competencies in the three domains of counselor awareness of biases and assumptions, counselor awareness of client's worldview, and use of culturally appropriate intervention strategies. These are but a few examples adapted from the AMCD Multicultural Counseling Competencies documents (Arredondo et al., 1996; Sue et al., 1992).

Culturally skilled counselors:

- can actively engage in an ongoing process of challenging their own attitudes and beliefs when these do not support respecting and valuing of differences introduced by people of Mexican, Cuban, Puerto Rican, Dominican, Central and South American heritage.

- can recognize their sources of comfort/discomfort with differences that exist between themselves and Latino clients who have a similar or different phenotype.
- can describe at least two different models of identity development and their implications for counseling with people of, for example, Mexican descent or different generational status.
- are knowledgeable about the role of the extended family and kinship systems for Latinos.
- understand the experiences that differentially affect migrant farm worker families, adolescents who grow up in border towns, and individuals who live in specific ethnic-dominated communities, for example, Little Havana in Miami, Florida.
- can identify sociopolitical issues that affect people of Latino heritage, including anti-bilingual education legislation, racial profiling, detainment of undocumented immigrants, and other forms of political, societal, and institutional oppression.
- can describe how they have incorporated Latino ethnic-specific developmental, gender, religious/spiritual, and personality considerations into case conceptualization.
- are familiar with the limitations of standardized assessment tools and can recommend instruments that are culturally, linguistically, and ethically appropriate.

New Challenges

To write about Latino-centered counseling from an academic perspective is but one way to view the landscape of "*Latinismo*" and what it portends for the profession. Teaching about Latinos in counseling has provided evidence of new issues at an individual, family, group, and societal level that may not have been so apparent. Through a combination of fieldwork, research studies, current events, futuristic trends, and the extensive experience of clinicians, primarily Latinos working with Latinos, we believe it is possible to articulate an agenda of short- and long-term issues that require professional attention. Many of these issues are influenced by external forces—sociopolitical, economic, and sociocultural—that cannot be controlled but that nevertheless impinge on the lives of all people in the United States. Concomitantly, these same issues require more exploratory and empirical research that will broaden the knowledge and practice base. Indeed, sharing clinical data is important because it highlights diversified Latino characteristics and perspectives.

Individual and Family-Centered Issues

Latinos, as has been previously discussed, are a youthful population with the highest fertility rates and family size. Several phenomena require attention: the teenage mother and father; cross-ethnic marriages or partnerships (including teens who do not marry) that result in more biracial children;

changing gender roles and functions influenced by acculturation across the life span; intrafamily dynamics and stressors due to differences in rates of acculturation, phenotype, educational attainment, and economics; and the consequences of societal and workplace bias and discrimination in family relationships.

Imposing strength versus deficit perspectives to understand individuals and families is an essential framework. Accordingly, this allows counselors to suspend preconceived thinking, often in the form of stereotypes, and to consider the multidimensionality of individuals and families who are continuously evolving and moving between different contexts. An example follows.

Although the trend is slight, more Latinos are pursuing a four-year college education. High school students are involved in church-related activities; take on roles as peer mediators, student government leaders, and other school offices; participate in civic organizations; and seemingly bridge the bicultural world with greater flexibility than previous generations based on language flexibility and technological access. Counselors need to be mindful of the strengths of students or youth in schools and of those who come to counseling with families.

In a course titled Counseling Latinos, graduate students generated a list of Latino/a strengths. These were derived from interviews with individuals across the life span. Among the strengths were the following:

- A worldview that emphasizes harmony, unity, cooperation, and a cyclical view of life
- A greater sense of personal identity compared to Anglo Americans
- Resiliency derived from religion and family
- A pioneer spirit in the face of adversity and structural barriers
- Resiliency among immigrants to do more beyond the norm in their home country
- A sense of debt and responsibility to one's cultural heritage
- Celebration through of dance and music, which brings a sense of life force and energy
- A sense of "coolness" about being Latino, expressed especially by teenagers

Acculturation and Ethnic Identity Development Processes

The heterogeneity of the Latino population has been emphasized throughout this text. For counselors, this requires more detailed attention to within- and across-ethnic group differences and similarities. The case examples have also provided a glimpse into family differences and the need to take an idiosyncratic approach to each individual. Acculturation and ethnic identity development are affected by multiple contexts, for example, neighborhood, school, society, and so forth, and other factors including age, gender, educational level, phenotype, and, for immigrants, country of origin. Counseling interventions will likely need to draw from a menu of therapeutic models, a range of culturally flexible competencies that apply to more acculturated and less acculturated Latinos as well, and more family/systemic versus individual approaches.

Bilingual, Monolingual, and Other Language Variations

The Spanish language is the unifying thread among people of Latino heritage. In the United States, Spanish is and will continue to be the second-most prevalent language. This presents an opportunity for educators and practitioners alike, as well as a challenge to our ethical practice. Ethical guidelines indicate that counselors should not practice out of their sphere of preparation; yet, this occurs regularly with limited-English speaking clients.

Cultural competencies recommend that counselors

- learn Spanish or develop a working knowledge of Spanish in a technical sense,
- develop techniques that will allow clients to speak Spanish to express emotions, even if the counselor does not understand,
- learn the limitations and appropriate use of interpreters and translated materials,
- use standardized assessments sparingly, if at all, that are not in the language of the client, and
- develop strategies for noncognitive assessments.

Spirituality, Health Care, and Mental Health Interconnectedness

Recent texts (Flores & Carey, 2000; Ramirez, 1998) and other Latino-centered literature provide considerable discussion about the role of spirituality and religion as core to the belief system and meaning making for many people of Latino heritage. Counselors, in particular, must expand their interview protocols to explore these dimensions and how they influence an individual's outlook on presenting issues and/or other aspects of their lives.

For example, rituals and other practices of Catholic Latinos reinforce cultural traditions. These include the use of *padrinos* and *madrinas* for baptism, confirmation, a young woman's *quinceañera,* marriage, and so forth. If people believe that spirits and other external forces bring bad luck through *mal ojo* (evil eye), they may prefer to seek out a *curandera/o* rather than follow through with the counselor. When it comes to illness, some families may prefer to shield the person who is ill from the truth, a practice not uncommon among non-Latinos as well. For clinicians, it is important not to view this as dysfunctional family behavior but rather to respect it as the family practice or preference.

Cultural Competence in Mental Health Practice

The majority of contemporary clinicians have received ethnocentric preparation. This means that a focus on multicultural and culture-specific guidelines, research, and experiences was not included. As a result, counselors come to counseling with a worldview suggesting that clients should be goal-oriented, highly verbal and expressive of their needs, reflective and insightful, and respectful of time and interpersonal boundaries. Although these values are instilled in the counselor training preparation, their generalization to all counseling situations is impossible. A family under duress because a parent has been deported will likely be experiencing grief and seeking ways to get legal assistance. Thus, a collaborative approach whereby the counselor can provide names of attorneys or agencies that provide legal counsel may be the goal to pursue. Simply stated, if clients have here-and-now needs or crises occurring, they will expect the counselor to be responsive to those needs. If, on the other hand, a counselor is expecting clients to be insightful about their crisis, this may lead to undue frustration. Unfortunately, clients who do not live up to the counselor's expectation are often labeled "resistant"; worse yet, those clients typically do not return to counseling.

These examples suggest that counselors must evaluate the principles, theories, and research that guide their practice and simultaneously self-assess in terms of the Multicultural Counseling Competencies and those that are more Latino-specific. Innovative services, which include the counselor working in collaboration with spiritual healers, going into the family home, or involving other supportive services from members of the kinship system to a community cultural broker, must be considered. When working with some Latino clients and families, practitioners may need to do more "out of the box" thinking to meet the client halfway. Throughout the book, we have emphasized looking beyond the ethnic/cultural label that is imposed to examine other aspects such as developmental status. By increasing the lenses through which they hypothesize about presenting issues, clinicians may more readily avoid the stereotype or blame the culture trap. Historically, researchers, clinicians, and others have blamed an individual's cultural background as the problem or source of the problem for presenting issues. Ethnic minority individuals in the past were labeled *culturally disadvantaged* or *culturally deprived.*

Cultural Competence in Mental Health Settings

Latino-serving agencies can determine their effectiveness on behalf of clients through assessment procedures that inform them about policies, procedures, and other practices that may be impeding issue relief for their clients. To be in theory and practice a culturally competent agency requires a self-study that examines practices such as intake forms and the language used, preparation of culturally competent clinicians, availability of Spanish-speaking clinicians or trained interpreters, bilingual signage throughout the institution, supervision by people knowledgeable about Latino cultural competencies, and the involvement of community members on advisory boards and so forth. With the myriad social issues affecting all families in the United States, it is incumbent on the agency administration to ensure that their clinicians are as well prepared as possible to know legislation and other institutional barriers that may affect the lives of their Latino clients. To be relevant, competent, and ethical, agency leadership, including the board of directors, must become a learning organization and move itself to initiatives for change through a focus on multiculturalism and diversity (Arredondo, 1998).

Latino Professional Networks and Organizations

Although a small percentage of educators, clinicians, and researchers in counseling and psychology are Latinos, there do exist organizations that provide access to information, resources, and Latino professionals themselves. These groups include the National Hispanic Psychological Association, the Latino Interest Network of the American Counseling Association (ACA), and the Latino Executives of the Child Welfare League of America. Latino psychology conferences emerged in the late 1990s, and national organizations such as ACA and the American Psychological Association have given more space in their publications and time at their national conferences to a Latino focus. More must be done, particularly through the recruitment and retention of Latinos in the helping professions. This is but one of many strategies to address the Latino reality in the United States.

Appendix A
Selected Measures of Acculturation

Acculturation Rating Scale for Mexican Americans (ARSMA). Cuellar, I., Harris, L. C., & Jasso, R. (1980). An acculturation scale for Mexican American normal and clinical population. *Hispanic Journal of Behavioral Sciences, 2,* 199-217.

Acculturation Rating Scale for Mexican Americans (ARSMA-II). Cuellar, I., Arnold, B., & Maldonado, R. (1995). Acculturation rating scale for Mexican Americans-II: A revision of the original ARSMA scale. *Hispanic Journal of Behavioral Sciences, 17,* 275-304.

Acculturation Scale (Mexicans, Cubans, Puerto Ricans and Central Americans). Marín, G., Sabogal, F., Marín B. V., Otero-Sabogal, R., & Perez-Stable, E. J. (1987). Development of a short acculturation scale for Hispanics. *Hispanic Journal of Behavioral Sciences, 9,* 183-205.

Behavioral Acculturation Scale (Cubans). Szapocznik, J., Scopetta, M. A., Kurtines, W., & Arnalde, M. A. (1978). Theory and measurement of acculturation. *Interamerican Journal of Psychology, 12,* 113-130.

Brief Acculturation Scale for Hispanics (Mexicans and Puerto Ricans). Norris, A. E., Ford, K., & Bova, C. A. (1996). Psychometrics of a brief acculturation scale for Hispanics in a probability sample of urban Hispanic adolescents and young adults. *Hispanic Journal of Behavioral Sciences, 18,* 29-38.

Children's Acculturation Scale (Mexicans). Franco, J. N. (1983). An acculturation scale for Mexican American children. *Journal of General Psychology, 108,* 175-181.

Psychological Acculturation Scale (PAS). Tropp L. R., Erkut, S., Garcia Coll, C., Alarcon, O., & Vazquez Garica, H. A. (1999). Psychological acculturation: Development of a new measure for Puerto Ricans on the U.S. mainland. *Educational and Psychological Measurement, 59,* 351-467.

Appendix B
Glossary of Terms

People and Places

Amorcito: Darling, dear (my love). (*Oxford Spanish Dictionary,* p. 34).

Boricua: In the 1960s, as working-class youth and students became politically aware of Puerto Rico's status issues, they began an effort to establish an identity by returning to their pre-Colombian indigenous roots and adopted the name *Boricua* to identify themselves. (Oboler, pp. 57-58)

Borínquen: "Great land of the valiant and noble Lord." Original Arawak name for the island of Puerto Rico (Coll y Toste, 1972).

Brujos: Practitioners of witchcraft or healing rituals; sorcerers. (Roeder, p. 318)

Cacique: During precolonial times, this referred to a chieftain or regional lord of the indigenous groups. In modern times, it denotes a regional political boss, often a landowner who controls all issues from behind the scenes; the *cacique* maintains interests of the ruling party (particularly in Mexico, an unofficial local representative of PRI [ruling party until July 1999]). (Ross, p. 267)

Campesino: Country person, peasant-like. Farmworker. *(Oxford Spanish Dictionary)*

Chicano: Believed to be derived from the word Mexicano. Although the term has been used for centuries, the Mexican American movement in the 1960s reimagined their history through the story of *Aztlán,* heralding Mexican Americans' Aztec roots, and popularized the term to refer to themselves (Oboler, pp. 57-58, 67-68).

Cielo/lito: Angel, sweetheart, darling (my little heaven). *(Oxford Spanish Dictionary)*

NOTE: This glossary was prepared by Solmerina Aponte. She obtained a B.A. in education and Latin American literature from Central University of Bayamón, Puerto Rico, an M.A. in Latin American and Caribbean studies from the State University of New York (SUNY) at Albany, Albany, New York, and an M.A. in modern art and contemporary art history, specializing in Latin American art, from the National Autonomous University of Mexico. She is currently a doctoral student in Latin American and Caribbean Studies at SUNY at Albany. She is a New York State-certified secondary school teacher and a certified court interpreter for the State of New York.

Constitucionalistas: Supporters of the *constitutional* aspect of democracy (e.g., division of powers, full respect of individual rights). (Boron, p. 156)

Criollo: Creole. First generation of children born to European colonizers (particularly Spaniards) in the Americas. (Samora & Vandel-Simon, p. 28)

Curanderos/as: Spiritual folk healers; Indian medicine men/women, especially in Mexican and Mexican American folk medicine. Word has connotation that healer has supernatural powers. (Roeder, p. 319)

Espiritistas: Religion based on the belief that good as well as evil spirits have a direct influence in aspects that affect an individual's life; common especially in Spanish-speaking Caribbean. Communication with spirits of the dead can be used for emotional and physical healing purposes. Rituals are performed to appease the spirits and ensure good outcomes of actions (Roeder, p. 320)

Guajiro/a: In Cuba, same as *jíbaro;* peasant. *(Oxford Spanish Dictionary)*

Jíbaro/a: Land laborer, farm worker in Puerto Rico, mountain dweller. Sometimes a pejorative term used to refer to a rustic, crude, uneducated person; hick *(Oxford Spanish Dictionary)*

Marielitos: Wave of Cuban immigrants to Miami in 1980. (Romero, p. 288).

Mestizo; mestizaje: Person of mixed race, particularly of Indian and white blood *(Oxford Spanish Dictionary)*

La Migra: Familiar or pejorative Mexican name for Immigration and Naturalization Service and/or officials. U.S.-Mexico Border Police. *(Oxford Spanish Dictionary)*

M'ijo/ja/jita/jito: Sweetie, darling, my child *(Oxford Spanish Dictionary)*

Mojados: "Wetbacks"; pejorative term for Mexican immigrant farm workers. (Desipio & de la Garza. p. 6)

Moreno: In Spain, a dark-haired person. Term derived from the word *moor.* In the Caribbean, dark-skinned, dark-haired person. *(Oxford Spanish Dictionary)*

Mulato: Today, any person of mixed white and black blood. Initially, a pejorative term from the Spanish language meaning mule to refer to the offspring born of a white and a black parent

Muñeco/a: Sweetie, honey (doll). *(Oxford Spanish Dictionary)*

Negro/a/ita/ito: Term of endearment usually for children or spouses. Literally, black, dark. *(Oxford Spanish Dictionary)*

Nuyorican: Cultural identity that defines the blending of U.S. and Puerto Rican culture, product of migrant experience of Puerto Ricans in New York. (Stavans, pp. 17, 41-43)

Pachucos: Mexican American adolescent members of juvenile gangs between the 1930s and 1950s. Commonly called by the media *zoot suiters* because of their particular style of dress. Later, many youths adopted the manner of dress, speaking style, unique stride, and anti-establishment attitude but were not gang members. (DeLeón, 2001)

Parteras: Midwives (Roeder, p. 323)

Pochos: Person of Mexican origin who speaks Spanish interspersed with English. Frequently a pejorative term. (*Oxford Spanish Dictionary*)

Quisqueya: "Place of the High Lands." Original Arawak name for the central region of the island of Haytí (Haiti), renamed island of Hispaniola by Columbus (today, Dominican Republic). (Coll y Toste, 1972)

Santeros: Practitioners of African-derived religion *Santería.* (Agun, 1996). *Santeros* also make wood carvings of religious icons, which is considered a craft.

Sobadore/as: Healers who administer rubs and massages with ointments and pumices to treat illness. Term derived from the verb sobar, to rub. (Roeder, p. 323)

Taíno: Arawak word meaning *good.* Name Spanish conquistadors believed Arawak inhabitants of the Caribbean islands called themselves (due to misunderstanding of the Arawak language) and conquistadors referred to them as such. Term is still used today. (Coll y Toste, 1972)

Tejanos: Texans. (*Oxford Spanish Dictionary*)

Trigueño/a: Literally, wheat-colored. Tan or dark skin color. *(Oxford Spanish Dictionary)* [Other terms also used to refer to dark skin: *quemadito* or tanned, (p. 522) and *indio* or Indian-color.]

Yerberos: Healers who prescribe herbs for medicinal purposes. (Roeder, *Chicano Folk Medicine,* p. 323)

Values

Cariño, Cariñoso/a: Affectionate. (*Oxford Spanish Dictionary,* p. 111).

Caudillismo: Dominance of chief executive in governmental system, i.e. *peronismo, castrismo.* (Rossi & Plano. *Latin America: A Political Dictionary,* p. 59)

Dignidad: Dignity; pride. Rank or high position. *(Oxford Spanish Dictionary)*

Fatalismo: Fatalism. Culturally, it is the belief that some things are meant to happen regardless of individual's intervention; events are a result of luck, fate, or powers beyond one's control. (Comas-Díaz, "Hispanic Latino Communities," *Journal of Training & Practice in Professional Psychology* pp. 14-35)

Hembrismo: Celebration of female attributes. Female equivalent for machismo. Glorification and exaggeration of attitudes and actions considered to be appropriate of feminine women, i.e. sensuality, manipulative and deceiving, possessiveness (Lumsden, 1996)

Machismo: Exaltation of masculinity. Glorification and exaggeration of attitudes and actions considered appropriate characteristics of masculine men, such as strength, sexual prowess, and bravery. (Stavans, pp. 108-111)

Marianismo: Cult of the feminine spiritual superiority. Teaches that women are morally superior and spiritually stronger than men. Tendency of Latino women to try to attain image of ideal woman using the Virgin Mary as role model. (Yeager, p. 3)

Personalismo: Dominant, charismatic person in the political life of a country. People give allegiance to a political leader rather than to constitutional institutions, political organizations, or ideals.

Sinvergüenza: Literally, person with no shame. Term that describes person who behaves inappropriately toward others. Crook, rascal, naughty. (*Oxford Spanish Dictionary*)

Historical Events

Bracero Program: An agreement signed by the governments of Mexico and the United States in which both countries would allow Mexican nationals to enter the United States for temporary periods under stipulated conditions. (Samora & Vandel-Simon, pp. 138-141)

Cinco de Mayo: Anniversary of the triumph of the Mexican army over invading French troops in the town of Puebla, Mexico. Day commemorated by the Mexican American population in the United States. (*Todo México, Encyclopedia of Mexico: 1985,* p. 327)

Día de los Muertos: November 1-2. Catholic feast day on which deceased family members and ancestors are remembered. In Mexico, traditional ornate celebration in which Aztec traditions of veneration of the dead are intertwined with Catholic day of observance on November 1. (Vigil, p. 39)

Encomiendas: (Colonial) forced labor system in which the governor of the islands allocated Indian labor to the mines or the fields. A certain amount of Native Indians were entrusted to a Spanish conquistador as merit pay for his contribution to the Spanish Conquista. In exchange for the gift, the Indians allocated to his care had to be instructed in the Catholic faith. (Bethell, pp. 17-19)

Treaty of Guadalupe Hidalgo: Peace treaty between the United States and Mexico, signed in 1848, which settled the Mexican American War. It established provisions for future relations between the two countries by increasing the territory of the United States. (Samora & Vandel-Simon, pp. 98-100)

Family

Comadre: Name given to mother and godmother, which defines relationship of *compadrazco* between them. Affectionate term mother and godmother use to refer to and to address each other. In some Latin American communities, affectionate term used to address a town's elderly woman. (*Oxford Spanish Dictionary*)

Compadrazco: Godparentage. Family relationship established through the baptism of a child. Family bond is created between parents and godparents of the child. Godparents become surrogate parents in the event of the death of the parents. Also, close bond established between people and/or families. (Vigil, p. xi)

Compadre: Name given to father and godfather, which defines the relationship of *compadrazco* between them. Affectionate term father and godfather use to address each other. In some Latin American communities, affectionate term used to address a town's elderly man. (*Oxford Spanish Dictionary*)

Familismo: Extension of family beyond nuclear family boundaries. (Comas-Díaz, "Hispanic Latino Communities," *Journal of Training and Practice in Professional Psychology,* pp. 14-35)

Traditions

Bautismo: Baptism, christening. (*Oxford Spanish Dictionary*)

Boda: Wedding. (*Oxford Spanish Dictionary*)

Charreada: In Mexico, spectacle of horsemanship and rodeo riding. (*Oxford Spanish Dictionary*)

Quinceañera: A girl's 15th birthday celebration. Traditionally, a girl's formal presentation to society to announce her availability for marriage. (Erickson, pp. 80-81)

Musical Expressions

Bachata: (Dominican Republic) Dominicanized Cuban bolero-son musical rhythm associated with barrio and rural culture. Lyrics are usually composed of street slang and make ironic commentaries on bitter realities. (Austerlitz, pp. 111-114)

Merengue: Traditional musical rhythm and dance originated in the Dominican Republic; Afro-Caribbean rhythm. (Austerlitz, pp. 2-8)

Rancheras: From the ranch. Mexican folk music. (*Oxford Spanish Dictionary*)

Salsa: Literal translation means seasoned sauce made with tomatoes. In some regions, it is elaborated with hot or spicy peppers. In music, blend of Cuban and Puerto Rican rhythms, such as mambo, African rhythms, and jazz. These musical rhythms were developed by Cuban and Puerto Rican musicians (mainly percussionists) in New York City in the early 1960s. (Padilla, pp. 28-45)

Religion and Traditional/Folk Health Beliefs

Altares: Altars; shrines decorated with objects as offerings to God, the saints, or departed loved ones, particularly in Mexico during the Day of the Dead celebration on November 1. (Vigil, p. 41)

Ataque de nervios: A nervous breakdown accompanied by hysteria. Usually women claim to be afflicted by this ailment. (Oquendo, Horwath & Martinez, pp. 367-376)

Empacho: Stomach ailment; gastrointestinal upset; a form of indigestion in which food clings to the stomach or intestinal tract causing sharp pain, nausea, and weakness. Usually caused by overeating, drinking bad water, or chilling. (Roeder, p. 323)

Espiritismo: Religion in which communication with the spirit of the dead is sought for guidance and healing purposes. (Roeder, p. 323)

Limpias: Cleansing ritual; ritual purifying or sweeping using holy water, an egg, or a small broom made with herbs. Symptoms of illnesses are relieved by ridding patient of evil influences. Usually performed by a *santero* or an *espiritista.* (Roeder, pp. 321-322)

Mal de ojo: The evil eye. (Roeder, p. 322)

Mal puesto: Illness caused by curse, witchcraft. (Roeder, p. 322)

Promesas: A vow of penitence offered to God to cure an ailment or to have a prayer or request granted.

Santería: Religion initially practiced by descendants of African slaves. Syncretic religion that integrates African animist religion and Catholic faith, in which African deities and Catholic saints are believed to be endowed with certain powers. Deities are believed to be vengeful, and rituals are performed to appease the saints. (Harris, pp. 210-211)

Santo: Saint. (*Oxford Spanish Dictionary*)

Susto: Sudden fright. Illness brought on by fright or a frightening experience, which is believed can jar the soul from the body. It is believed that treatment is required to return the soul to the body. (Roeder, p. 324)

Virgen de la Guadalupe: Patron Madonna of Mexico. Cult figure for large number of the Mexican population. Dark-skinned Virgin who is believed to have appeared before the Indian, Juan Diego, with the purpose of instructing him to spread the word of Christianity among the indigenous people. Image Catholic Church used to substitute for Aztec earth-mother deity. (Poole, 1995).

References for Glossary

Algun, E. *Los secretos de la santería).* Miami, FL: Ediciones Universal.

Austerlitz, Paul. *Merengue: Dominican Music and Dominican Identity.* (1997). Philadelphia, PA: Temple University Press.

Bethell, Leslie. (Ed.) (1987). *Colonial Spanish America.* New York: Cambridge University Press.

Boron, Atilio. A. (1995). *State, Capitalism, and Democracy in Latin America. Boulder, CO: Lynne Rienner.*

Coll y Toste, *Dictionary of the Taíno-Indigenous People of the Caribbean.* Clásicos de Puerto Rico, 2nd ed. Puerto Rico: Ediciones Latinoamericans.

Comas-Díaz. (1990). "Hispanic Latino communities: Psychological implications." *Journal of Training and Practice in Professional Psychology, 4*(1), 14-35.

DeLeón, *Ethnicity in the Sunbelt: Mexican Americans in Houston.* (2001). College Station: Texas A&M University Press.

Desipio, L., & de la Garza, R. O. (1998.) *Making Americans, remaking America: Immigration and immigrant policy.*.Boulder, CO: Westview Press.

Erickson, P. (1998). *Latin Adolescent Childbearing in East Los Angeles)* Austin, TX: University of Texas Press.

Harris, I. (Ed.) (1994). *Longman Guide to Living Religions.*). Harlow, Essex, UK: Longman.

Lumsden, I. (1996). *Machos, Maricones, and Gays: Cuba and Homosexuality.<D Philadelphia, PA: Temple University Press.*

Oboler, S. (1977). *Ethnic labels, Latino lives: Identity and the politics of (re)presentation in the United States. Minneapolis: University of Minnesota Press.*

Oquendo, Horwath, & Martinez, (1977). *Culture, medicine, and psychiatry.* Boston, D. Reidel.

Padilla, F. M. *Hispanic Journal of Behavioral Science, 11,* 28-45) (1989). Salsa music as an expression of Latino consciousness and unity.

Poole, S. (1995). *Our Lady of Guadalupe: The origins and sources of a Mexican national symbol, 1531-1797.* Tucson: University of Arizona Press.

Roeder, B. A. (1988). *Chicano Folk Medicine from L.A. California.* Berkeley: University of California Press.

Romero, M., Hondagneu-Sotelo, P., & Ortiz, V. (1997). *Challenging fronteras: Structuring Latina and Latino lives in the U.S.: An anthology of readings. New York: Routledge, 1997.*

Rossi, E. E., & Plano, J. C. (1992). *Latin America: A Political Dictionary.* Santa Barbara, CA: ABC-CLIO.

Samora, J., & Vandel-Simon, P. (1993). *A history of the Mexican-American people.* Notre Dame, IN: University of Notre Dame Press.

Shadows of tender fury: The letters and communiqués of Subcomandante Marcos and the Zapatista Army of National Liberation. (1995). Translated by Frank Bardacke, Leslie Lopez, and the Watsonville, California, Human Rights Committee; introduction by John Ross; afterword by Frank Bardacke. New York: Monthly Review Press.

Stavans, I. (1995). *The Hispanic condition: Reflections on culture and identity in America..* New York, NY: HarperCollins.

Todo México. (1985). Encyclopedia Britanica de México.

Vigil, A. (1998). *Una Linda Raza: Cultural and artistic traditions of Hispanics.* Golden, CO: Fulcrum.

Yeager, G. M. (Ed.). (1994). *Confronting change, challenging tradition: Women in Latin American history. Wilmington, DE: Scholarly Resources.*

Appendix C
Culture-Centered Clinical Interview

Name_____ Date _____

Date of Birth_____Gender ____ Ethnicity_____ Race_____

Marital Status ☐ Child ☐ Married ☐ Divorced ☐ Separated ☐ Widowed

Present in Interview_____ Referral _____

Review: Counseling process: ☐ Consent ☐ Confidentiality

Presenting Problem (Complaints, behaviors, symptoms)
 Duration
 Precipitating event
 Stressors

Counseling Objectives (As expressed by client)
 Objectives
 Help-seeking style

History

Psychological/Psychiatric History (Dates, providers, testing results, findings)

Medical History (Past and present diagnoses, hospitalizations, medications)

Developmental History (if applicable)

Educational and Vocational (History and current functioning)

Social Functioning and Relationships (History and current functioning)
 Primary social network: ☐ Same ethnicity ☐ Mixed ☐ Other
 Friends/relationships:
 Work/school:
 Leisure activities_____

SOURCE: Adapted from Gallardo-Cooper (2001).

Family History (Past and current structure; mental illness/substance abuse)

Family Kinship Network

Immigration History

Pre-Migration: _____

Precipitating Events: _____

Migration Experience: _____

Post-Migration: _____

Cultural Dimensions

Place of Nativity _____ Generation Status _____

Places of residence: _____

Native Culture Contact (Frequency): ☐ High   ☐ Moderate   ☐ Low

Socio-Political Dimensions (Political, economics, ethno-cultural support)

Language Dimensions

Language spoken during interview_____ Preferred _____

First Language _____   ☐ Read and write _____

Second Language _____   ☐ Read and write _____

At what age introduced?_____

How?_____

Language spoken at home: _____at work_____

Language of self-talk, prayer :_____ Language of emotions_____

Code Switching   Themes associated with code switching_____

Psycho-Cultural Dimensions

Ethnic Identity:_____

Acculturation Level: ☐ Integrated ☐ Assimilated ☐ Marginalized ☐ Rejecting

Acculturation Stress:_____

Sources of Stress

☐ Residency   ☐ Immigration   ☐ Voc/Educational   ☐ Language

☐ Oppression   ☐ Racism   ☐ Prejudice   ☐ Economic

☐ Gender   ☐ Ethno-support ☐ Familial   ☐ Marital

☐ Other _____

Spiritual Dimensions

Religion:_____ ☐ Practicing ☐ Non-Practicing

Church Name/Spiritual Guide _____

   Folk Healers _____

   Spiritual Attributions _____

Other Relevant Information

Assessments

Substance Abuse Assessment (History, frequency, current use, drug preferences)

Risk Assessment

Suicide:	☐ History	_____
	☐ Current	_____
Homicide:	☐ History	_____
	☐ Current	_____
Victim:	☐ History	_____
	☐ Current	_____
Perpetrator:	☐ History	_____
	☐ Current	_____

Risk Plan

Observations during interview

Mental Status

Assets and Barriers to Treatment

   Personal Strengths _____

   Cultural Strengths _____

   Personal Barriers _____

   Cultural Barriers _____

   Community Resources _____

Clinical and Cultural Impressions

Preliminary Diagnoses

    Axis I

    Axis II

    Axis III

    Axis IV

    Axis V

Culture Bound Syndromes

Initial Treatment Plan

    Individual

    Systemic/Ecological

    Cultural Accomodations

    Referral

    Community Resources

Signature   **Date**

Appendix D

Selected Bibliotherapy Resources

Reference	Title	Type
Alvarez, J.	*How the García Girls Lost Their Accent* (1992)	Fiction
	!Yo! (1997)	Fiction
Augenbraum, H., & Stavans, I. (Eds.)	*Growing Up Latino: Memoirs and Stories* (1993)	Anthology
Carlson. L. (Ed.)	*Cool Salsa: Bilingual Poems on Growing Up Latino in the United States*** (1995)	Anthology/ Juvenile
Castillo-Speed, L. (Ed.)	*Latinas: Women's Voices From the Borderlands* (1995)	Anthology
Cisneros, S.	*The House on Mango Street* (1991)*	Fiction
	*Women Hollering Creek: And Other Stories** (1992)	Anthology
García, C.	*Dreaming in Cuban** (1993)	Fiction
Gonzalez, R. (Ed.)	*Muy Macho: Latino Men Confront Their Manhood* (1996)	Anthology
Gonzalez, R., & Ruiz, A.	*My First Book of Proverbs/ Mi Primer Libro de Dichos*** (1995)	Nonfiction for children
López, T. A. (Ed.)	*Growing Up Chicana* (1995)	Anthology
Marquez, A., & Anaya, A. (Eds.)	*Cuentos Chicanos: A Short Story Anthology* (1984)	Anthology

* Spanish edition available.
** Spanish and English used in edition.

Nava, Y. (Ed.)	*It's All in the Frijoles: 100 Famous Latinos Share Real-Life Stories, Time Tested Dichos, Favorite Folktales, and Inspiring Words of Wisdom* (2000)	Self-Help
Rodríguez, G.	*Raising Nuestros Niños: Bringing Up Latino Children in a Bicultural World* (1999)	Self-help
Santiago, E.	*When I Was Puerto Rican** (1994)	Auto-biography
	Almost a Woman* (1999)	Auto-biography
Santiago, E., & Davidow, J. (Eds.)	*Las Christmas: Favorite Latino Authors Share Their Holidays Memories* (1999)	Anthology
Serros, M.	*How to be a Chicana role model* (2000)	Fiction
Stavans, I.	*The Hispanic condition: Reflections on culture and identity in America* (1996)	Nonfiction
Treviño Hart, E.	*Barefoot heart: Stories of a migrant child* (1999)	Auto-biography

References

Abalos, D. T. (1986). *Latinos in the United States: The sacred and the political.* Notre Dame, IN: University of Notre Dame Press.

Abreu, J. M., & Gabarain, G. (2000). Social desirability and Mexican American counselor preferences: Statistical control for a potential confound. *Journal of Counseling Psychology, 47,* 165-176.

Acosta-Belén, E., & Santiago, C. (1995, Spring). Merging borders: The remapping of America. *The Latino Review of Books, 1*(1), 2-12.

Acosta-Belén, E., & Sjostrom, B. R. (Eds.). (1988). *The Hispanic experience in the United States.* New York: Praeger.

Alderete, E., Vega, W. A., Kolody, B., & Aguilar-Gaxiola, S. (1999). Depressive symptomatology: Prevalence and psychosocial risk factors among Mexican migrant farm workers in California. *Journal of Community Psychology, 27,* 457-471.

Altarriba, J., & Santiago-Rivera, A. L. (1994). Current perspectives on using linguistic and cultural factors in counseling the Hispanic client. *Professional Psychology: Research and Practice, 25,* 388-397.

Ambrose, H. J., Flores, M. T., & Carey, G. (2000). Healthcare today: Treating Hispanic families and children with chronic illness. In M. T. Flores & G. Carey (Eds.), *Family therapy with Hispanics* (pp. 229-250). Boston: Allyn & Bacon.

American Psychological Association. (1990). *Guidelines for providers of psychological services to ethnic, linguistic, and culturally diverse populations.* Washington, DC: Author.

American Psychological Association. (1999). *Guidelines for psychotherapy with gay, lesbian, and bisexual clients.* Washington, DC: Author.

American Psychological Association. (in press). *Guidelines for multicultural counseling proficiency for psychologists: Implications for education and training, research, and clinical practice.* Washington, DC: Author.

Anderson, W. T., Anderson, R. A., & Hovestadt, A. J. (1988). Intergenerational family therapy: A practical primer. In P. E. Keller & S. R. Heyman (Eds.), *Innovations in clinical practice: A source book* (Vol. 7, pp. 175-188). Sarasota, FL: Professional Resource Press.

Angel, J. (1998). *Nuestros padres:* Elder care in Hispanic families. *Hispanic, 11,* 18-23.

Angel, J. L., & Angel, R. J. (1998). Aging trends: Mexican Americans in the southwestern USA. *Journal of Cross-Cultural Gerontology, 13*(3), 281-290.

Angel, R., & Angel, J. (1997). *Who will care for us? Aging and long-term care in multicultural America.* New York: New York University Press.

Arbona, C. (1990). Career counseling research and Hispanics: A review of the literature. *The Counseling Psychologist, 18,* 300-323.

Arbona, C. (1998). Psychological assessment: Multicultural or universal. *The Counseling Psychologist, 6,* 911-921.

Arcaya, J. M. (1996). The Hispanic male in group therapy. In M. P. Andronico (Ed.), *Men in groups: Insights, intervention, and psychoeducation work* (pp. 151-161). Washington, DC: American Psychological Association.

Arcia, E., & Johnson, A. (1998). When respect means to obey: Immigrant Mexican mothers' values for their children. *Journal of Child and Family Studies, 7,* 79-95.

Arciniega, M., Casaus, L., & Castillo, M. (1987). *Parenting models and Mexican Americans: A process analysis.* Albuquerque, NM: Pajarito.

Armas, G. (2001, May 8). Hispanic population exceeds predictions. *The Daily Gazette,* pp. 1A, 6A.

Arredondo, P. (1998). Integrating multicultural counseling competencies and universal helping conditions in culture-specific contexts. *The Counseling Psychologist, 26,* 592-601.

Arredondo, P. (2000, November/December). Suggested "best practices" for increasing diversity in APA Divisions. *The APA/Division Dialogue,* pp. 1-3.

Arredondo, P., & Glauner, T. (1992). *Personal dimensions of identity model.* Boston: Empowerment Workshops.

Arredondo, P., & Santiago-Rivera, A. (2000). *Latino dimensions of personal identity* (adapted from Personal Dimensions of Identity Model). Unpublished manuscript.

Arredondo, P., Toperek, R., Brown, S. P., Jones, J., Locke, D. C., Sanchez, J., & Stadler, H. (1996). Operationalization of the multicultural counseling competencies. *Journal of Multicultural Counseling and Development, 24,* 42-78.

Arredondo-Dowd, P. (1981). Personal loss and grief as a result of immigration. *Personnel and Guidance Journal, 59,* 376-378.

Arroyo, J. A. (1996). Psychotherapist bias with Hispanics: An analog study. *Hispanic Journal of Behavioral Sciences, 18,* 21-28.

Atkinson, D. R., Morten, G., & Sue, D. W. (1983). *Counseling American minorities: A cross cultural perspective* (2nd ed.). Dubuque, IA: William C. Brown.

Baca Zinn, M. (1979). Chicano family research: Conceptual distortions and alternative directions. *The Journal of Ethnic Studies, 7,* 59-71.

Baca Zinn, M. (1982). Urban kinship and Midwest Chicano families: Evidence in support of revision. *De colores, 6,* 85-98.

Bacigalupe, G. (2000). El Latino. In M. T. Flores & G. Carey (Eds.), *Family therapy with Hispanics: Toward appreciating diversity* (pp. 283-311). Needham Heights, MA: Allyn & Bacon.

Bailey, D. B., Skinner, D., Rodriguez, P., & Correa, V. (1999). Awareness, use, and satisfaction with services for Latino parents of young children with disabilities. *Exceptional Children, 65*(3), 367-381.

Bamford, K. W. (1991). Bilingual issues in mental health assessment and treatment. *Hispanic Journal of Behavioral Sciences, 13*(4), 377-390.

Baptiste, D. A. (1987). Family therapy with Spanish-heritage immigrant families in cultural transition. *Contemporary Family Therapy, 9,* 229-251.

Baptiste, D. A. (1990). Therapeutic strategies with Black-Hispanic families: Identity problems of a neglected minority. *Journal of Family Psychotherapy, 1,* 15-38.

Barker, P. (1985). *Using metaphors in psychotherapy.* New York: Brunner/Mazel.

Barón, A., & Constantine, M. G. (1997). A conceptual framework of conducting psychotherapy with Mexican-American college students. In J. G. Garcia & M. C. Zea (Eds.), *Psychological interventions and research with Latino populations* (pp. 108-124). Needham Heights, MA: Allyn & Bacon.

Battle, J. J. (1997). Academic achievement among Hispanic students from one versus dual-parent households. *Hispanic Journal of Behavioral Sciences, 19,* 156-170.

Bean, R. A., Perry, B. J., & Bedell, T. M. (2001). Developing culturally competent marriage and family therapists: Guidelines for working with Hispanic families. *Journal of Marital and Family Therapy, 27,* 43-54.

Berg, I. K., & Miller, S. D. (1992). *Working with the problem drinker: A solution-focused approach.* New York: Norton.

Bernal, G., Bonillo, J., & Bellido, C. (1995). Ecological validity and cultural sensitivity for outcome research for the cultural adaptation and development of psychosocial treatments with Hispanics. *Journal of Abnormal Child Psychology, 23,* 67-82.

Bernal, G., & Flores-Ortiz, Y. (1982). Latino families in therapy: Engagement and evaluation. *Journal of Marital and Family Therapy, 8*(3), 357-365.

Bernal, M. E., & Knight, G. P. (Eds.). (1993). *Ethnic identity: Formation and transmission among Hispanics and other minorities.* Albany: State University of New York Press.

Betancourt, H., & López, S. R. (1993). The study of culture, ethnicity, and race in American psychology. *American Psychologist, 48,* 629-637.

Beyebach, M., Rodríguez Morejón, A., Palenzuela, D. L., & Rodríguez-Aras, J. L. (1996). Research on the process of solution-focused therapy. In S. D. Miller & B. L. Duncan (Eds.), *Handbook of solution-focused brief therapy* (pp. 299-334). San Francisco: Jossey-Bass.

Birman, D. (1998). Biculturalism and perceived competence of Latino immigrant adolescents. *American Journal of Community Psychology, 26,* 335-354.

Blacher, J., Shapiro, J., & López, S. (1997). Depression in Latina mothers of children with mental retardation: A neglected concern. *American Journal of Mental Retardation, 101,* 483-496.

Blackhall, L. J., Murphy, S. T., Frank G., Michel, V., & Azen, S. (1995). Ethnicity and attitudes toward patient autonomy. *Journal of the American Medical Association, 274,* 820-825.

Blank, S., & Torrecilla, R. S. (1998). Understanding the living arrangements of Latino immigrants: A life course approach. *International Migration Review, 32,* 3-19.

Boswell, T. (1994). *A demographic profile of Cuban Americans.* Miami, FL: Cuban American Policy Center, Cuban American National Council.

Bracero, W. (1998). Intimidades: Confianza, gender, and hierarchy in the construction of Latino-Latina therapeutic relationships. *Cultural Diversity and Mental Health, 4,* 264-277.

Bradford, D. T., & Muñoz, A. (1993). Translation in bilingual psychotherapy. *Professional Psychology: Research and Practice, 24,* 52-61.

Brofenbrenner, U. (1979). *The ecology of human development: Experiments by nature and design.* Cambridge, MA: Harvard University Press.

Brook, J., Whiteman, M., Balka, E. A., Win, P. E., & Gursen, M. D. (1997). African American and Puerto Rican drug use: A longitudinal study. *Journal of the American Academy of Child and Adolescent Psychiatry, 36,* 1260-1268.

Burnette, D. (1999). Physical and emotional well-being of custodial grandparents in Latino families. *American Journal of Orthopsychiatry, 69,* 305-318.

Canino, I. A., & Spurlock, J. (2000). *Culturally diverse children and adolescents: Assessment, diagnosis, and treatment* (2nd ed.). New York: Guilford.

Carey, G., & Manuppelli, L. (2000). Culture class or not? In M. T. Flores & G. Carey (Eds.), *Family therapy with Hispanics: Toward appreciating diversity* (pp. 79-123). Boston: Allyn & Bacon.

Carter, B., & McGoldrick, M. (1999). *The expanded family life-cycle: Individual, family, and social perspectives.* Needham Heights, MA: Allyn & Bacon.

Carter, R. T. (1995). *The influence of race and racial identity in psychotherapy.* New York: John Wiley.

Cervantes, R. C., Padilla, A. M., & Salgado de Snyder, V. N. (1991). The Hispanic stress inventory: A culturally relevant approach to psychosocial assessment. *Psychological Assessment, 3,* 438-447.

Cervantes, R. C., Salgado de Snyder, V. N., & Padilla, A. M. (1989). Post-traumatic stress disorder among immigrants from Central America and Mexico. *Hospital and Community Psychiatry,*
40, 615-619.

Cheung, F. K., & Snowden, L. R. (1990). Community mental health and ethnic minority populations. *Community Mental Health Journal, 26,* 277-291.

Clauss, C. S. (1998). Language: The unspoken variable in psychotherapy practice. *Psychotherapy,*
35, 188-196.

Coleman, L. K., Wampold, B. E., & Casali, S. L. (1995). Ethnic minorities' ratings of ethnically
similar and European American counselors: A meta-analysis. *Journal of Counseling Psychology, 42,* 55-64.

Comas-Díaz, L. (1981). Puerto Rican *espiritísmo* and psychotherapy. *American Journal of
Orthopsychiatry, 51,* 636-645.

Comas-Díaz, L. (1985). Cognitive and behavioral group therapy with Puerto Rican women: A
comparison of content themes. *Hispanic Journal of Behavioral Sciences, 7,* 273-283.

Comas-Díaz, L. (1987). Feminist therapy with Hispanic/Latina women: Myth or reality? *Women
and Therapy, 6,* 39-61.

Comas-Díaz, L. (1988). Hispanics. In L. Comas-Díaz & E. E. Griffith (Eds.), *Clinical guidelines in
cross-cultural mental health* (pp. 183-268). New York: John Wiley.

Comas-Díaz, L. (1996). LatiNegra: Mental health issues of African Latinas. In M.P.P. Root (Ed.),
The multiracial experience: Racial borders as the new frontier (pp. 167-190). Thousand Oaks,
CA: Sage.

Comas-Díaz, L. (1997). Mental health needs of Latinos with professional status. In J. G. Garcia &
M. C. Zea (Eds.), *Psychological interventions and research with Latino populations* (pp. 142-
165). Needham Heights, MA: Allyn & Bacon.

Comas-Díaz, L., & Duncan, J. W. (1985). The cultural context: A factor in assertiveness training
with mainland Puerto Rican women. *Psychology of Women Quarterly, 9,* 463-475.

Costantino, G., Colón-Malgady, G., Malgady, R., & Pérez, A. (1991). Assessment of attention
deficit disorder using a thematic apperception technique. *Journal of Personality Assessment,
57,* 87-95.

Costantino, G., Flanagan, R., & Malgady, R. G. (2001). Narrative assessment: TAT, CAT, and
TEMAS. In L. A. Suzuki, J. G. Ponterotto, & P. Meller (Eds.), *Handbook of multicultural
assessment: Clinical, psychological, and educational applications* (2nd ed., pp. 217-236).
San Francisco, CA: Jossey-Bass.

Costantino, G., Malgady, R. G., & Rogler, L. H. (1986). Cuento therapy: A culturally sensitive modality for Puerto Rican children. *Journal of Consulting and Clinical Psychology, 54,* 639-645.

Costantino, G., & Rivera C. (1994). Culturally sensitive treatment modalities for Puerto Rican
children, adolescents, and adults. In R. G. Malgady & O. Rodriguez (Eds.), *Theoretical and
conceptual issues in Hispanic mental health* (pp. 181-226). Malabar, FL: Krieger.

Council of National Associations for the Advancement of Ethnic Minority Issues. (2000). *Guidelines for research in ethnic minority communities.* Washington, DC: American Psychological
Association.

Crohn, J. (1998). Intercultural couples. In M. McGoldrick (Ed.), *Re-visioning family therapy:
Race, culture, and gender in clinical practice* (pp. 295-308). New York: Guilford.

Croker, J., & Major, B. (1989). Social stigma and self-esteem: The self-protective properties of
stigma. *Psychological Review, 96,* 608-630.

Cross, W. E. (1991). *Shades of Black: Diversity in African American identity.* Philadelphia: Temple
University Press.

Cuellar, I., Harris, L. C., & Jasso, R. (1980). An acculturation scale for Mexican American normal
and clinical populations. *Hispanic Journal of Behavioral Sciences, 2,* 199-217.

Currier, R. I. (1966). The hot-cold syndrome and symbolic balance in Mexican and Spanish-
American folk medicine. *Ethnology, 5,* 251-263.

Dana, R. H. (1993). *Multicultural assessment perspectives for professional psychology*. Boston: Allyn & Bacon.

D'Andrea, M., & Arredondo, P. (2000, April). Convergence of multiple identities presents new challenges. *Counseling Today*, pp. 12, 40.

D'Andrea, M., & Daniels, J, (1995). Promoting multicultural and organizational changes in the counseling profession: A case study. In J. B. Ponterotto, J. M. Casas, L. A. Suzuki, & C. M. Alexander (Eds.), *Handbook of multicultural counseling* (pp. 17-33). Thousand Oaks, CA: Sage.

Deater-Deckard, K., & Scarr, S. (1996). Parenting stress among dual-earner mothers and fathers: Are there gender differences? *Journal of Family Psychology, 10,* 45-59.

de los Angeles Torres, M. (1998). Transnational political and cultural identities: Crossing theoretical borders. In R. F. Bonilla, E. Melendez, R. Morales, & M. de los Angeles Torres (Eds.), *Borderless borders: U.S. Latinos, Latin Americans, and the paradox of interdependence* (pp. 169-182). Philadelphia: Temple University Press.

Dicen que prosperidad en E.E. U.U. se debe a la familia. (2000, September 2). *El Nuevo Día Interactivo: Noticias desde Puerto Rico*. [On-line]. Available: www.endi.com

Diez de Leon, C. (2000). Acculturation and family therapy with Hispanics. In M. T. Flores & G. Carey (Eds.), *Family therapy with Hispanics: Toward appreciating diversity* (pp. 283-311). Needham Heights, MA: Allyn & Bacon.

Driscoll, A., & Henderson, T. (March 31, 2001). In Dade, Latin percentage highest in nation. *Miami Herald*.

Echeverry, J. J. (1997). Treatment barriers: Accessing and accepting professional help. In J. G. Garcia & M. C. Zea (Eds.), *Psychological interventions and research with Latino populations* (pp. 94-107). Needham Heights, MA: Allyn & Bacon.

Ellickson, P. L., & McGuigan, K. A. (2000). Early predictors of adolescent violence. *American Journal of Public Health, 90,* 566-572.

Erikson, E. H. (1968). *Identity: Youth and crisis*. New York: Norton.

Espín, O. M. (1987). The psychological impact of migration on Latinas: Implications for psycho-therapeutic practice. *Psychology of Women Quarterly, 11,* 489-503.

Espín, O. M. (1997). *Latina realities: Essays on healing, migration, and sexuality*. Boulder, CO: Westview.

Espín, O. M. (1999). *Women crossing boundaries: A psychology of immigration and transformation of sexuality*. New York: Routledge.

Estrada, L. F. (2000). *Children: A demographic profile*. Unpublished manuscript, UCLA School of Public Policy and Social Research.

Fabbro, F. (1999). *The neurolinguistics of bilingualism*. East Sussex, UK: Psychology Press Ltd.

Falicov, C. J. (1986). Cross-cultural marriages. In N. S. Jacobson & A. S. Gurman (Eds.), *Clinical handbook of marital therapy* (pp. 429-450). New York: Guilford.

Falicov, C. J. (1998). *Latino families in therapy: A guide to multicultural practice*. New York: Guilford.

Falicov, C. J. (1999). Latino life cycle. In B. Carter & M. McGoldrick (Eds.), *The expanded life cycle: Individual, family, and social perspectives* (pp. 141-152). Boston, MA: Allyn & Bacon.

Featherstone, V. (1996). A feminist critique of family therapy. *Counseling Psychology Quarterly, 9,* 15-23.

Fischer, A. R., Jome, L. M., & Atkinson, D. R. (1998). Back to the future of multicultural psycho-therapy with a common factors approach. *The Counseling Psychologist, 26,* 602-606.

Fitzgerald, L. F., & Nutt, R. (1986). The Division 17 principles concerning the counseling/psychotherapy of women: Rationale and implementation. *The Counseling Psychologist, 14*(1), 180-216.

Flaskerud, J. H. (1986). The effects of culture-compatible intervention on the utilization of mental health services by minority clients. *Community Mental Health Journal, 22,* 127-141.

Flores, M. T., & Carey, G. (2000). *Family therapy with Hispanics: Toward appreciating diversity*. Boston: Allyn & Bacon.

Flores-Ortíz, Y. (2000). Injustice in Latino families: Considerations for family therapists. In M. T. Flores & G. Carey (Eds.), *Family therapy with Hispanics: Toward appreciating diversity* (pp. 251-263). Boston: Allyn & Bacon.

Flores-Ortíz, Y., & Bernal, G. (1990). Contextual family therapy of addiction with Latinos. In G. W. Saba, B. M. Karrer, & K. V. Hardy (Eds.), *Minorities and family therapy* (pp. 123- 142). Binghamton, NY: Haworth.

Florsheim, P., Tolan, P. H., & Gorman-Smith, D. (1996). Family process and risk of externalizing behavior problems among African American and Hispanic boys. *Journal of Consulting and Clinical Psychology, 64,* 1222-1230.

Frank, J. D., & Frank, J. B. (1991). *Persuasion and healing: A comparative study of psychotherapy* (3rd ed.). Baltimore: John Hopkins University Press.

Frauenglass, S., Routh, D. K., Pantin, H. M., & Mason, C. A. (1997). Family support decreases influences of deviant peers on Hispanic adolescents' substance use. *Journal of Clinical Child Psychology, 26*(1), 15-23.

Fukuyama, M. A. (1990). Taking a universal approach to multicultural counseling. *Counselor Education and Supervision, 36,* 6-17.

Gallardo-Cooper, M. (1998, March). Treatment strategies. In P. Arredondo (Chair), *Latino identity.* Learning institute conducted at the meeting of the American Counseling Association, Indianapolis, IN.

Gallardo-Cooper, M. (1999, March). Latino perspectives. In S. Kromash (Chair), *Cultural/ spiritual diversity: A social worker's guide to sensitive practice.* Symposium conducted at the National Association of Social Workers, Melbourne, FL.

Gallardo-Cooper, M. (2000). *Bilingual mental health practice: An emerging specialty.* Unpublished manuscript, Melbourne, FL.

Gallardo-Cooper, M. (2001a). *Culture-centered clinical interview.* Unpublished manuscript.

Gallardo-Cooper, M. (2001b, March). *The Latino parent-child relationship across the life- span.* Learning institute presented at the meeting of the American Counseling Association, San Antonio, TX.

Garcia Coll, C., Lamberty, G., Jenkins, R., McAdoo, H. P., Crnie, K., Wasik, B. H., & Vázquez García, H. (1998). An integration model for the study of developmental competencies in minority children. In M. E. Hertzig & E. A. Farber (Eds.), *Annual progress in child psychiatry and child development: 1997* (pp. 437-463). Philadelphia: Brunner/Mazel.

García-Preto, N. (1996a). Latino families: An overview. In M. McGoldrick, J. Giordano, & J. K. Pearc (Eds.), *Ethnicity and family therapy* (2nd ed., pp. 141-154). New York: Guilford.

García-Preto, N. (1996b). Puerto Rican families. In M. McGoldrick, J. Giordano, & J. K. Pearce (Eds.), *Ethnicity and family therapy* (pp. 183-199). New York: Guilford.

García-Preto, N. (1998). Latinas in United States: Building two bridges. In M. McGoldrick (Ed.), *Re-visioning family therapy: Race, culture, and gender in clinical practice* (pp. 330-346). New York: Guilford.

Garvin, G. (2000, January 2). Latin America the main source of immigrants to United States. *The Miami Herald* [Online], http:onlinetest.herald.com/content/archive/specialreport/docs/020096. html

Garzon, F., & Siang-Tan, T. (1992). Counseling Hispanics: Cross-cultural and Christian perspectives. *Journal of Psychology and Christianity, 11*(4), 379-390.

Gil, A. G., Vega, W. A., & Biafora, F. (1998). Temporal influences of family structure and family risk factors on drug abuse initiation in a multiethnic sample of adolescent boys. *Journal of Youth and Adolescence, 27,* 373-393.

Gil, R. M., & Vazquez, C. I. (1996). *The Maria paradox.* New York: Perigee.

Glickauf-Hughes, C., Hughes, G. B., & Wells, M. (1986). A developmental approach to treating dual-career couples. *The American Journal of Family Therapy, 14,* 254-263.

Gloria, A. M., & Rodríguez, E. R. (2000). Counseling Latino university students: Psycho-sociocultural issues for consideration. *Journal of Counseling and Development, 78,* 145-154.

Gómez, M. Y. (1999). The grandmother as an enlightened witness in the Hispanic culture. *Psychline: Inter-Transdisciplinary Journal of Mental Health, 3,* 15-19.

Gonzalez, J. (2000). *Harvest of empire: The history of Latinos in America.* New York: Viking.

Gonzalez-Wippler, M. (1989). *Santería, the religion: A legacy of faith, rites, magic.* New York: Harmony Books.

Gottman, J. M. (1998). Psychology and the study of marital processes. *Annual Review of Psychology, 49,* 169-197.

Gregory, D. (1978). Transcultural medicine: Treating Hispanic patients. *Behavioral Medicine, 5,* 22-29.

Grossman, J., & Shigaki, I. S. (1994). Investigation of familial and school-based risk factors for Hispanic Head Start children. *American Journal of Orthopsychiatry, 64,* 456-467.

Guerin, P. J. (Ed.). (1976). *Family therapy: Theory and practice.* New York: Garder Press.

Gutierrez, L. M. (1990). Working with women of color: An empowerment perspective. *Social Work, 35,* 149-153.

Hakuta, K., & Garcia, E. E. (1989). Bilingualism and education. *American Psychologist, 44,* 374-379.

Hardiman, R. (1982). White identity development: A process-oriented model for describing the racial consciousness of White Americans. *Dissertation Abstracts International, 43,* 104A. (University Microfilms No. 82-10330)

Hardy, K. V. (1990). The theoretical myth of sameness: A critical issue in family therapy training and treatment. In G. W. Saba, B. M. Karrer, & K. V. Hardy (Eds.), *Minorities and family therapy* (pp. 17-33). New York: Haworth.

Hardy, K. V., & Laszloffy, T. A. (1995). The cultural genogram: Key in training culturally competent family therapists. *Journal of Marriage and Family Therapy, 21,* 227-237.

Hartman, A. (1995). Diagrammatic assessment of family relationships. *Families in Society, 76,* 111-122.

Harwood, A. (1971). The hot-cold theory of disease. *Journal of the American Medical Association, 216,* 1153-1158.

Hayes-Bautista, D. (1978). Chicano patients and medical practitioners: A sociology of knowledge, paradigms of lay professional interaction. *Social Science and Medicine, 12,* 83-90.

Hayghe, H. V., & Bianchi, S. M. (1994). Married mothers' work patterns: The job-family compromise. *Monthly Labor Review, 117,* 24-30.

Hazuda, H. P., Stern, M., & Haffner, S. (1988). Acculturation and assimilation among Mexican Americans: Scales and population based data. *Social Science Quarterly, 69*(3), 687-706.

Heller, T., Markwardt, R., Rowitz, L., & Farber, B. (1994). Adaptation of Hispanic families to a member with mental retardation. *American Journal of Mental Retardation, 99,* 289-300.

Helms, J. E. (1984). Toward a theoretical explanation of the effects of race on counseling: A Black and White model. *The Counseling Psychologist, 12,* 153-165.

Helms, J. E. (1995). An update of Helms' White and people of color racial identity models. In J. G. Ponterotto, J. M. Casas, L. A. Suzuki, & C. M. Alexander (Eds.), *Handbook of multicultural counseling* (pp. 181-191). Thousand Oaks, CA: Sage.

Hernández, M. (1996). Central American families. In M. McGoldrick, J. Giordano, & J. K. Pearce (Eds.), *Ethnicity and family therapy* (pp. 214-224). New York: Guilford.

Hernández, M., & McGoldrick, M. (1999). Migration and the life cycle. In B. Carter & M. McGoldrick (Eds.), *The expanded family life-cycle: Individual, family, and social perspectives* (pp. 169-184). Boston: Allyn & Bacon.

Hernández, P. (2000, August). The TEMAS life story group: Narrative inpatient therapy. In W. Bracero (Chair), *TEMAS therapy: TEMAS narratives as cultural discourse and therapeutic metaphors.* Symposium conducted at the meeting of the American Psychological Association, Washington, DC.

Hernández, R., Rivera-Batiz, F., & Agodini, R. (1995). *Dominican New Yorkers: A socioeconomic profile* (Dominican Research Monographs). New York: City College of New York, The Dominican Studies Institute.

Heubusch, K., & Dortch, S. (1996). Meet the new Hispanic family. *American Demographics* [On-line], 18. Available: Academic Search Elite.

Ho, M. (1987). *Family therapy with ethnic minorities.* Thousand Oaks, CA: Sage.

Ho, M. (1990). *Intermarried couples in therapy.* Springfield, IL: Charles C Thomas.

Hoberman, H. M. (1992). Ethnic minority status and adolescent mental health service utilization. *Journal of Mental Health Administration, 19,* 246-267.

Holcomb-McCoy, C., & Myers, J. E. (1999). Multicultural competence and counselor training: A national survey. *Journal of Counseling & Development, 77,* 294-302.

Hong, Y., Morris, M. W., Chiu, C., & Benet-Martínez, V. (2000). Multicultural minds: A dynamic constructivist approach to culture and cognition. *American Psychologist, 55,* 709-720.

Hurtado, A. (1995). Variations, combinations, and evolutions: Latino families in the United States. In R. Zambrana (Ed.), *Understanding Latino families: Scholarship, policy, and practice* (pp. 40-61). Thousand Oaks, CA: Sage.

Hurtado, A., Rodriguez, J., Gurin, P., & Beals, J. L. (1993). The impact of Mexican descendants' social identity on the ethnic socialization of children. In M. E. Bernal & G. Knight (Eds.), *Ethnic identity: Formation and transmission among Hispanics and other minorities* (pp. 131-162). Albany: SUNY Press.

Immigration and Naturalization Service. (2000, August 22). *Statistics illegal alien resident population* [On-line]. Available: http://www.ins.usdoj.gov/text/aboutins/statistics/ illegalalien/index.htm

Inclán, J. E. (1990). Understanding Hispanic families: A curriculum outline. *Journal of Strategic & Systemic Therapies, 9,* 64-82.

Inclán, J. E., & Hernandez, M. (1992). Cross-cultural perspectives and codependence: The case of poor Hispanics. *American Journal of Orthopsychiatry, 62*(2), 245-255.

Inclán, J. E., & Herron, D. G. (1998). Puerto Rican adolescents. In J. T. Gibbs & L. H. Huang (Eds.), *Children of color* (pp. 240-263). San Francisco: Jossey-Bass.

Jasinski, J. L. (1998). The role of acculturation in wife assault. *Hispanic Journal of Behavioral Sciences, 20*(2), 175-191.

Javier, R. (1989). Linguistic considerations in the treatment of bilinguals. *Psychoanalytic Psychology, 6,* 87-96.

Jenkins, J. H., & Schumacher, J. G. (1999). Family burden of schizophrenia and depressive illness: Specifying the effects of ethnicity, gender, and social ecology. *British Journal of Psychiatry, 174,* 31-38.

Johnson, J. J. (1986). *Life events as stressors in childhood and adolescence* (Developmental Clinical Psychology and Psychiatry, Vol. 8). Beverly Hills, CA: Sage.

Johnston, C. (1996). Parent characteristics and parent-child interactions in families of nonproblem children and ADHD children with higher and lower levels of oppositional-defiant behavior. *Journal of Abnormal Child Psychology, 24,* 85-101.

Keefe, S. E., & Padilla A. M. (1987). *Chicano ethnicity.* Albuquerque: University of New Mexico Press.

Koss-Chioino, J. (1999). Depression among Puerto Rican women: Culture, etiology, and diagnosis. *Hispanic Journal of Behavioral Sciences, 21,* 330-350.

Koss-Chioino, J. O., & Vargas, L. M. (1999). *Working with latino youth: Culture, development, and context.* San Francisco: Jossey-Bass.

Kratochwill, T. R., & Sheridan, S. M. (1990). Advances in behavioral assessment. In T. R. Gutkin & C. R. Reynolds (Eds.), *Handbook of school psychology* (pp. 328-364). New York: John Wiley.

Krauth, L. D. (1995, December). Single-parent families: The risk to children. *Family Therapy News*, p. 14.

Kuehl, B. P. (1995). The solution-focused genogram: A collaborative approach. *Journal of marital and Family Therapy, 21,* 239-250.

Kunkel, J. H. (1997). The analysis of rule-governed behavior in social psychology. *Psychological Reports, 47,* 698-715.

La Roche, M. J. (1999). The association of social relations and depression levels among Dominicans in the United States. *Hispanic Journal of Behavioral Sciences, 21,* 420-430.

Latinos in America: A journey in stages. (2000, January 15). *The Washington Post* [Online], www.washingtonpost.com/wp-dyn/article/a51043-2000jan 15.html

Leong, T. L., Wagner, N. S., & Tata, S. P. (1995). Racial and ethnic variations in help-seeking attitudes. In J. G. Ponterotto, J. M. Casas, L. A. Suzuki, & C. Alexander (Eds.), *Handbook of multicultural counseling* (pp. 415-438). Thousand Oaks, CA: Sage.

Lequerica, M. (1993). Stress in immigrant families with handicapped children: A child advocacy approach. *American Journal of Orthopsychiatry, 63*(4), 545-552.

Leslie, L. A., & Leitch, M. L. (1989). A demographic profile of recent Central American immigrants: Clinical and service implications. *Hispanic Journal of Behavioral Sciences, 11*(4), 315-329.

Levine, E. S., & Padilla, A. M. (1980). *Crossing cultures in therapy: Pluralistic counseling for the Hispanic.* Belmont, CA: Wadsworth.

Lichter, D. T., & Landale, N. S. (1995). Parental work, family structure, and poverty among Latino children. *Journal of Marriage and the Family, 57,* 346-354.

Lijtmaer, R. M. (1998). Psychotherapy with Latinas. *Feminism & Psychology, 8,* 537-543.

Locke, D. C. (1992). *Increasing multicultural understanding: A comprehensive model.* Newbury Park, CA: Sage.

López, E. C., & Gopaul-McNicol, S. (1997). English as a second language. In G. G. Bear, K. M. Minke, & A. Thomas (Eds.), *Children's needs: Vol. 2. Development, problems, and alternatives* (pp. 523-531). Bethesda, MD: National Association of School Psychologists Publications.

López, S. R., Grover, K. P., Holland, D., Johnson, M. J., Kain, C. D., Kanel, K., Mellins, C. A., & Rhyne, M. C. (1989). Development of culturally sensitive psychotherapists. *Professional Psychology Research and Practice, 20,* 369-376.

Lopez-Baez, S. (1999). Marianismo. In J. S. Mio, J. E. Trimble, P. Arredondo, H. E. Cheatham, & D. Sue (Eds.), *Key words in multicultural interventions: A dictionary* (p. 183). Westport, CT: Greenwood.

Lorenzo-Hernandez, J. (1998). How social categories may inform the study of Hispanic immigration. *Hispanic Journal of Behavioral Sciences, 20*(1), 39-59.

Lyle, R. R., & Faure, F. (2000). Life-cycle development, divorce, and the Hispanic family. In M. T. Flores & G. Carey (Eds.), *Family therapy with Hispanics: Toward appreciating diversity* (pp. 185-203). Boston: Allyn & Bacon.

Magaña, S. M. (1999). Puerto Rican families caring for an adult with mental retardation: Role of familism. *American Journal of Mental Retardation, 104,* 466-482.

Magilvy, J. K., Congdon, J. G., Martinez, R. J., Davis, R., & Averill, J. (2000). Caring for our own: Health care experiences of rural Hispanic elders. *Journal of Aging Studies, 14,* 171-190.

Malgady, R. G., & Costantino, G. (1998). Symptom severity in bilingual Hispanics as a function of clinician and language of interview. *Psychological Assessment, 10,* 120-127.

Malgady, R., Costantino, G., & Rogler, L. (1984). Development of a Thematic Apperception Test (TEMAS) for urban Hispanic children. *Journal of Consulting and Clinical Psychology, 52,* 986-996.

Malgady, R. G., & Rodriguez, O. (Eds.). (1994). *Theoretical and conceptual issues in Hispanic mental health.* Melbourne, FL: Robert E. Krieger.

Malgady, R. G., Rogler, L. H., & Costantino, G. (1990a). Culturally sensitive psychotherapy for Puerto Rican children and adolescents: A program of treatment outcome research. *Journal of Consulting and Clinical Psychology [Special Series on Treatment of Children], 58,* 704-712.

Malgady, R. G., Rogler, L. H., & Costantino, G. (1990b). Hero/heroine modeling for Puerto Rican adolescents: A preventive mental health intervention. *Journal of Consulting and Clinical Psychology, 58,* 469-474.

Marcos, L. R. (1976). Bilinguals in psychotherapy: Language as an emotional barrier. *American Journal of Psychotherapy, 30,* 552-560.

Marcos, L. R. (1994). The psychiatric examination of Hispanics: Across the language barrier. In R. Malgady & O. Rodriguez (Eds.), *Theroetical and conceptual issues in Hispanic mental health* (pp. 143-153). Malbar, FL: Krieger.

Marcos, L. R., & Alpert, M. (1976). Strategies and risks in psychotherapy with bilingual patients. *American journal of Psychiatry, 133,* 1275-1278.

Marcos, L. R., Alpert, M., Urcuyo, L., & Kesselman, M. (1973). The effects of interview language on the evaluation of psychopathology in Spanish-American schizophrenic patients. *American Journal of Psychiatry, 130,* 549-553.

Marcos, L. R., & Urcuyo, L. (1979). Dynamic psychotherapy with the bilingual patient. *American Journal of Psychotherapy, 33,* 331-338.

Marín, G. (1992). Issues in the measurement of acculturation among Hispanics. In K. F. Geisinger (Ed.), *Psychological testing of Hispanics* (pp. 235-251). Washington, DC: American Psychological Association.

Marín, G. (1993). Influence of acculturation on familialism and self-identification among Hispanics. In M. E. Bernal & G. P. Knight (Eds.), *Ethnic identity: Formations and transmission among Hispanics and other minorities* (pp. 181-196). Albany: State University of New York Press.

Marín, G., & Marín, B. V. (1991). *Research with Hispanic populations.* Newbury Park, CA: Sage.

Marín, G., Sabogal, F., Marín, B. V., Otero-Sabogal, R., & Perez-Stable, E. (1987). Development of a short acculturation scale for Hispanics. *Hispanic Journal of Behavioral Sciences, 9,* 183-205.

Marín, G., & Triandis, H. C. (1985). Allocentrism as an important characteristic of the behavior of Latin Americans and Hispanics. In R. Diaz-Guerrero (Ed.), *Cross-cultural and national studies in social psychology* (pp. 85-104). Amsterdam: North Holland.

Markides, K. S., Ray, L. A., Stroup-Behnam, C. A., & Trevino, F. (1990). Acculturation and alcohol consumption in the Mexican American population of the southwestern US: Findings from HHANES 1982-1984. *American Journal of Public Health, 80,* 42-46.

Marsella, A. J., & Yamada, N. M. (2000). Culture and mental health: An introduction and overview of foundations, concepts, and issues. In I. Cuellar & F. A. Paniagua (Eds.), *Handbook of multicultural and mental health assessment and treatment of diverse populations* (pp. 3-24). New York: Academic Press.

Martínez, C. (2000). Conducting the cross-cultural clinical interview. In I. Cuellar & F. A. Paniagua (Eds.), *Handbook of multicultural mental health assessment and treatment of diverse populations* (pp. 311-322). New York: Academic Press.

Martinez, R. J. (1999). Close friends of God: An ethnographic study of health in older Hispanic adults. *Journal of Multicultural Nursing and Health, 5,* 40-45.

Mary, N. L. (1990). Reactions of Blacks, Hispanics, and White mothers to having a child with handicaps. *Mental Retardation, 28*(1), 1-5.

Massey, D., Zambrana, R. E., & Alonzo-Bell, S. (1994). Contemporary issues in Latino families: Future directions for research, policy, and practice. In R. E. Zambrana (Ed.), *Understanding Latino families: Scholarship, policy, and practice* (pp. 190-204). Thousand Oaks, CA: Sage.

Masud-Piloto, F. (1988). *With open arms.* Totowa, NJ: Rowan & Littlefield.

McGoldrick, M., & Carter, B. (1998). Self in context: The individual life cycle in systemic perspective. In B. Carter & M. McGoldrick (Eds.), *The expanded life cycle: Individual, family, and social perspectives* (pp. 27-45). Boston: Allyn & Bacon.

McGoldrick, M., & García-Preto, N. (1984). Ethnic intermarriage: Implications for therapy. *Family Process, 23,* 347-364.

McGoldrick, M., Gerson, R., & Schellenberger, S. (1999). *Genograms in family assessment.* New York: Norton.

McMiller, W. P., & Weisz, J. R. (1996). Help seeking preceding mental health clinic intake among African-American, Latino, and Caucasian youths. *Journal of the American Academy of Child and Adolescent Psychiatry, 35,* 1086-1094.

Mena, F. J., Padilla, A. M., & Maldonado, M. (1987). Acculturative stress and specific coping strategies among immigrant and later generation college students. *Hispanic Journal of Behavioral Sciences, 9,* 207-255.

Microtraining Associates. (1999). *Culturally competent counseling & therapy, Part III: Innovative approaches to counseling Latina/o people* [Film]. (Available from Microtraining and Multicultural Development, PO Box 9641, North Amherst, MA 01059-9641)

Miller-Jones, D. (1989). Culture and testing. *American Psychologist, 44,* 360-366.

Minuchin, S. (1974). *Families and family therapy.* Cambridge, MA: Harvard University Press.

Mirandé, A (1985). *The Chicano experience: An alternative perspective.* Notre Dame, IN: University of Notre Dame Press.

Mock, M. R. (1998). Clinical reflections on refugee families: Transforming crisis into opportunities. In M. McGoldrick (Ed.), *Re-visioning family therapy: Race, culture, and gender in clinical practice* (pp. 347-359). New York: Guilford.

Molina, C., Zambrana, E. E., & Aguirre-Molina, M. J. (1994). The influence of culture, class, and environment on health care. In C. W. Molina & M. Aguirre-Molina (Eds.), *Latino health in the US: A growing challenge.* Washington, DC: American Public Health Association.

Molina, C. W., & Aguirre-Molina, M. (Eds.). (1994). *Latino health in the US: A growing challenge.* Washington, DC: American Public Health Association.

Moncher, M. S., Holden, G. W., Schinke, S. P., & Palleja, J. (1990). Behavioral family treatment of the substance abusing Hispanic adolescent. In E. L. Feindler & G. R. Kalfus (Eds.), *Adolescent behavioral therapy handbook* (pp. 329-349). New York: Springer.

Montalvo, B., & Gutiérrez, M. J. (1989). Nine assumptions for work with ethnic minority families. *Journal of Psychotherapy and the Family, 6,* 35-52.

Moore, J., & Pachon, H. (1985). *Hispanics in the United States.* Englewood Cliffs, NJ: Prentice Hall.

Moore Hines, O., Garcia-Preto, N., McGoldrick, M., Almeida, R., & Weltman, S. (1999). In B. Carter & M. McGoldrick (Eds.), *The expanded life cycle: Individual, family, and social perspectives* (pp. 27-45). Boston: Allyn & Bacon.

Morales, E. (1996). Gender roles among Latino gay and bisexual men: Implications for family and couple relationships. In J. Laird & R. J. Green (Eds.), *Lesbians and gays in couples and families: A handbook for therapists* (pp. 272-297). San Francisco: Jossey-Bass.

Murphy, J. J., & Duncan, B. L. (1997). *Practical solutions to school problems: A brief intervention.* New York: Guilford.

Nava, Y. (Ed.). (2000). *It's all in the frijoles: 100 famous Latinos share real-life stories, time-tested dichos, favorite folktales, and inspiring words of wisdom.* New York: Fireside.

Negy, C. (2000). Limitations of the multicultural approach to psychotherapy with diverse clients. In I. Cuellar & F. A. Paniagua (Eds.), *Handbook of multicultural mental health assessment and treatment of diverse populations* (pp. 439-453). New York: Academic Press.

Negy, C., & Snyder, D. K. (2000). Relationship satisfaction of Mexican American and non-Hispanic White American interethnic couples: Issues of acculturation and clinical intervention. *Journal of Marital and Family Therapy, 26,* 293-304.

Novas, H. (1994). *Everything you needed to know about Latino history.* New York: Plume.

Office of Management and Budget. (1978, May 4). Directive 15: Race and ethnic standards for federal statistics and administrative reporting. *Federal Registry, 43,* 19269.

Oquendo, M., Horwath, E., & Martinez, A. (1989). Ataque de nervios: Proposed diagnostic criteria for a culture-specific syndrome. *Culture, Medicine, and Psychiatry, 16,* 367-376.

Oropesa, R. S. (1996). Normative beliefs about marriage and cohabitation: A comparison of non-Latino Whites, Mexican Americans, and Puerto Ricans. *Journal of Marriage & the Family, 58,* 49-62.

Ortiz, V. (1995). The diversity of the Latino family. In R. E. Zambrana (Ed.), *Understanding Latino families: Scholarship, policy, and practice* (pp. 18-38). Thousand Oaks, CA: Sage.

Pabón, E. (1998). Hispanic delinquency and the family: A discussion of sociocultural influences. *Adolescence, 33,* 941-951.

Padilla, A. M. (1994). Bicultural development: A theoretical and empirical examination. In R. G. Malgady & O. Rodriguez (Eds.), *Theoretical and conceptual issues in Hispanic mental health* (pp. 19-51). Malabar, FL: Krieger.

Padilla, A. M. (Ed.). (1995). *Hispanic psychology: Critical issues in theory and research.* Thousand Oaks, CA: Sage.

Padilla, A. M., Cervantes, R. C., Maldonado, M., & Garcia, R. E. (1988). Coping responses to psychosocial stressors among Mexican and Central American immigrants. *Journal of Community Psychology, 16*(4), 418-427.

Paniagua, F. A. (1996). Cross-cultural guidelines in family therapy practice. *Family Journal, 4,* 127-138.

Paniagua, F. A. (1998). *Assessing and treating culturally diverse clients: A practical guide.* Thousand Oaks, CA: Sage.

Paniagua, P. (2001). *A casebook for mental health professionals.* Thousand Oaks, CA: Sage.

Papp, P. (Ed.). (2000). *Couples on the fault line: New directions for therapists.* New York: Guilford.

Pedersen, P. (1999). *Multiculturalism as a fourth force.* Philadelphia: Taylor & Francis.

Penn, C. D., Hernández, S. L., & Bermúdez, M. (1997). Using a cross-cultural perspective to understand infidelity in couples therapy. *The American Journal of Family Therapy, 25,* 169-185.

Perel, E. (2000). A tourist's view of marriage: Cross-cultural couples—challenges, choices, and implications. In P. Papp (Ed.), *Couples on the fault line* (pp. 180-204). New York: Guilford.

Pérez-Foster, R. P. (1998). *The power of language in the clinical process: Assessing and treating the bilingual person.* Northvale, NJ: Jason Aronson.

Pernani, D., Paulesu, E., Galles, N. S., Dupoux, E., Dehaene, S., Bettinardi, V., Cappa, S. F., Fazio, F., & Mehler, J. (1998). The bilingual brain: Proficiency and age of acquisition of the second language. *Brain, 121,* 1841-1852.

Phinney, J. S. (1993). A three-stage model of ethnic identity in adolescence. In M. E. Bernal & G. P. Knight (Eds.), *Ethnic identity: Formation and transmission among Hispanics and other minorities.* Albany: State University of New York Press.

Planos, R., Zayas, L. H., & Busch-Rossnagel, N. A. (1997). Mental health factors and teaching behaviors among low income Hispanic mothers. *Families in Society, 78,* 4-12.

Poma, P. (1983). Hispanic cultural influences on medical practice. *Journal of the National Medical Association, 75,* 941-946.

Ponterotto, J. G. (1987). Counseling Mexican Americans: A multimodal approach. *Journal of Counseling and Development, 65,* 308-312.

Ponterotto, J. G. (1988). Racial consciousness development among white counselors' trainees: A stage model. *Journal of Multicultural Counseling and Development, 16,* 146-156.

Ponterotto, J., & Pedersen, P. B. (1993). *Preventing prejudice: A guide for counselors and educators.* Newbury Park, CA: Sage.

Poston, W. C. (1990). The biracial identity development model: A needed addition. *Journal of Counseling and Development, 69,* 152-155.

Preciado, J., & Henry, M. (1997). Linguistic barriers in health education and services. In J. G. Garcia & M. C. Zea (Eds.), *Psychological interventions and research with Latino populations* (pp. 235-254). Needham Heights, MA: Allyn & Bacon.

Quintana, S. M. (1995). Acculturative stress: Latino immigrants and the counseling profession. *The Counseling Psychologist, 23,* 68-73.

Quintana, S. M., & Vega, E. M. (1999). Mexican American children's ethnic identity, understanding of ethnic prejudice, and parental ethnic socialization. *Hispanic Journal of Behavioral Sciences, 21,* 387-404.

Ramirez, M. (1998). *Multicultural/multiracial psychology: Mestizo perspectives in personality and mental health.* Northvale, NJ: Jason Aronson.

Ramírez, O. (1998). Mexican American children and adolescents. In J. T. Gibbs & L. H. Huang (Eds.), *Children of color* (pp. 217-239). San Francisco: Jossey-Bass.

Ramos-McKay, J. M., Comas-Díaz, L., & Rivera, L. A. (1988). Puerto Ricans. In L. Comas-Díaz & E.E.H. Griffith (Eds.), *Clinical guidelines in cross-cultural mental health* (pp. 204-232). New York: John Wiley.

Ramos-Sánchez, L., Atkinson, D. R., & Fraga, E. D. (1999). Mexican Americans' bilingual ability, counselor bilingualism cues, counselor ethnicity, and perceived counselor credibility. *Journal of Counseling Psychology, 46,* 125-131.

Ranson, M. A. (2000, August). TEMAS psychoeducational group therapy with Latina mothers of at-risk children. In W. Bracero (Chair), *TEMAS therapy: TEMAS narratives as cultural discourse and therapeutic metaphors.* Symposium conducted at the meeting of the American Psychological Association, Washington, DC.

Rhodes, J. E., Contreras, J. M., & Mangelsdorf, S. C. (1994). Natural mentor relationships among Latina adolescent mothers: Psychological adjustment, moderating processes, and the role of early parental acceptance. *American Journal of Community Psychology, 22(2),* 211-227.

Rhodes, J. E., Gingiss, P. L., & Smith, P. B. (1994). Risk and protective factors for alcohol use among pregnant African-American, Hispanic, and White adolescents: The influence of peers, sexual partners, family members, and mentors. *Addictive Behaviors, 19,* 555-564.

Rivera-Arzola, M., & Ramos-Grenier, J. (1997). Anger, ataques de nervios, and la mujer Puertorriqueña: Sociocultural considerations and treatment implications. In J. G. Garcia & M. C. Zea (Eds.), *Psychological interventions and research with Latino populations* (pp. 125-141). Needham Heights, MA: Allyn & Bacon.

Rivera-Batiz, F., & Santiago, C. (1994). *Puerto Ricans in the United States: A changing reality.* Washington, DC: National Puerto Rican Coalition.

Rivera-Batiz, F., & Santiago, C. (1996). *Island paradox: Puerto Rico in the 1990s.* New York: Russell Sage Foundation.

Roberts, R. E., & Chen, Y. (1995). Depressive symptoms and suicidal ideation among Mexican-origin and Anglo adolescents. *Journal of the American Academy of Child and Adolescent Psychiatry, 34,* 81-90.

Robinson, L. (1998, May 11). Hispanics don't exist. *U.S. News & World Report,* pp. 27-32.

Robinson, T. L., & Howard-Hamilton, M. F. (2000). *The convergence of race, ethnicity, and gender: Multiple identities in counseling.* Upper Saddle River, NJ: Prentice Hall.

Rogler, L. H. (2000). Methodological sources of cultural insensitivity in mental health research. *American Psychologist, 54,* 424-433.

Rogler, L. H., Malgady, R. G., Costantino, G., & Blumenthal, R. (1987). What do culturally sensitive mental health services mean? The case of Hispanics. *American Psychologist, 42,* 565-570.

Rogoff, B., & Morelli, G. (1989). Perspectives on children's development from cultural psychology. *American Psychologist, 44,* 343-348.

Romero, A. J. (2000). Assessing and treating Latinos: Overview of research. In I. Cuellar & F. Paniagua (Eds.), *Handbook of multicultural mental health* (pp. 209-223). New York: John Wiley.

Romero, A. J., Cuéllar, I., & Roberts, R. E. (2000). Ethnocultural variables and attitudes toward cultural socialization of children. *Journal of Community Psychology, 28,* 79-89.

Root, M.P.P. (Ed.). (1992). *Racially mixed people in America.* Newbury Park, CA: Sage.

Rosado, J. W., & Elias, M. J. (1993). Ecological and psychoeducational mediators in the delivery of services for urban, culturally diverse Hispanic clients. *Professional Psychology: Research & Practice, 24,* 450-459.

Rotter, J. C., & Casado, M. (1998). Promoting strengths and celebrating culture: Working with Hispanic families. *The Family Journal: Counseling and Therapy for Couples and Families, 6*(2), 132-136.

Rovira, L. I. (1984). *Spanish proverbs: A survey of Spanish culture and civilization.* Lanham, MD: University Press of America.

Rozensky, R. H., & Gómez, M. Y. (1983). Language switching in psychotherapy with bilinguals: Two problems, two models, and case examples. *Psychotherapy: Theory, Research, and Practice, 20,* 152-160.

Ruiz, A. S. (1990). Ethnic identity: Crisis and resolution. *Journal of Multicultural Counseling and Development, 18,* 29-40.

Sabogal, F., Marín, G., Otero-Sabogal, R., Marín, B., & Perez-Stable, E. (1987). Hispanic familism and acculturation: What changes and what doesn't? *Hispanic Journal of Behavioral Sciences, 9,* 397-412.

Saldaña, D. (1996). Acculturative stress: Minority status and distress. *Hispanic Journal of Behavioral Sciences, 16,* 116-128.

Salgado de Snyder, V. N. (1999). Latina women: Constructing a new vision from within. *Hispanic Journal of Behavioral Sciences, 21,* 229-235.

Sánchez, B., & Reyes, O. (1999). Descriptive profile of the mentorship relationships of Latino adolescents. *Journal of Community Psychology, 27,* 299-302.

Sánchez-Ayéndez, M. (1989). Puerto Rican elderly women: The cultural dimension of social support networks. *Women and Health, 14,* 239-252.

Santiago-Rivera, A. (1995). Developing a culturally sensitive treatment modality for bilingual Spanish-speaking clients: Incorporating culture and language in therapy. *Journal of Counseling and Development, 74,* 12-17.

Santiago-Rivera, A. L. (1999). Central American. In J. S. Mio, J. E. Trimble, P. Arredondo, H. E. Cheatham, & D. Sue (Eds.), *Key words in multicultural interventions: A dictionary* (pp. 39-40). Westport, CT: Greenwood.

Santiago-Rivera, A. L., & Altarriba, J. (2001). *The role of language in therapy with bilingual Spanish-speaking clients: Past contributions, contemporary perspectives, and future directions.* Manuscript submitted for publication.

Santiago-Rivera, A. L., & Esterman, K. (1999, August). *Why multicultural family therapy?* Paper presented at the meeting of the American Counseling Association, San Diego, CA.

Schrauf, R. W. (1999). Mother tongue maintenance among North American ethnic groups. *Cross-Cultural Research, 33,* 175-192.

Sciarra, D. T. (1999). Intrafamilial separations in the immigrant family: Implications for cross-cultural counseling. *Journal of Multicultural Counseling and Development, 27,* 31-41.

Sciarra, D. T., & Ponterotto, J. G. (1991). Counseling the Hispanic bilingual family: Challenges to the therapeutic process. *Psychotherapy, 28,* 473-479.

Seijo, R., Gómez, H., & Freidenberg, J. (1991). Language as a communication barrier in medical care for Hispanic patients. *Hispanic Journal of Behavioral Sciences, 13,* 363-376.

Sesin, M. C. (2000, August). Healing open wounds: The paintings of Frida Kahlo in group therapy with Latinas. In W. Bracero (Chair), *TEMAS therapy: TEMAS narratives as cultural discourse and therapeutic metaphors.* Symposium conducted at the meeting of the American Psychological Association, Washington, DC.

Shank, M. S., & Turnball, A. P. (1993). Cooperative family problem solving: An intervention with single-parent families of children with disabilities. In G.H.S. Singer & L. E. Powers (Eds.), *Families, disability, and empowerment: Active coping skills and strategies for family interventions* (pp. 231-254). Baltimore, MD: Brooks.

Sluzki, C. E. (1998). Migration and the disruption of the social network. In M. McGoldrick (Ed.), *Re-visioning family therapy: Race, culture, and gender in clinical practice* (pp. 360-369). New York: Guilford.

Smart, J. F., & Smart, D. W. (1994). The rehabilitation of Hispanics experiencing acculturative stress: Implications for practice. *The Journal of Rehabilitation, 60,* 8-12.

Smart, J. F., & Smart, D. W. (1995a). Acculturative stress of Hispanics: Loss and challenge. *Journal of Counseling and Development, 73,* 390-396.

Smart, J. F., & Smart, D. W. (1995b). Acculturative stress: The experience of the Hispanic immigrant. *The Counseling Psychologist, 23,* 25-42.

Sodowsky, G. R., Taffe, R. C., Gutkins, T. B., & Wise, S. L. (1992). Development of the Multicultural Counseling Inventory: A self-report measure of multicultural competencies. *Journal of Counseling Psychology, 46,* 137-148.

Speight, S. L., & Vera, E. M. (1997). Similarity and difference in multicultural counseling: Considering the attraction and repulsion hypotheses. *The Counseling Psychologist, 25,* 280-298.

Stevens, E. P. (1973). The prospect for a women's liberation movement in Latin America. *American Journal of Marriage and the Family,* 231-320.

Sue, D. W. (1978). Eliminating cultural oppression in counseling: Toward a general theory. *Journal of Counseling Psychology, 25,* 419-428.

Sue, D. W., Arredondo, P., & McDavis, R. J. (1992). Multicultural counseling competencies and standards: A call to the profession. *Journal of Counseling and Development, 70,* 477-483.

Sue, D. W., Bernier, J., Durran, M., Feinberg, L., Pedersen, P., Smith, E., & Vasquez-Nuttall, E. (1982). Position paper: Cross-cultural counseling competencies. *The Counseling Psychologist, 10,* 45-52.

Sue, D. W., & Sue, D. (1990). *Counseling the culturally different: Theory and practice.* New York: John Wiley.

Sue D. W., & Sue, D. (1999). *Counseling the culturally different.* New York: John Wiley.

Suro, R. (1999). Mixed doubles. *American Demographics, 21,* 56-62.

Szapocznick, J. (1994, August). *Hispanic families: Contributions to a psychology for all people.* Invited address presented at the meeting of the American Psychological Association, Los Angeles, CA.

Szapocznick, J., & Kurtines, W. (1980). Acculturation, biculturalism, and adjustment among Cuban Americans. In A. M. Padilla (Ed.), *Acculturation: Theory, models, and some new findings* (pp. 139-159). Boulder, CO: Westview.

Szapocznick, J., & Kurtines, W. M. (1993). Family psychology and cultural diversity: Opportunities for theory, research, and application. *American Psychologist, 48,* 400-407.

Szapocznick, J., Kurtines, W. M., Foote, F., Pérez-Vidal, A., & Hervis, O. (1986). Conjoint versus one-person family therapy through one person with drug-abusing adolescents. *Journal of Consulting and Clinical Psychology, 54,* 395-397.

Szapocznick, J., Kurtines, W. M., Santisteban, D. A., Patín, H., Scopetta, M., Mancilla, Y., Aisenberg, S., Pérez-Vidal, A., & Coatsworth, J. D. (1997). The evolution of a structural ecosystemic theory for working with Latino families. In J. G. Garcia & M. C. Zea (Eds.), *Psychological interventions and research with Latino populations* (pp. 166-190). Boston: Allyn & Bacon.

Szapocznick, J., Kurtines, W. M., Santisteban, D. A., & Rio, A. T. (1990). Interplay of advances between theory, research, and application in the treatment interventions aimed at behavior problem children and adolescents. *Journal of Consulting and Clinical Psychology, 58,* 693-703.

Szapocznick, J., Pérez-Vidal, A., Brickman, A. L., Foote, F. H., Santisteban, D., Hervis, O., & Kurtines, W. M. (1988). Engaging adolescent drug abusers and their families in treatment: A strategic structural systems approach. *Journal of Consulting and Clinical Psychology, 56,* 552-557.

Szapocznick, J., Rio, A. T., Murray, E., Cohen, R., Scopetta, M., Rivas-Vázquez, A., Hervis, O., Posada, V., & Kurtines, W. M. (1989). Structural family versus psychodynamic child therapy for problematic Hispanic boys. *Journal of Consulting and Clinical, 57,* 571-578.

Szapocznick, J., Santisteban, D., Kurtines, W. M., Pérez-Vidal, A., & Hervis, O. (1984). Bicultural effectiveness training: A treatment intervention for enhancing intercultural adjustment in Cuban American families. *Hispanic Journal of Behavioral Sciences, 6*(4), 317-344.

Szapocznick, J., Santisteban, D., Rio, A., Pérez-Vidal, A., Kurtines, W., & Hervis, O. (1986). Bi-cultural effectiveness training (BET): An intervention modality for families experiencing intergenerational/intercultural conflict. *Hispanic Journal of Behavioral Sciences, 11,* 4-27.

Szapocznick, J., Scopetta, M. A., Aranalde, M. A., & Kurtines, W. M. (1978). Cuban value struc-ture: Treatment implications. *Journal of Consulting and Clinical Psychology, 46,* 961-970.

Szapocznick, J., Scopetta, M. A., King, O. (1978). Theory and practice in matching to the special characteristics and problems of Cuban immigrants. *Journal of Community Psychology, 6,* 112-122.

Szapocznick, J., Scopetta, M. A., Kurtines, W. M., & Aranalde, M. A. (1978). Theory and mea-surement of acculturation. *Interamerican Journal of Psychology, 12,* 113-130.

Teti, D. M., Gelfand, D. M., Messinger, D. S., & Isabella, R. (1995). Maternal depression and the quality of early attachment: An examination of infants, preschoolers, and their mothers. *Developmental Psychology, 31,* 364-376.

Tiet, Q. Q., Bird, H. R., Davies, M., Hoven, C., Cohen, P., Jensen, P. S., & Goodman, S. (1998). Adverse life events and resilience. *Journal of the American Academy of Child and Adolescent Psychiatry, 37,* 1191-1200.

Titelman, P. (1998a). Family systems assessment based on Bowen theory. In P. Titelman (Ed.), *Clinical applications of Bowen family systems theory* (pp. 51-116). New York: Hawthorne.

Titelman, P. (1998b). Overview of the Bowen theoretical-therapeutic system. In P. Titelman (Ed.), *Clinical applications of Bowen family systems theory* (pp. 7-49). New York: Hawthorne.

Todd, T. (2000). Solution-focused strategic parenting of challenging teens: A class for parents. *Family Relations, 49,* 165-168.

Toppelberg, C. O. (1997). Minority help seeking [Letter to the editor]. *Journal of the American Child and Adolescent Psychiatry, 36,* 443-444.

Torres-Rivera, E. (1999). Group work with Latino clients: A psychoeducational model. *Journal of Specialists in Group Work, 24,* 383-402.

Torres-Saillant, S., & Hernández, R. (1998). *The Dominican Americans.* Westport, CT: Greenwood.

Trevino, F. M., & Sumaya, C. (1993). Increasing the representation of Hispanics in the health professions. *Public Health Reports, 108,* 551-558.

Triandis, H. C., Marín, G., Lisansky, J., & Betancourt, H. (1984). *Simpatía* as a cultural script of Hispanics. *Journal of Personality and Social Psychology, 47,* 1363-1375.

Trostle, S. L. (1988). The effects of child-centered group play sessions on social-emotional growth of three- to six-year-old bilingual Puerto Rican children. *Research in Childhood Edu-cation, 3,* 93-106.

U.S. Bureau of the Census. (1990). *1990 census population* (Public use microdata sample). Washington, DC: Government Printing Office.

U.S. Bureau of the Census. (1993). *Hispanic Americans today* (Current Population Reports, P23-183). Washington, DC: Government Printing Office.

U.S. Bureau of the Census. (1999). *The Hispanic population in the United States: March 1999* (Current Population Reports, P 20-535). Washington, DC: Government Printing Office.

U.S. Bureau of the Census. (2001a). *The Hispanic population: Census brief* (C2KBR/01-3). Washington, DC: Government Printing Office.

U.S. Bureau of the Census. (2001b). *The Hispanic population in the United States: Population characteristics: March 2000* (Current Population Survey, P20-535). Available: www.census. gov/population/socdemo/hispanic.html

Vasquez, M. (1994). Latinas. In L. Comas-Díaz & B. Greene (Eds.), *Women of color: A portrait of heterogeneity* (pp. 114-138). New York: Guilford.

Vega, W. A., Gil, A. G., Warheit, G. J., Zimmerman, R. S., & Apospori, E. (1993). Acculturation and delinquent behavior among Cuban American adolescents: Toward an empirical model. *American Journal of Community Psychology, 21*(1), 113-125.

Warda, M. R. (2000). Mexican Americans perceptions of culturally competent care. *Western Journal of Nursing Research, 22,* 203-224.

Wasserstein, S. B. (1998). Hurricane Andre parent conflict as a moderator of children's adjustment. *Hispanic Journal of Behavioral Sciences, 20,* 212-224.

Wehrly, B., Kenney, K. R., & Kenney, M. E. (1999). *Counseling multiracial families.* Thousand Oaks, CA: Sage.

Wilson, M. N., Kohn, L. P., & Lee, T. S. (2000). Cultural relativistic approach toward ethnic minorities in family therapy. In J. F. Aponte & J. Wohl (Eds.), *Psychological intervention and cultural diversity* (pp. 92-109). Needham Heights, MA: Allyn & Bacon.

Wolin, S., & Bennett, L. (1984). Family rituals. *Family Process, 23,* 401-420.

Wrenn, C. G. (1962). The culturally encapsulated counselor. *Harvard Educational Review, 32,* 444-449.

Yoshioka, M. (2000). Substantive differences in the assertiveness of low-income African American, Hispanic, and Caucasian women. *The Journal of Psychology, 134,* 243-259.

Zambrana, R. (Ed.). (1995). *Understanding Latino families: Scholarship, policy, and practice.* Thousand Oaks, CA: Sage.

Zavala, M. V. (2000). Puerto Rican identity: What language has to do with it? In S. Nieto (Ed.), *Puerto Rican students in U.S. schools* (pp. 115-135). Mahwah, NJ: Lawrence Erlbaum.

Zayas, L. H., Kaplan, C., Turner, S., Romano, K., & Gonzàlez-Ramos, G. (2000). Understanding suicide attempts by adolescent Hispanic females. *Social Work, 45,* 53-63.

Zea, M. C., Diehl, V. A., & Porterfield, K. S. (1997). Central American youth exposed to war violence. In J. G. Garcia & M. C. Zea (Eds.), *Psychological interventions and research with Latino populations* (pp. 39-55). Boston: Allyn & Bacon.

Zea, M. C., Mason, M. A., & Murguía, A. (2000). Psychotherapy with members of Latino/ Latina religions and spiritual traditions. In P. S. Richards & A. E. Bergin (Eds.), *Handbook of psychotherapy and religious diversity* (pp. 397-419). Washington, DC: American Psychological Association.

Zea, M. C., Quezada, T., & Belgrave, F. Z. (1997). Limitations of an acultural health psychology for Latinos: Reconstructing the African influence on Latino culture and health-related behaviors. In J. G. Garcia & M. C. Zea (Eds.), *Psychological interventions and research with Latino populations* (pp. 255-266). Needham Heights, MA: Allyn & Bacon.

Zepeda, M., & Espinosa, M. (1988). Parental knowledge of children's behavioral capabilities: A study of low income parents. *Hispanic Journal of Behavioral Sciences, 10,* 149-159.

Zúñiga, M. E. (1992a). *Dichos* as metaphorical tools for resistant Latino clients. *Psychotherapy, 28,* 480-483.

Zúñiga, M. E. (1992b). Families with Latino roots. In E. W. Lynch & M. J. Hanson (Eds.), *Developing cross-cultural competence: A guide for working with young children and their families* (pp. 151-179). Baltimore, MD: Brooks.

Index

About the Authors

Azara L. Santiago-Rivera, Ph.D., is Associate Professor and holds academic appointments in the Department of Latin American and Caribbean Studies and the Department of Educational and Counseling Psychology, Division of Counseling Psychology, at the State University of New York at Albany, Albany, New York. She earned a doctorate in counseling from Wayne State University, Detroit, Michigan. She is a national certified counselor and has held leadership positions within the counseling profession. She served as vice president of the Latino Interest Network of the Association of Multicultural Counseling and Development (AMCD) and as president of Counselors for Social Justice (CSJ) within the American Counseling Association. Her publications and research interests include bilingual therapy, health and the environment, and stress and coping. She has presented on these topics at major conferences and has published in such journals as the *Journal of Professional Psychology: Research and Practice and the Journal of Counseling and Development.*

Patricia Arredondo, Ed.D, is Associate Professor in the Division of Psychology in Education at Arizona State University, Tempe, Arizona. She earned a doctorate in counseling psychology at Boston University, Boston, Massachusetts. She is a licensed psychologist and began her professional career as a teacher. She has held leadership positions within the counseling field and is renowned for her contributions in the development of multicultural counseling competencies, with such publications as the "Operationalization of the Multicultural Counseling Competencies" (with R. Toporek, S. P. Brown, J. Jones, D. C. Locke, J. Sanchez, and H. Stadler) appearing in the *Journal of Multicultural Counseling and Development.* Dr. Arredondo's research interests and publications include managing diversity in the workplace, racism, Latino/Hispanic health issues, gender issues, and the impact of migration on psychological health. She has authored several books and has written articles for *Business Week, Latina Magazine,* and *Counseling Today.* She has served in numerous leadership positions including president of the Association of Multicultural Counseling and Development (AMCD) of the American Counseling Association and president of the Society for the Psychological Study of Minority Issues, Division 45 of the American Psychological Association.

Maritza Gallardo-Cooper, Ph. D., is a school psychologist and marriage family therapist with more than 25 years experience as a clinician in the private sector, practicing in Texas, Puerto Rico, and Florida. She obtained her doctorate from the University of Florida. Dr. Gallardo-Cooper has developed and directed a variety of mental health treatment programs in Florida. Currently, she is the outpatient program director for a large behavioral health consortium in Florida, a position she has held for the past 12 years. She was a member of the Hispanic Task Force in the 1978 President's Commission on Mental Health and has presented in numerous professional training programs at the local, state, and national level in areas such as child and family therapy, marital interventions, Latino psychology, and organizational development. Her research interests focus on brief therapy models, treatment outcome, biculturalism, and bilingual assessment and intervention therapy.